Contents

We deliberately haven't put answers in this book — because there are lots of valid ways to answer essay questions. Instead, we've put in a section about how to do well in your exam — which includes some sample 'A' grade exam answers.

D0620256

Culture and Identity

There are lots of different theories about how society shapes individuals — or how individuals shape society. You need to have a decent idea of what functionalism, Marxism and interpretivism are. **These two pages are for AQA and OCR.**

Functionalism Says the Individual is the Product of Society

Emile Durkheim (1858-1917) was one of the founders of sociology. In his view, society is made up of various **institutions**, each of which has a useful **function**. So, Durkheim and his followers are known as **functionalists**. They looked at **how society was structured** — you can call functionalism a **structural theory**. Functionalists looked at how institutions in society work, and how they **affect individuals**. Here are some examples:

1)   **The Family** — has the function of socialising children.
2)   **Education** — has the function of preparing young people for adult society.
3)   **Religion** — has the function of uniting society through shared beliefs.

Functionalists believe that the **structures** of society are set up to allow society to **run as smoothly as possible**. Durkheim was keen on the idea that individuals **internalise** the **norms** and **values** (the rules and ideas) of society. This means those norms and values **become a part of who you are** — your personality and your **identity**. The result is **consensus**, which means everyone sharing the **same norms and values**.

Durkheim called the **shared norms and values** that **hold society together** the "**collective consciousness of society**".

> **Definitions**
>
> **Structure** — the way **society operates as a whole**. Individuals have **almost no control** over this.
> **Identity** — an individual's **mental picture** of herself / himself.
> **Norms** — ways of **behaving** and / or **thinking** that are seen as **normal** in society.
> **Values** — **beliefs** about what things are **important** and what things are **right** and **wrong**.
> **Culture** — The **combined** effect of **norms** and **values** — a **way of life**.

Not Everyone Agrees with Functionalist Thinking

1)   **Interpretivists** (also called **interactionists**) focus on the **individual** more than functionalists do. They say functionalism is **wrong to ignore the individual**. They think that individuals can choose how to behave, and aren't simply responding to social forces.

2)   **Marxists** say functionalism ignores the **unequal power** of some groups. Marxists say the rich have the most influence in defining the norms, values and beliefs in society. They think structures in society are set up to **serve the interests of the rich**, not to keep society ticking along as smoothly as possible.

3)   **Postmodernists** say **functionalism is outdated** because it's based on the idea that there's only one dominant or shared culture. Postmodernists argue that today there's a **complex and diverse range** of cultural norms and values.

Marxism Says the Individual is the Product of Economic Forces

Karl Marx

Karl Marx (1818-1883) was another of the founders of sociology. He focused on the **effects of capitalism**. He thought that the **economic system (infrastructure)** of a society determined the beliefs and values of that **society (the superstructure)**.

> **Marxists** believe that the most important force in society is **class conflict**
>
> 1)   In **capitalist societies**, workers are employed to produce goods which are sold by their employers at a **profit**.
> 2)   Only a bit of this profit ends up in the workers' wages — most of it's **kept by the employer**.
> 3)   Marx said that if workers were allowed to **notice the unfairness** of this, they'd revolt. So, to **avoid revolution**, the **capitalist system shapes the superstructure** to make sure that the workers accept their lot in life.
> 4)   **Institutions** like the family, education and religion **lead individuals** into **accepting** the **inequalities of capitalism**.

In other words, Marxists think people are **socialised** into a **culture** based on their **social class**. They think people's **identity** depends on their **class position** in the capitalist system.

Not Everyone Agrees with Marx either...

1)   **Functionalists** say Marx put too much emphasis on the role of **economic structures** in shaping ideas and beliefs.
2)   **Interpretivists** say he placed too much emphasis on **class** and not enough on individuals.
3)   **Postmodernists** say social class doesn't have such an important influence on individual identity any more. They say people are defined by the choices they make, not by whether they're a worker or a boss.

Culture and Identity

Interpretivists Say Individual Actions are Most Important

Many sociologists say that culture is actually determined by the **behaviour and interaction of individuals**. Theories like this are called **action theories** because they emphasise the **action** of individuals, as opposed to **structural theories** like functionalism and Marxism, which are all about the big structures of society.

Interpretivist (or **interactionist**) theories start with the idea that all individuals **interpret** society around them — people **try to make sense** of society. Interpretivists say that culture comes from **people's own ideas** of how people **interact** with each other.

Interpretivists don't say structures aren't important, but they do suggest that each of us **responds** to social structures in our **own way**. We aren't just products of socialisation — we all have **free will** and make **choices**. An important thing here is that the **results of individual choice** can be **large-scale social change**. For example, **Jonathan Gershuny (1992)** made an interpretivist analysis of gender roles in the home.

It's always good to bring an example in.

1) Some **women decided** they wanted to **work outside the home**. That's the **individual choice** bit.

2) Male partners then took on **more childcare** and housework. It became **acceptable** for men to adopt roles in the family that had been considered **feminine**. That's the **large-scale social change** bit.

Labelling Theory Says We're Given Labels which Affect our Behaviour

The **classic example** of labelling theory is the **self-fulfilling prophecy** of educational failure. This is where a child is **labelled** as a bad student and then goes on to actually **become** a bad student.

Very **strong labels**, e.g. "**criminal**" or "**pervert**", can take on what's called **master status**, which means they replace an individual's other labels. Someone labelled a criminal could be seen as just a criminal, and **nothing else**.

It's important to remember that labelling theory is a kind of **interpretivism** — it says that the **individual** can choose to accept or reject labels. In other words, being called a failure will only turn you into a failure if you choose to accept the label.

What do you know... Not Everyone Agrees with the Interpretivists either...

Marxists say interpretivists don't pay enough attention to **conflict** or to the fact that some social groups are more **powerful** than others. **Functionalists** say they don't acknowledge the importance of the **socialisation process**.

To **sum up** — here's a nice table showing the **main ideas** of functionalism, Marxism and interpretivism.

Functionalism	Marxism	Interpretivism
Dominant in 1940s and 1950s	Dominant in 1960s and 1970s	Influential in the 1970s
Culture is produced by social structure to create consensus.	Culture is produced by social structure to disguise class conflict.	Culture isn't produced by social structure. Culture is produced by individuals.

Practice Questions

Q1 What's the basic difference between structural and interpretivist approaches?

Q2 Which theorist believed in consensus?

Q3 Which theorist believed in class conflict?

Exam Question

Q1 Explain what is meant by "labelling theory". (2 marks)

Students of the world unite — all you have to lose is your brains...

*Social structure, social action, consensus and conflict are key sociological ideas. If you understand them, many other topics will make a lot more sense. So **learn these pages**. Make sure you can jot down a few sentences about what functionalists, Marxists and interpretivists think about the relationship between individuals and society. Then you'll know you've learnt it.*

Different Types of Culture

In the UK, there's more than one type of culture and there are lots of ways to look at culture — folk vs urban, high vs low, popular culture, global culture... **These pages are for AQA and OCR.**

Culture is a *Way Of Life*

Culture means the **language**, **beliefs**, **shared customs**, **values**, **knowledge**, **skills**, **roles** and **norms** in a society. It's the way of life of a **social group** or **society**. Culture is **socially transmitted**. That means it's **passed on** through **socialisation**.

> A **subculture** is an identifiable **group** within a culture whose members share **values** and **behaviour patterns** which are **different** from **mainstream norms**, e.g. youth subcultures like punks and goths (there's more about these in Section 7). Subcultures can be a form of **resistance** to mainstream culture.

Mass Culture replaces *Folk Culture*

Folk culture is the culture of **pre-industrial society**. It includes things like folk dances, folk songs, fairy tales, old wives' tales, traditional folk medicine and agricultural rituals. It's mainly passed on through word of mouth. Sociologists have looked at the ways **culture changes** as people move from **villages** into **towns** and **cities**.

Just try and tell me folk culture is dead... I dare ya, punk...

1) **Robert Redfield (1947)** said that "**folk societies**" were based on strong extended families, **supportive communities** and a **local culture**. In **urban** societies these were **not present**.

2) **Georg Simmel (1950)** argued that **urban societies** showed a **reduced sense of community**, and that urban people were more **individualistic** and **selfish**.

3) Theorists from the **Frankfurt School** said that this reduced sense of community was linked to the development of a **mass culture**. They said that the **media** had become a **strong agent of socialisation**, and it was wiping out the differences between local cultures. Instead, it looked more and more like there was just **one big culture**, shared by **everyone**.

4) These days, the term **mass culture** is used not just to describe the effects of the **media**, but also to refer to **fashion** and other types of **consumption**, e.g. if you eat lunch in a famous burger chain, you're taking part in mass culture.

You can also *Divide* culture up into *"High Culture"* and *"Low Culture"*

The **elite** (better educated, with more money and power) tend to have a **distinct culture** from the **masses**.

1) Shakespeare, opera, sophisticated restaurants and arty French films are the type of things that are associated with "**high culture**".

2) Meanwhile, the masses enjoy **low culture** — e.g. soap operas, reality TV, musicals, fast food and Hollywood films.

This is all linked to the ideas of "class taste", cultural deprivation and cultural capital — see p.58-59.

3) High culture is generally considered more **difficult to appreciate** and the audience is seen as **educated** and having "**good taste**". Aspects of high culture are seen as **good for society**, though they don't make much money compared to a lot of low culture, so the government often **subsidises** them.

4) In recent years a lot of **funding for high culture** has come from a **low culture source** — the National Lottery®. Some customers have been hostile to the idea that the lottery is used to pay for "arty" dance and theatre companies. They suggest it's **elitist culture** — most lottery punters **wouldn't get to see it** and probably **wouldn't like it** if they did.

Many sociologists say there's *No Such Thing* as *"Low Culture"*

1) The ideas of **mass culture** and **low culture** are very **negative**. Some sociologists have argued that this view is based on an **elitist perspective**. For example, **Bourdieu (1984)** says the **whole idea** of "high culture" is just a way of giving **status** to **elite groups** — he says that status is maintained by passing on **cultural knowledge**.

2) Marxists argue that high culture is just ruling class culture, and that the ruling class have imposed their idea of culture on the rest of society, and defined it as "better" than working class culture. Some Marxists argue that so-called "low culture" is just as **complex** and **sophisticated** as "high culture". For that reason, they prefer to use the term "**popular culture**", which is more of a positive idea.

3) Important work on popular culture has been done by the **Centre for Contemporary Cultural Studies** (**CCCS**). They analyse popular culture products like TV, magazines and youth fashions, finding **meanings** within them.

Popular Culture theorists emphasise that the *Audience* is *Active*

"**Mass**" and "**Low**" culture are both concepts that are based on the idea of a **passive audience**. They assume that the audience is being **manipulated** by the media and doesn't have much control.

"**Popular**" culture is a concept that is based on the idea of an **active audience**. This audience shapes and changes the culture. The CCCS has done a lot of research into the way this happens in youth fashions and subcultures.

Different Types of Culture

There's also a Global Culture

Giddens (1990) says that **technological change** has led to globalisation. Goods can be **transported** to anywhere in the world, and **information** can be quickly transmitted across the globe. This has meant that cultures that were once local have become global. For example, British and American pop music is everywhere. American and Indian films are popular internationally.

1) **Klein (2000)** and **Sklair (1995)** point out that a few large **transnational corporations** (TNCs), e.g. Coca-Cola®, NIKE and TimeWarner, are involved in the majority of cultural production, making cultural goods that are consumed all over the world. **Sklair** argues that TNCs and the global media have **more power** than individual **nation states**.

2) Critics of globalisation worry that these TNCs will replace the world's current **cultural diversity** (the differences in people's lifestyles because of the society they live in) with Western culture. They refer to cultural globalisation as **cultural imperialism**. **Klein (2000)** says there's already a trend towards **cultural homogeneity** (everyone having the same culture, wearing the same trainers, eating the same burgers, drinking the same fizzy drinks).

3) Supporters of cultural globalisation argue that it's a **two-way process**. Western culture is transmitted to new societies, and other identities and cultures get passed back to Western societies — e.g. through **Bollywood films** shown in Western mainstream cinemas. With the movement of people from different countries and cultures to other parts of the world, many countries are now **multicultural societies**. Postmodernists argue that this allows people to consume a **plurality** of cultures — this is called **multiculturalism**. They think that globalisation leads to **hybridity** (a **pick and mix**) of cultures rather than one culture being imposed on another.

A Cultural Industry is... an Industry that Creates Culture

1) In pre-industrial times, people mostly **made their own things**, or made things for their **community**. They made their own folk culture — singing folk songs, telling stories round the fire, even... morris dancing.

2) In our capitalist industrial society, we **buy cultural goods** that have been made by the **cultural industries**. Buying goods has become part of the culture of modern, Western society — it's known as **consumer culture**.

3) Some of the most important examples of **cultural industries** are the fashion industry and various media industries such as film, news, music, advertising, broadcasting and the magazine industry. All of these industries create and sell things that fit into people's **cultural lives** — the stuff they **think about**, and **talk about**, and in many cases the stuff that helps them to **define who they are**. Some theorists, e.g. **Featherstone (1991)**, call this "**symbolic consumption**" — see below.

Symbolic Consumption means Buying Things that help Define who you are

1) In modern industrial societies, **hardly anyone** buys any product based on its **function** alone.

2) For example, most **trainers** are just comfortable shoes — so choosing a pair should be pretty easy, right... yeah, right. The thing is, when most people choose a pair of trainers, they have to make sure that they're the **right brand** and the **right style**. You don't just buy the shoes, you buy what the shoes **stand for** — their "symbolic value". What you're actually buying is part of your **identity**.

3) That means that **most industries** in the modern world have actually become **cultural industries**. They're selling things that have some kind of "**cultural meaning**" attached. Any industry that makes things with a **brand image** that **means something** to people, or **stands** for something, is involved in **cultural production**.

Practice Questions

Q1 What is folk culture?
Q2 What is mass culture?
Q3 What is globalisation?
Q4 Give an example of symbolic consumption.

Exam Question

Q1 Explain and briefly evaluate why high culture is seen as superior to low culture. (24 marks)

If I watch X factor on top of Ben Nevis, does that make it high culture?

Culture is everywhere, apparently. Even something as simple as choosing Coke® over PEPSI®, or Burger King® to McDonald's, is seen by sociologists as a case of symbolic consumption. In fact, a sociologist would probably see this very book as a cultural product. You need to be familiar with the terms on these pages, because you'll need them to analyse different views of culture in the exam.

Theories of Culture

Some approaches focus on the idea that those in power use popular culture to control those who aren't. **For AQA only.**

Cultural Decline approaches suggest everything is *Getting Worse*

The idea that culture is getting worse isn't new. Back in **1869**, **Matthew Arnold** argued that **low culture** (he called it "philistine culture") was **taking over**. Later on, the literary critic **F.R. Leavis (1930)** wrote a great deal about the idea that high culture was in decline. Like Arnold, he felt that **low culture** was **dominant**, and that this was leading to **serious social damage**.

You can still find people expressing Leavis's sort of idea in books and newspaper columns.

A lot of cultural criticism doesn't come from sociologists, but from <u>art critics</u> *and* <u>literary critics</u>.

The **cultural decline argument** says there's a **cycle of degradation**. It goes like this:

1) **High culture** is **refined** and improves its audience as people.

2) **Low culture** has **bad values**. It encourages **swearing**, **violence**, **uncouth behaviour** and general **lack of respect**.

3) Society gets worse because almost **nobody** is exposed to **high culture** and almost **everybody** is exposed to **low culture**.

4) As **society gets worse**, **low culture** gets **even worse** in response, and in turn brings society down **even further**.

Many critics feel that this is a **snobbish** and **elitist** perspective, which encourages the idea that some people in society are **naturally superior** to others. For example, **Marxists** have mostly been pretty **unsympathetic** to the cultural decline argument. On the other hand, some influential Marxists were very **pessimistic** about **low/mass culture** too, but for different reasons.

Marxism says that the working class are *Oppressed* by *Capitalism* via *Culture*

1) Many Marxists say it's down to **ideology**. They say everyone is **tricked** into accepting the idea that everything about society is **just fine**. Marxists from the **Frankfurt School** decided that the **mass media** were the main way of transmitting **capitalist ideology**. (The Frankfurt School began as a group of sociological thinkers in 1930s Germany.)

2) They argued that mass culture **helped capitalism** to oppress the working classes by **destroying community** and **individuality**. It also encouraged **acceptance of authority** and **discouraged** people from **thinking for themselves**.

3) In this way, capitalism used **mass culture** to **prevent revolution** from ever happening.

Some examples the Frankfurt School pointed out were:

- **Hollywood films** that distracted ordinary people from social issues, giving them **false dreams** of **glamour** and **adventure**.

- **Newspaper horoscopes** which suggested that a person's life experiences were down to **luck** or **fate**, rather than social structures or personal actions.

- TV and radio **advertising** that reinforced the values of capitalism.

Marxists said capitalism creates **False Needs** *and* **Commodity Fetishism**

1) **Capitalism** is based on **selling things**. According to Frankfurt School sociologists **Adorno and Horkheimer (1944)** mass culture encourages you to think you **"need"** to **buy things** which you don't need at all, such as a cupboard full of shoes, or an iPod®. You **don't** actually **need** these things in the same way you need **food** and **water** and **oxygen**, but it's **good for capitalism** if you **think** you do. That's **false need**.

2) Another Marxist idea is **commodity fetishism**. This is where false needs create **obsessions** and **desires** about consumer goods — **"must-have"** objects. An example of this is when a new mobile phone comes out and everyone wants it. **Golding and Murdock (1991)** suggest that people buy products because capitalism promotes goods via the media.

3) **Adorno and Horkheimer** said commodity fetishism was like a **religion**.

4) According to them, the really clever trick is that **capitalism creates desires** that **only capitalism can satisfy**. This means we all end up thinking **capitalism** is a **good** thing, because it gives us **exactly what we want**.

Arnold liked his job, but had misunderstood when they had asked him to knead the bread.

So to sum up, the **Frankfurt School** took a **pessimistic** approach to mass culture:

- Mass culture is used to **dull the minds** of the **working classes**.

- Mass culture promotes **capitalist ideology**.

- **Commodity fetishism** encourages **economic activity**.

- The population are **passive victims** of mass culture.

Theories of Culture

Not All Marxists agree with the Frankfurt School

1) The Italian thinker **Antonio Gramsci** (1891-1937) said that the idea of a **single mass culture** was too **simplistic**.

2) **Gramsci (1971)** thought that capitalism creates a big **dominant culture**. He called this dominance **hegemony**.

3) Gramsci believed that **capitalism** had to **tolerate** some oppositional cultures, rather than stamp them out. By **allowing some opposition** to exist, he said, capitalism could create the **illusion** that it was a **fair** and **free** system.

4) He had a big influence on the work of Marxists like **Stuart Hall** of the **Centre for Contemporary Cultural Studies**. Hall says that **youth subcultures** help working class youths to **resist capitalist values**.

5) Hall, and other neo-Marxists who take a more positive, optimistic view of modern culture, prefer the term **popular culture** to mass culture.

Gramsci wrote most of his theories in prison, in the 1930s. His prison notebooks were published much later. That's why the date of publication is well after he died.

Hegemony — nothing to do with dominant hedges. Apparently.

Feminism links popular culture to Socialisation and Patriarchy

Where Marxists see the mass media as promoting **capitalism**, feminists have concentrated on representations of **gender roles**. During the 1970s and 1980s, many feminists researched the relationship between **popular culture** and **gender socialisation**.

Most of these studies suggested that popular culture **stereotypes** women into roles — such as housewife or sex object. These roles are then **reinforced** in society.

1) **Ferguson (1983)** and **McRobbie (1978)** studied magazines, and found that they promoted traditional female roles.

2) **Radical feminists**, such as **Andrea Dworkin (1981)** in her study of pornography, suggest that many images of women in popular culture encourage and justify **violence** against women.

3) More recently, some feminists have argued that popular cultural representations of women can also be **empowering**. For example, **Camille Paglia** has written a lot about Madonna's public image as a strong female role model.

Practice Questions

Q1 Explain what is meant by "cultural decline".
Q2 How do the Frankfurt School view popular culture?
Q3 What is commodity fetishism?
Q4 Explain how popular culture could be said to stereotype women.

Exam Question

Q1 Identify two ways in which popular culture has been linked to patriarchy by feminists. (4 marks)

Capitalism didn't tell me to want a new phone — the TV advert did...

According to the Frankfurt School, I didn't really need that Mina dress after all. If only Theodor Adorno could have texted me to tell me. Sigh. Anyway, make sure you know the nuts and bolts of these theoretical approaches, because you'll need them if you want to get top level marks. Without mentioning relevant theorists, you aren't going to win the examiner over.

Theories of Culture

*Get ready for some hardcore theory. This is the stuff that really shows those examiners that you know what you're talking about. Modernism, pluralism and postmodernism – it can look brain-bursting to start with, but once you get the key ideas, it all just falls into place. **For AQA only.***

Modernist sociologists believe society can be understood Scientifically

Modernism is a word that's used to mean many different things. In sociology it refers to the "**classical sociological**" approaches of **Marx** and **Durkheim**. Those two certainly didn't agree about everything, but they had some similar **beliefs** which meant that they can both be seen as modernist.

- They both believed that society was a **structure** — an organised system.
- They both believed that **social structures controlled individuals**, never the other way around.
- They both believed in the idea of **progress** — society improving over time.
- They both believed a **scientific approach** could explain society.

> Marxism and functionalism are also known as structuralist viewpoints because they focus on structure.

In Modernism there are Two Opposing Views of Culture

1) The **Marxist** perspectives start from the idea that culture creates **false consciousness**. Marxists believe culture is all set up to reinforce the **class structure** and to **distract** the working classes from realising that they're being **oppressed**. According to Marx, this helps prevent **revolution** from taking place.

2) Marx thought that the working classes would eventually **realise** that they were being tricked and the **false consciousness** created by capitalist culture would be replaced by **class consciousness**. Then **revolution** would come. The **Frankfurt School** perspective described on p.6 is a good example of Marxist modernism.

1) Durkheim's **functionalist** perspective describes culture as a kind of **social glue**. It bonds people together by creating shared interests and purposes.

2) It also helps to **socialise** people into appropriate behaviour. This prevents society from breaking down into chaos.

It should be pretty clear that **Marx** and **Durkheim** saw culture as doing basically the **same thing** — **controlling people**. The difference was, Marx thought that this was a bad thing, while Durkheim believed it was necessary and good.

Semiotic Analysis looks for Hidden Structures of Meaning

1) An important approach to popular culture is semiotics. This perspective is based on the ideas of the linguist **Ferdinand de Saussure** (1857-1913). Saussure was a **structuralist** — he thought that meaning was found in the **structure** of language, rather than in the **individual words** of a language.

2) According to semiotics, society is full of **signifiers** (words, symbols and images) — which create **meanings**.

3) Meanings can be either **denoted** or **connoted**. **Denoted** (or denotative) meanings are **obvious**. **Connoted** (or connotative) meanings are **suggested** — you don't see them right away, and may only notice them **subconsciously**.

4) For example, a **picture** of a gun **denotes** a gun. A picture of a gun **connotes** all sorts of things — **power**, **masculinity**, **death**, **gangsters**, **fear** and so on.

5) Quite a lot of **sociological work** on culture now involves **semiotic analysis**, looking for the **connotative** meanings of cultural objects. This can be from all kinds of perspectives. For example, **Dick Hebdige (1979)** took a **Marxist** approach to his semiotic analysis of **punk** (see p.92) while **Ann DuCille's (1996)** analysis of the Barbie™ doll was focused on **feminism** and **ethnicity**.

Theories of Culture

Pluralists say we have Power through Choice

Pluralists think that popular culture **reflects society**.

1) They argue that there is a **range of consumer goods** available which gives people lots of **choice**, e.g. different magazines, different brands of trainers, different films to go and see.

2) People have the **power to choose** the products they like — this is called **consumer power**. Consumers are **active**, not passive.

3) The cultural industry **takes notice** of what consumers want — it's in their interests to **create products** that people will **buy**.

4) Therefore, it is the **consumers** who **shape popular culture** — not the other way round.

However, not everyone agrees with the pluralists. For example, **Ien Ang (1991)** suggests that the **opinions** of consumers are largely **ignored** by the cultural industry.

The chin-flator 5000. Surely a must-have?

Postmodernism argues that Culture is Diverse

1) Postmodernists reject the idea that culture helps to unify people in society. Instead they argue that **culture is increasingly diverse**.

2) Postmodernists like **Stuart Hall (1992)** say that this diversity results in **fragmented identities**. People can **construct their identity** from a range of different cultures. Layers of identity can include nationality, gender, ethnicity, religion and political beliefs.

3) Hall links this with the rise of **new social movements** such as feminism, black power, and the green movement. He also links this with **globalisation** — as a response to cultural globalisation, people have constructed new identities such as "Black British", "British Muslim", "Somali living in London" etc.

4) The way people **use culture** reflects their **fragmented identity**. Some sociologists have looked at the way that British Asians pick and mix aspects of traditional **Indian** and **Pakistani** culture, black **hip-hop culture** and British **urban** culture to make a **hybrid culture**.

> Postmodernists say signifiers are more powerful than the things they signify
>
> 1) In other words, the **name** and **image** we give to something has more meaning than the thing itself.
>
> 2) There are lots of examples in popular culture — e.g. **brands**. Look at the counterfeit "label" goods on any street market in the country. The **only selling point** for a cheaply made, **fake Gucci watch** is the **name** on the product.
>
> 3) **Baudrillard (1981)** suggests that in the postmodern age **symbols** have become **commodities**, and that we no longer buy products for what they **are** but for the things they **represent**.

Practice Questions

Q1 What does modernism mean?
Q2 What is semiotic analysis?
Q3 What is consumer power?
Q4 What did Stuart Hall mean by "fragmented identities"?

Exam Question

Q1 Assess the view that culture helps to unify society. (24 marks)

What a load of Baudrillard...

The modernist viewpoints ought to be familiar — it's only old functionalism and Marxism all over again. Pluralists think ordinary people have some control over culture. Postmodernists are obsessed with symbolism. And scientologists think that people were brought to Earth by the alien ruler Xenu in a spacecraft 75 million years ago... Fortunately you don't need to revise that last lot.

Socialisation and Social Roles

Most sociologists believe you have to learn how to fit into society, e.g. learn how to behave and what to believe. This process is called socialisation. It begins in childhood and continues throughout life. As usual in Sociology, there are different views about how it all works... **These pages are for AQA and OCR.**

Socialisation is the passing on of Culture

1) **Culture** is a key term for this section. It means the **"way of life"** of a society — things like language, customs, knowledge, skills, roles, values and norms. Culture is **passed on** through **socialisation** from generation to generation.

2) **Norms** are **social rules** about **correct behaviour**. For example, by queuing in a shop or wearing formal clothes to a job interview, you're conforming to norms. **Laws** often reflect norms, but sometimes lawbreaking is the norm. Making illegal copies of CDs is a good example of this.

3) **Values** are more **generalised beliefs and goals**. Ideas like "freedom of speech", "respect for human life" or "equality" are all **values**.

4) **Culture, values and norms** are **not fixed**. They **vary** according to the time and place. For example, British culture is different from American culture, and today's culture is different from the culture of 30 years ago.

Sociologists say that through socialisation the **norms and values** of society are **internalised** — i.e. they become part of everyone's way of thinking.

There are two kinds of socialisation — **primary socialisation** and **secondary socialisation**.

There is only one Agent of Primary Socialisation — The Family

Primary socialisation comes first. In **early childhood**, individuals learn the **skills**, **knowledge**, **norms** and **values** of society. This all happens in three ways:

1) Children **internalise** norms and values by **imitating their parents / guardians**.

2) Children are **rewarded** for **socially acceptable behaviour**.

3) Children are **punished** for **socially "deviant" behaviour**.

> Children who are deprived of social contact during development often can't function as social adults. In 1970, an American girl known as "Genie" was discovered. She'd been locked up by her father for her first 13 years and never managed to recognise even basic social norms.

There are many Agents of Secondary Socialisation

Secondary socialisation comes after primary socialisation and **builds on it**. It's carried out by **various institutions**. The most important are **education**, **peer groups**, **religion**, **mass media** and **workplace**.

Education

The education system aims to pass on **knowledge and skills** such as reading and numeracy. Learning these skills is a part of socialisation, but sociologists suggest that **education socialises individuals** in **other ways** as well:

1) **Functionalists**, like **Durkheim**, believe that school **promotes consensus** by **teaching norms and values**. They also say children learn to value belonging to a **larger group** through things like school uniform and assembly. All this is important for **fitting into society**.

2) **Marxists**, such as **Bowles and Gintis (1976)** believe education operates a **hidden curriculum** that socialises pupils into **ruling class cultures** and encourages them to **accept exploitation**. The curriculum is the **content** of education. Marxists reckon there are two sorts — the acknowledged curriculum (maths, English, geography etc.) and the hidden curriculum (doing as you're told and not questioning authority).

Peer Groups

Peer groups are made up of people of **similar social status**. The peer group can **influence norms and values**. This can be towards **conformity** or **deviance**. **Youth subcultures** sometimes encourage **deviant** behaviour, like joyriding.

> Conformity = doing what society likes
> Deviance = doing what society doesn't like

Religion

Religion often provides **social norms and values**. Most religions oppose theft and murder, and teach respect for elders.

Mass Media

The **mass media** are **powerful** in shaping norms and values in the audience. Some sociologists (e.g. Althusser) argue that the media have now **replaced religion** in secondary socialisation.

Workplace

Workplace socialisation involves learning the norms and values that enable people to join the world of work, such as being on time and obeying the boss.

Socialisation and Social Roles

Individuals have Social Roles and Status

Like it says on the past few pages, **socialisation** is the process that turns individuals into members of a social culture. According to some sociological perspectives, an important result of socialisation is that each individual ends up with a number of **roles**. These are associated with different sorts of **status**. This is a bit tricky, so concentrate.

1)   Your **status** is your **position** in a **hierarchy**. You can have low status or high status. It's the respect and recognition others give to your position. The Queen is a **person**, but **being Queen** is a **status**.

2)   Your **roles** are the **behaviours and actions** you take on **because of your status**. In sociological terms, a role is a set of norms that go with a status. The Queen has to meet the public and show an interest, she has to speak to the nation on TV on Christmas Day and she has to travel abroad and meet leaders of other countries. These are all **roles**.

Status can be ascribed or achieved

Ascribed status is fixed at **birth**. For example the Queen (this is the last time with that example, I promise) **inherited her status** from her father (who was King, not Queen, obviously) when he died.

Head teachers, on the other hand, have **achieved** status. This means they've **earned** it through **education** and **work**. This is a **very important difference** for sociological arguments about gender, class and ethnic identities. It'll reappear on future pages, so be sure you understand it now.

Social Behaviour is Regulated by Social Control

1)   Socialisation puts **limits** on people's behaviour. The functionalist Durkheim called this **constraint**. If it weren't for internalised norms and values, people would **do what they liked**. Internalised norms and values are like having a **little police officer inside your head**, stopping you from doing wrong and crazy things.

2)   Functionalists say that socialisation creates a **consensus**, where everyone has the **same values and norms**.

3)   It's important for people to **conform** to the norms and values of society. When people conform to the expectations, they're **rewarded**. When people **don't conform** to social expectations, they're **punished**. Sociologists call these punishments **sanctions**. Sociologists call behaviour which doesn't conform to society's expectations **deviant**. (Learn those words, they'll be useful...)

There are **two types** of **social control**:

Formal social control — rules imposed by **agents of social control** such as the **police, the courts and the army**. E.g. if you stole some money, you could be punished with a prison sentence.

Informal social control — norms and values reinforced by the **family, education, media, workplace and peers**. E.g. if you refused to contribute to a friend's leaving present, you might get disapproving looks and comments from other people.

Society is Diverse

Functionalists say that there's a **consensus** of shared values and norms in society. It's true that many values and norms are shared across the whole of society, but there's actually a lot of **variation**. There are **many different cultures** in today's society — it's **multicultural**.

Postmodernists are big on the idea of **personal choice**. They say that in today's society people have a large amount of choice in their actions and behaviour — and in the values that they believe in.

Practice Questions

Q1   When in a person's life does socialisation occur: (a) in early childhood, (b) in adolescence, or (c) throughout life?

Q2   Give three ways in which primary socialisation occurs in the family.

Q3   Name five agents of secondary socialisation.

Q4   What is a role?

Q5   What is the difference between ascribed and achieved status?

Exam Question

Q1   Describe the concept of ascribed status. Illustrate your answer with examples.   (8 marks)

And I thought socialisation was just something to do down the pub...

Exam questions on this topic often ask you to discuss primary and secondary socialisation, norms and values. Learn what they are and make sure you can explain them all with examples of each one. Prepare some good examples in advance — they'll help you get the marks. Remember to use words like "deviance", "conformity" and "internalised values".

The Nature vs Nurture Debate

What makes you what you are — the genes you inherit from your parents, or the way you're brought up in society? This question's called the nature vs nurture debate, and people have been arguing about it for years...
These pages are for OCR — but AQA students will find them useful extra background.

The **Nature** argument says your **Behaviour** is a result of your **Genes**

1) The idea that **human behaviour** is all down to **biology** is popular with many scientists and psychologists.

2) This point of view is called **biological determinism** and it is often linked to **heredity** — the **passing on** of **characteristics** from one generation to the next.

3) Everyone **agrees** that you can **inherit physical characteristics** like the shape of your nose and the colour of your hair from your parents — these things are controlled by the genes that you inherit. But it's **debatable** whether you can inherit **personality traits** like an angry temper or musical ability. Biological determinists think you can.

> **Here are some examples of biological determinists:**
>
> 1) The criminologist **Caesare Lombroso (1876)** believed that a tendency to be a criminal was **innate** (that means you're born with it). According to Lombroso, you can identify criminals by such "physical defects" as fleshy lips, bald heads and long arms. He held these views way, way back in the **nineteenth century**...
>
> 2) The psychologist **Hans Eysenck (1971)** thought that intelligence was inherited.
>
> 3) Another psychologist, **Simon Baron-Cohen (2003)**, proposed that most men have '**male brains**' and most women have '**female brains**'. According to Baron-Cohen, this **biological difference** makes men more likely to be good at working with computers, and women more likely to be good at dealing with people. His argument can be contrasted with **feminist perspectives** (see the bottom of this page and page 16).

Biological Determinism has been used for **Evil Purposes**

1) Historically, biological determinist ideas have been used in some very **unpleasant** ways to justify treating some **people** as **inferior** to others.

2) For example, the **slave trade** was built on the idea that black people were less human than whites. In the 1930s, the **Nazis** claimed that certain races were '**genetically inferior**' and should be destroyed.

3) This is one reason why **sociologists** are usually quite **uncomfortable** with 'nature' as an explanation for human behaviour.

The **Nurture** argument says your **Behaviour** is a result of your **Environment**

1) Most sociologists prefer the idea that it's **society** that shapes your behaviour and personality.

2) According to this **social determinist** perspective, your genes will have little or no effect. Your **family environment**, **friends**, **religion**, **schooling** and the effects of the **mass media** will all help to make you into the person you are. This process is called socialisation (see p.10-11).

3) Some of the best-known arguments for social determinism have come from feminist thinkers.

> 1) The anthropologist **Margaret Mead (1935)** found that in the **tribal societies** of New Guinea, **male** and **female roles** were completely unlike those in European society. In the Arapesh tribe, men were strongly involved in childcare and behaved very gently. The Mundugumor women weren't interested in their children and behaved very aggressively. Mead argued that this showed that it is **not 'natural'** for women to be maternal and gentle, or for men to be aggressive.
>
> 2) The philosopher **Simone de Beauvoir (1949)** argued that so-called '**feminine' behaviour** was not innate. She said that it is **learned in childhood**, and that women keep behaving in a 'feminine' way because that's what society expects of them.

It's useful to **compare** these views on gender with the **biological determinism** of Simon Baron-Cohen.

The Nature vs Nurture Debate

It's **Tricky** to **Decide** which side of the **Debate** is **Right**

1) Like most debates about human behaviour, there are lots of **theories** out there, but **finding evidence** is extremely **difficult**.

2) The commonest **methods** used by psychologists and geneticists are **twin studies** and **adoption studies**.

> **Twin studies** involve (you guessed it) studying twins. The idea is that **identical twins** are **genetically** the **same**, and so by looking at their adult **personalities** you can **test** whether or not behaviour is determined by biology. For example, if identical twins who grew up apart have very different personalities then it suggests that **nurture** has had a **big influence**.

> **Adoption studies** look at the behaviour and personalities of people who **grew up away** from their **biological parents**. For example, if an adopted child is similar in character to his or her biological parents (rather than to their adopted parents), it might suggest that **nature** has a **big influence**.

There are **Lots** of **Variables**

1) No study can 'prove' either side of the nature/nurture debate because there are **too many variables**.

2) Biologically, any person's **genetic make-up** is very **complicated**. Think about it — two parents, four grandparents, eight great-grandparents, sixteen great-great-grandparents, and so on back to the dawn of time. If you're not like your mother, maybe you're a bit more like your great-great-great-great-grandmother.

3) **Social influences** are just as **complicated**. Your **behaviour** and **interests** might not be similar to your father's, but **parents** are **only one influence** on you. Perhaps you've been shaped by your friends, or by TV, or by a book you've read.

The **Answer** is probably **Between** the **Two Sides**

1) There's **no clear evidence** one way or the other. It's likely that people are formed by a **mixture** of **biological** and **social** influences.

2) For example, if parents are intelligent, they probably pass on the **biological potential** to be intelligent to their children. But they will also probably encourage their children to read and give them educational toys — they will **nurture** them in a way that encourages them to be academic.

3) Whenever you have to discuss two opposing ideas, this sort of compromise can be a good way to conclude your answer.

Practice Questions

Q1 What does the word 'innate' mean?

Q2 Who suggested that there are 'male brains' and 'female brains'?

Q3 How do the male and female roles that Mead observed in New Guinean tribes contribute to the nurture argument?

Q4 What two types of study are commonly used to investigate the nature/nurture debate?

Q5 Why can't any study 'prove' which side of the nature/nurture debate is 'right'?

Exam Question

Q1 Define the concept of biological determinism. Illustrate your answer with examples. (8 marks)

Sociologists think society is important — no shock, Sherlock...

The history of biological determinism is a bit scary sounding. Fortunately, we've moved on from the era when you could be accused of being a criminal because you had long arms and a bald head... Don't discount the 'nature' side of the debate completely though. It's likely that biology does affect people's personalities and behaviours a bit — as does society.

Class Identities

Societies are usually divided up into different social classes. Which social class a person belongs to is part of their identity. **These pages are for AQA and OCR.**

'Identity' is a tricky concept in Sociology

Identity can be a bit of a slippery concept, so best to nail it down right at the start...

1) At a basic level, your **personal identity** is the sort of stuff that would appear on an identity card — name, age, physical appearance, distinguishing marks, place of birth. These are **easily checked**, hard to change **facts** about who you are.

2) In **Sociology**, identity has a **deeper meaning**. It refers to the **way we see ourselves**, and the **way others see us**. This sort of identity comes from things that are more **complicated**, and sometimes **less fixed**, than the basic identity card stuff. Social class, ethnicity, friendships, work, gender, age and sexuality are all factors that contribute to your **social identity**.

3) Your social identity is often linked to **roles you perform** in society (e.g. daughter, student, volunteer, best friend) as well as the **social groups** you are a part of (e.g. female, middle class, Asian, teenager).

Societies are Stratified — Divided into Layers

Stratification is the division of societies into **layers**. The **richest** and **most powerful** are at the **top**, the **poorest** and **most powerless** are at the **bottom**. In between are lots of **strata** (which means layers, like the layers in rock) organised in a **hierarchy**. **Social class** is the main stratification system in **modern, Western capitalist societies**, such as the **contemporary UK**.

Powerful and rich

Powerless and poor

Stratification

There are Four Key Classes

For the **census** the **government** uses a scale called the **National Statistics Socio-Economic Classification** (NS-SEC). It has **eight classes** based on the **jobs** people do:

- higher management and professional
- lower management and professional (e.g. teacher, nurse)
- intermediate (jobs without managerial responsibilities, mostly in service industries)
- small employers and self-employed (e.g. restaurant-owner, plumber)
- lower supervisory and technical (e.g. builder's foreman, salesfloor supervisor)
- semi-routine (skilled services and manual work)
- routine (usually unskilled work)
- never worked / long-term unemployed.

However, sociologists usually talk about just **four basic social classes**:

1) The **upper class** are **wealthy** and **powerful**. The original upper class was the **landowning aristocracy**. Their wealth is **passed on from generation to generation**. People who have made a lot of money from business or from the entertainment industry are also sometimes considered to be upper class.

2) The **middle class** earn their money from **non-manual work**. Teachers, doctors, managers and pretty much anyone who **earns their living sitting in an office** are middle class. The middle class is **getting bigger** because there are **more non-manual jobs** these days, and fewer manual jobs.

3) The **working class** make their money from **manual work**. Farm labourers and factory workers are working class. The working class have **poorer life chances** than the middle class.

4) The **underclass** get their money from **state benefits**. They include the long-term unemployed and the homeless. The underclass have **the poorest life chances**.

Sociologists have most often focused on the division between the **middle class** and the **working class**. Marx divided society into just two classes — the **proletariat** (the workers) and the **bourgeoisie** (the bosses).

Class Identities

Class Culture Affects Identity

Sociologists often link **identity** to **social class**. **Who you are** is connected to your **class culture** and **class identity**.

1) **Barry Sugarman (1970)** argued that middle class and working class children are socialised into **different norms and values**. **Middle class** children are encouraged to plan for the future (**deferred gratification**) whereas **working class children** are encouraged to live for the moment (**immediate gratification**). Deferred gratification is a big part of studying and training for a **professional career**.

2) **Charles Murray (1994)**, a New Right thinker, suggested that **certain values keep people poor**, for example believing in the **acceptability** of living on **state benefits**. He argued these values are **passed on** from one generation to the next.

3) **John Scott (1991)** looked at the ways the **upper class** use the **public school system** (this means the **top private schools** like Eton and Rugby) to create **social networks** which then follow through into **high status universities** (such as Oxford).

4) In the state education system, **middle class children** tend to form **pro-school subcultures** (such as homework clubs) and are more likely to be placed in top sets. **Working class children** are more likely to be **anti-school** and to find themselves in lower sets (for further detail on this, see pages 58-59).

Bourdieu said the Upper Class use Cultural Capital

1) **Pierre Bourdieu** argued that the upper class **maintains its position** (on top, that is) by passing on **cultural capital**. This means the **knowledge** and **social skills** you need to fit in to the top strata of society. It includes things like knowing **which knife and fork to use**, the **"right" way to speak** and also an appreciation of **high culture** such as opera and ballet.

2) He also said that **middle class** families try to **develop cultural capital** in their own children in order to **improve** their class position. These parents **encourage** their children to read "good" books, experience theatres, go to art galleries and so on.

3) By contrast, he said that **working class** families **don't develop** this form of **cultural capital**.

Many Sociologists say Class Isn't the Most Important Influence any more

1) Most sociologists agree that identity used to be based on how and where people **earned their money** (social class). Many **postmodernists** say that these days identity is based on how and where people **spend** their money (consumption).

2) They also claim that people's **leisure activities** are **no longer class based**.

3) Traditional **working class** activities included things like **bingo**, **darts** and the **pub**. The **middle classes** were associated with **DIY**, **dinner parties**, **golf** and **bridge**.

4) Nowadays, lifestyles are based more on **individual choice** rather than class background. Middle class people do traditional working class leisure activities and vice versa.

Postmodernists also argue that there isn't any difference between high and low culture any more — globalisation means people have access to a range of media images in an instant, resulting in a mass culture (see p.4).

1) **New Right** theorist **Peter Saunders (1990)** argues that today an individual's identity **isn't** based on social class. He claims that the old **divisions** between social classes have **disappeared** in our modern, **equal opportunities** society.

2) **Marshall (1988)** suggests that the working class still see themselves as working class, but they are more **fragmented** than in the past due to the **loss of traditional industries**. This has meant that traditional working class identities have weakened.

Practice Questions

Q1 What are the four social classes usually discussed in sociology?
Q2 What does the term 'immediate gratification' mean?
Q3 Briefly outline Charles Murray's views about culture and poverty.
Q4 According to Marshall, why have working class identities become fragmented?

Exam Questions

Q1 Explain what is meant by the term 'cultural capital'. (2 marks)

Some very classy pages to revise...

Most sociologists are keen on figuring out what makes the working class different from the middle class. Agents of socialisation like the family and workplace (see p.10) are a common explanation. Postmodernists, on the other hand, argue that social class doesn't really exist in this twenty-first century world.

Gender Identities

Gender is about masculinity and femininity (as opposed to straightforward biological boy/girl differences).
These pages are for AQA and OCR.

Sex *is* Not the Same *as* Gender

In sociology, **sex** means the **biological differences** between men and women. **Gender** means the aspects of **masculinity** and **femininity** that are **not biological** but **cultural**. They are **learned through socialisation**.

Sociologists focus on **gender**. One reason for this is that there are **gender inequalities** in education and employment that **can't be explained** by the **biological** differences between men and women.

The **Family** *is the* Primary Agent *of* **Gender Socialisation**

Ann Oakley's (1974) research led her to identify **four** ways in which **family life** usually teaches children the **norms** and **values** associated with **masculinity** and **femininity**.

1) **Manipulation** — parents **often encourage** "normal" behaviour and interests for the child's sex and **discourage** what's seen as **deviant**. This **manipulates** the child's self-image — the child becomes interested in "normal" behaviours. For example, girls are often dressed up in pretty dresses so that being pretty becomes important to them. Girls are sometimes told off for being "unladylike" — shouting, playing loudly, getting mucky.

2) **Canalisation** — parents often **channel** their **children's interest** in particular directions. **Boys** may be given **construction toys** like LEGO® and **aggressive toys** like toy guns. **Girls** may be given **beauty toys** like toy jewellery and make-up, **mothering toys** like dolls and prams, or **housewife toys** like toy kitchens.

3) **Verbal appellation** — parents may **use language and names** to **define what's appropriate**. For example, "you're an angel" (girl) versus "you're a cheeky monkey" (boy), or "what a beautiful little girl" versus "what a big strong boy".

4) **Different activities** — parents may involve children in **different aspects** of the **household**. For example, girls help wash the dishes, boys help wash the car.

School *is a* Secondary Agent *of Gender Socialisation...*

For more on the experiences of boys and girls at school see p.62-63.

1) Girls and boys are treated **differently** in **education**. Sociologists say that education passes on **gender stereotyped assumptions** about how males and females should behave. Remember that gender stereotyped assumptions can **disadvantage boys** as well as girls.

2) There are still **gender differences** in **subject choice**. Boys are more likely to study science subjects (especially physics) and I.T. at AS / A2 level. Girls tend to dominate in art and English literature.

3) **Skelton (2002)** argues that schools both create gender stereotypes and maintain those learnt at home.

...and so is the **Media**

1) The **mass media** help to build gender roles. For example, **females** in Hollywood films are often presented as **weak,** in need of rescuing by a strong male hero.

2) **Angela McRobbie (1978)** has argued that teenage female magazines **reinforce conventional notions of femininity**, emphasising the importance of getting and keeping a man, being "beautiful" and so on.

Awww, kittens

3) **Wolf (1990)** suggests that **advertising** tends to present an unobtainable **'ideal image'** for women, reinforcing the notion that women should **look good** for **men**.

4) **Joan Smith**, in her 1997 book *Different for Girls*, also argued that **culture creates** and **perpetuates** gender differences.

Gender Stereotypes *can Affect* **Employment Opportunities**

1) **Traditional gender roles** can have an **impact** upon the **opportunities** and **experiences** of men and women in the workplace and at home. According to Social Trends 38 (2008) **19% of men** are employed as **managers or senior officials**, compared to **11% of women**.

2) It is still difficult for women to reach the **top levels** of traditionally 'male' professions. For example, the majority of **judges** are male.

Gender Identities

Gender Roles Are Changing — for Females...

1) In the **1970s**, when Sue Sharpe first researched **teenage girls' attitudes**, she found they valued **marriage** and **motherhood**. When she repeated the research in the **1990s**, she found that this generation of teenage girls stressed their **career ambitions**.

2) **Diana Gittins (1993)** looked at the **rising divorce rate** and said this was evidence that women's **attitudes to marriage** had changed a great deal. They were much **less willing** to **accept** relationships they weren't happy with. This was a sign that the old **passive female gender roles** were a **thing of the past**.

3) One important factor is the fact that more women **go out to work**, and earn good money. It is now more common for women to be the **biggest earners** or only earners in their household than it was in the past. The increase in office-based work is referred to as the **feminisation of the workforce**.

4) There has also been an **increase** in **female deviant behaviour** — for example girl gangs, as studied by **Ann Campbell (1984)**.

...And for Males

1) Research by **Jonathan Gershuny (1992)** shows that **childcare** and **housework** are **shared** between men and women much more than in the past. The so-called **"new man"** does the dishes and changes the baby's nappies. Statistics show an increase in the number of **househusbands** — men who stay at home, cook, clean and care while their female partners go out to work.

2) One cause of men staying at home might be the **loss of traditional jobs** and **roles** for men. **Heavy industry has declined** and the majority of jobs now require **traditionally feminine skills** such as communication. Boys aren't socialised to have these skills as much as girls are, but girls are now socialised to be ambitious and dominant — traditionally masculine traits.

3) **Máirtín Mac an Ghaill (1994)** says these changes have led to a **crisis of masculinity** where **men no longer know** what their **role** should be. This idea says that men are **shut out** from their **traditional** roles, and **not adequately socialised** to be able to **fit into new roles**.

Masculinity in the Media has Become Feminised

1) **Rutherford (1996)** points out that images of men in the media are now being used in traditionally female ways — i.e. to be ogled at. Male stripper groups like the Chippendales are a good example. He also looks at the marketing of **men's cosmetics and toiletries**. There are far **more** of these products now than in the past, and the images used to advertise them are often of **half-naked male models**. These are signs that men's roles have moved closer to women's. Rutherford calls this the **feminisation of masculinity**.

2) **Wilkinson (1997)** suggested that increasingly male and female **values** are **coming together**, with both men and women **creating** their **own identities**.

> Findings like this have led some sociologists to believe that **traditional ideas** of **masculinity** and **femininity** are now in **decline**. **Postmodernists** say that **both men and women** now see **consumption** and **leisure** as the **key factors** in shaping their **identity**, rather than masculinity and femininity.

Practice Questions

Q1 What is the difference between sex and gender?

Q2 Name two secondary agents of gender socialisation.

Q3 What did Rutherford mean by the "feminisation of masculinity"?

Exam Questions

Q1 Define the concept of gender. Illustrate your answer with examples. (8 marks)

Q2 Outline and explain how two agents of socialisation influence femininity. (16 marks)

I never liked pink much anyway...

With these pages, you need to learn about traditional masculinity and femininity AND how these gender roles are changing as society changes. As usual, those postmodernists claim nothing matters any more except shopping and leisure. Wasters.

Ethnic Identities

British society includes many different ethnic groups. Ethnicity can be an important part of identity. Not to forget gender, religion, class, nationality and occupation. One thing you can say for identity — it ain't simple... **For AQA and OCR.**

Sociologists Use the Term Ethnicity, not Race

Race is a way of classifying people by **visible biological features**, like skin colour or bone structure. The idea of race is linked to **racism**, the idea that some races are inferior to others.

That's one reason most sociologists agree **ethnicity** is a better term to use when you're talking about society. People from the same **ethnic group share** the **same culture** and **socialisation**.

Ethnic Minorities have Different Cultural Features

Ethnic minorities in the UK are mostly people whose families came here from former colonies like **Jamaica** and **India** in the **1950s and afterwards**. Statistics from the **2001 census** say **7.9% of the population** are from ethnic minorities.

> Ethnic minorities have distinctive cultural features from their countries and cultures of origin. This means stuff like values, customs, religion, diet, language and clothing. These cultural features give each ethnic minority its ethnic identity.

It's a long time since the 1950s, so Britain's ethnic minorities have been through a lot of **changes**. The way **ethnic identity changes over time**, from one generation to the next, is something a lot of sociologists study (see below).

Culture based on **shared origin** is still an **important influence** on **ethnic identity** though. Some ethnic groups work hard to keep distinctive cultural features going. For example, **Modood et al (1997)** suggested that cultural origins still play a key role in influencing the behaviour of Asians, particularly the older generation.

Children are Socialised into an Ethnic Identity

Quite a few studies have looked at the way **parents pass on ethnic identity** to their children. This is primary socialisation — the socialisation that takes place as part of family life.

1) **Rosemary Hill (1987)** found **the family** was very **important** in the Leicester Asian community. She also said that some children learned "Western" ideas about marriage, education, work and so on from white peers. Hill thought this led to **generational conflict** between parents and children from ethnic minorities.

2) **Roger Ballard (1994)** disagreed. He found that young Asians **negotiated** the two aspects of their lives (home and outside the home). That meant that at **home** they'd behave in **traditional** ways to fit in with their parents, but **outside** the home they'd "**act Western**".

3) **Shaun Hides (1995)** studied the use of **artefacts** in ethnic minority homes. He was interested in the way things like **furniture**, **pictures**, **ornaments** and **religious items** helped **reinforce** ethnic identity. Hides found that the wearing of **traditional dress** was a really important part of this. **Women** wore traditional dress **more often** than men, and Hides concluded that **women** had the most **important role** in keeping ethnic identity going.

Ethnic Identity is Also Created by Secondary Socialisation

1) **Racism** in British society can affect secondary socialisation. For example, studies by **David Gillborn (1990)** and **Cecile Wright (1992)** suggest that Afro-Caribbean pupils are often **labelled** as a **problem** by teachers. This can lead to a **self-fulfilling prophecy** where pupils form an **anti-school subculture** because that's what the school seems to **expect** them to do.

2) The **peer group** is important too. Academic **Tony Sewell** said in an interview in **2000** that he thinks young Afro-Caribbean males are too influenced by popular culture. He believes that they encourage each other to be interested in **expensive consumer goods** (e.g. cars, the latest mobile phones, clothes) instead of **education**.

Some Sociologists Say that Ethnic Identities are a Response to Racism

1) When **Afro-Caribbean** and **Asian** families first arrived in Britain, they faced a lot of **prejudice** from the white population.

2) Some people from ethnic minorities felt there **wasn't any point** trying to **integrate** into the mainstream.

3) One way minorities responded to **discrimination** in work, housing and education was to **hold on** to their **ethnic identity** and **resist** full assimilation into the mainstream.

4) **Cashmore and Troyna (1990)** show how people in ethnic minorities turned to **each other** for **support**, for example in religious groups like the (mostly black) **Pentecostal Church**.

Ethnic Identities

New Ethnic Identities are Emerging

1) **Stuart Hall (1996)** talks about **new ethnicities** which are very **varied**. He says that the **old ideas** of condensing ethnicity to **white / black** are being **challenged**. There are lots of **different kinds** of Asian ethnicity and black ethnicity. Hall also points out that for ethnic minority people, **gender** identity, **class** identity and **sexuality** can actually be **as important** or **more important** than ethnic identity.

2) Many sociologists argue that **young people** from **ethnic minority** backgrounds are developing **hybrid identities** — based on a mixture of influences. **Paul Gilroy (1987)** examined how black and white culture has become mixed together. **Maria Gillespie (1995)** looked at how young Sikhs brought bits of **mainstream popular culture** together with **Punjabi traditions**.

3) **Tariq Modood (1997)** found that **ethnic identities** were **changing**. Things like wearing **ethnic clothes** were **less important** for young people than for their parents. **Younger** people were more likely to be **political** and upfront about their **ethnic identity**. On the other hand, second generation immigrants were **more likely** to **see themselves** as **British** or partly British than first generation immigrants.

4) **Basit's (1997)** study suggested that ethnic identities are **dynamic** and **changeable**. Basit's interviews with British Asian schoolgirls suggested that they **combine elements** of both British and Asian cultures. They created their identity based on their Asian culture's **ethnicity**, **language** and **religion**, but in the **context** of a **British society**. This made their identity particularly **unique**, as the girls' parents thought that their daughters would not feel as **comfortable** if they were to go to Pakistan or Bangladesh to live, because of the **impact of British culture** upon them.

Celtic Identity is another type of Ethnic Identity

1) **Historically**, the **Celts** were tribes living in Europe during the Iron Age. We know about them mainly from Roman historians and archaeology.

2) The places most associated with Celtic culture today include **Scotland**, **Wales**, **Ireland**, **Cornwall**, the **Isle of Man**, and **Brittany** in France. **Languages** in these areas (e.g. Gaelic and Welsh) are related to **ancient Celtic languages** — and are a key feature of modern Celtic identity.

3) Ancient **Celtic art** is also distinctive and continues to influence artists today. Sports such as **hurling** are thought to have ancient Celtic origins.

4) Celtic culture and identity can be used to reinforce **regional or national identity**. For example, Celtic culture can be seen as **part of Welsh national identity** — and something that **differentiates** Wales from England.

Practice Questions

Q1 What's the difference between 'race' and 'ethnicity'?
Q2 What makes ethnic minorities distinctive from the mainstream population?
Q3 What are hybrid identities?
Q4 Briefly outline the view that ethnic identities are a response to racism.
Q5 What are Stuart Hall's views about the emergence of new ethnicities?
Q6 Give three aspects of modern Celtic identity.

Exam Questions

Q1	Outline and explain two ways the family may influence ethnic identities.	(16 marks)
Q2	Explain and briefly evaluate why new ethnic identities are emerging.	(24 marks)

So many identities, so little time...

Sociology is full of these "hot button" topics. Debates about racism, identity and multiculturalism come up in the newspapers and on the radio fairly often. For you as a sociology student, the important thing is to know the main theories about how ethnic identity is learnt by socialisation — and to know some key studies so you can quote them in your answers.

National Identities

Yup. Yet more aspects of identity. **These pages are for AQA. OCR people go straight on to p.22.**

National Identity is about Feeling you Belong to a Country and its People

Durkheim said that national identity (nationalism) has an important function. It makes **individuals** feel that they **belong** to a **larger group**. **Benedict Anderson (1983)** reckons that **nationalism has replaced religion** in giving people's lives meaning.

National identity can have **negative** effects. It can be used to **exclude** certain groups. For example, if someone defines being British as being **white**, then they are **excluding black and Asian British people**. When an organisation excludes ethnic minorities like this, it's called **institutional racism**.

1) **Symbols** and **rituals** are important to national identity. The symbols of a nation's identity include things like its **currency**, its **flag**, and its **national anthem**.

2) Every nation has its own **national rituals**. These are events when people are **expected** to **think** about what it **means** to be English, or Scottish or French, and so on. A good example from Britain is **Remembrance Sunday** when there are processions and ceremonies to remember British soldiers who died fighting in wars.

National Identity is a Product of Socialisation

Schudson (1994) says that individuals are **socialised** into a **national culture** and identity by agents of socialisation such as **education** and the **mass media**. For example, the National Curriculum says all children must learn about Shakespeare. The **hidden curriculum** also contributes by having school celebrations for national events such as the **Queen's Jubilee**, or letting pupils watch "important" national football matches at school.

The **media** are also very important in building up national identity. They do this by **broadcasting national rituals** — things like Royal funerals or the state opening of Parliament.

Stuart Hall (1992) writes about the way each country has its own collection of **stories** about itself. National identity is about **learning** and **sharing** these tales of **wars won**, **great sporting victories** and so on. These are **passed on** from one generation to the next.

Traditional National Identity is on the Decline

Some sociologists suggest that during the last 20 years, people have found it **harder** to **identify** with Britishness. British national identity isn't as strong as it was, and some would say it **doesn't exist** any more. There are a few reasons for this:

1) **Big business** is now **international**, and companies like the McDonald's fast food chain appear all around the world. People in Britain are often **working for companies** based in **Japan**, or **Germany** or the **USA**. Some **British companies** have been **bought by corporations** from **overseas**. Sociologists call this breaking down of national boundaries **globalisation**.

2) Mainstream **TV**, **fashion**, **music** and **film** are often dominated by **American products**. Many people think that the result of this is that Britain and other countries are **losing their own cultures**.

3) Britain today is **multi-ethnic**. It contains many **different** groups, religions and languages.

4) Britain has strong **regional differences**. Scotland, Wales and Northern Ireland have strong national identities of their own. Under the New Labour government, regional identities have been given a boost by **devolution** — regions being given **more political power** by central government, e.g. the creation of the National Assembly for Wales in 1998.

New National Identities are Being Formed

The old "Britishness" is partly being replaced by a **new multicultural national identity**. Things like food, fashion and music bring together **British traditions** with **multicultural influences** from **inside Britain** and **international influences** from the **rest of the world**. Our new "national dish", chicken tikka masala, is an example of this.

There are some **obstacles** to the creation of this new British identity, one of which is **racism**. A lot of the traditional British identity was based on the idea that the British were **different from** (and **better than**) the rest of the world. Some people may prefer this traditional view of "Britishness" and be **resistant** to the idea that British society and identity is changing.

Sexuality and Identity

Sexuality is another part of Identity

1) **Sexuality** means a person's **sexual orientation** — whether they are heterosexual, homosexual or bisexual. It also implies **sexual desire**. It is something which **society** can seek to **control**.

2) **Attitudes** towards sexuality **vary** between different cultures and over time. **Jeffrey Weeks (1986)** argued that sexuality is a **social** and **historical construct** — taking on **different meanings** depending on the society and time period.

3) In the past in the UK, **monogamous heterosexual relationships** were the **norm** in **mainstream culture** — and people who tried to live differently were often treated **very negatively**. People with different sexual orientations sometimes formed **subcultures** (see p.4) — **alternatives** to the mainstream.

4) **Agents of socialisation** such as religion, the media and education can **pass on attitudes** about sexuality.

Religion passes on ideologies that control sexuality

1) Religion tends to **promote** a **norm** of **heterosexuality** and **marriage**. Many religions forbid homosexuality and sex outside of marriage, e.g. Catholicism.

2) **Feminists** argue that religion **oppresses female sexuality** by imposing a **strict norm** of staying a **virgin until marriage**, only having sex to have babies and being **sexually passive**.

3) **Functionalists** think that the **control** and channelling of **sexuality** is crucial to the continuation of society. They think it's important to have a **stable family** for kids to be born into, and a monogamous sexual relationship between husband and wife to keep society stable.

4) The **New Right** claim that a **moral decline** caused by **secularisation** has encouraged homosexuality, abortion and pornography. They say these are **threats to social order**.

5) **Postmodernists** think this is all old hat and that religion doesn't have that big an influence on sexuality any more. They say individuals have choice in the **construction** of their **identity** — including **sexual identity**.

Representations of sexuality in the media can be stereotyped

1) **Homosexual** relationships and **heterosexual** relationships are often treated differently in the media. For example, **Coronation Street** and **EastEnders** have both had storylines involving a **gay kiss** which got widespread media attention. You don't get much outcry in the papers when a **man and woman** kiss on a soap opera.

2) There was a **prejudiced** aspect to **early media reporting** of **HIV/AIDS**. It was initially openly characterised as a "gay disease". Some tabloid newspapers in the 1980s referred to AIDS as a "gay plague".

3) Increasingly though, the way that the **media has represented gay people** is **more positive**, for example the television series *Queer as Folk*, and the films *Beautiful Thing* and *Brokeback Mountain*.

Social attitudes towards sexuality are reflected in the law

1) Homosexuality used to be **illegal** in the UK. It was **decriminalised** in England and Wales in **1967** — but the **age of consent was 21**, higher than for heterosexual people.

2) In 1988, **Section 28** came into force. It **prevented** local authorities from **"promoting"** homosexuality, i.e. presenting gay relationships as acceptable. The scope of this law was ambiguous — but many **teachers** thought it meant they **weren't allowed** to **talk about homosexuality** with pupils.

3) Over the last decade, there have been moves towards **equality** — for example, Section 28 was repealed in 2003, the **age of consent** for gay men was **lowered to 16** in 2000, **civil partnerships** for gay couples were introduced in 2005, and the **Equality Act (Sexual Orientation) 2007** made it illegal to discriminate against gay men and women in the provision of goods and services. This reflects **changing attitudes** in **society**.

Practice Questions

Q1   Give one example of a national symbol and one example of a national ritual.

Q2   Give three agents of socialisation that can pass on attitudes about sexuality.

Exam Question

Q1   Suggest two ways national identity has changed.   (4 marks)

I'm having an identity crisis...

People don't just have one identity — they have blimmin' loads. Class, gender, ethnicity, nationality, sexuality... and there's more over the page. So gird your loins, square your shoulders and chin up — another 4 pages and you'll have polished off this section.

Age and Identity

The identity topic rolls on... Two more aspects of identity are age and disability.
Page 22 is for AQA and OCR. But page 23 is for AQA only.

Attitudes about Age *Vary* between *Cultures* and *Change Over Time*

1) Views about age **aren't universal** — they **change over time**, and vary between **different societies** and cultures. **Age** can be seen as a **social construct**.

2) Age is part of social **identity**. People are **socialised** to accept the **norms** and **values** of the **society** they live in. So the way a society **views** certain **age groups** affects **people's behaviour** and **treatment of each other**.

3) Assumptions about at **what age** someone becomes an **"adult"**, or at what age someone is **"old"** can vary between different societies and cultures.

4) For example, in **modern, British society** children are treated **differently** from **adults**. They have to go to school, they aren't allowed to do certain activities (e.g. smoking), and they are viewed as needing constant protection and care. But back in 1800, many children in the UK were treated like **mini-adults** and **worked full-time** as soon as they were physically able to do so (see p.42-43).

5) People who are **similar ages** and have lived through the same **cultural and political events** are often referred to as being from the same **generation**. It can be part of an individual's **identity** that they **feel part of a generation** — e.g. the 60s generation.

6) The **law** affects how different age groups are treated. For example, legally **65** is the **retirement age** in the UK. People over 70 **can't** do **jury service**.

7) **Bradley (1997)**, however, argues that age is **less important** to identity than other factors like class, gender and ethnicity. This is because people know that their age identity is **temporary** — they're not going to be a child, teenager or middle aged forever.

A social construct is something that's accepted as true in a particular society — but which isn't a scientific fact.

Her cooking wasn't up to much, but if you're going to insist on hiring a two-year-old chef...

The *Media* sometimes present *Stereotyped* views of different *Age Groups*

1) The way the media represent different age groups can **influence** social attitudes — and **reflect** them.

2) Some sociologists have found evidence of **ageist** attitudes in media products. **Simon Biggs (1993)** studied the way older people are presented on television entertainment programmes. He found they were often in stereotyped roles, e.g. "forceful", "vague" or "difficult" — especially in sitcoms.

3) **Lambert (1984)** found that **older men** were often portrayed in **positions of power**, e.g. newsreaders. But this was not the case for older women.

4) There are also media stereotypes of **young people**. Children are often represented as **innocent**. Teenage characters in TV soaps are often **a bit wild** — prone to drug-taking, petty crime, binge drinking and unplanned pregnancy.

Marxists think *Attitudes* to *Age* are influenced by *Capitalism*

1) Marxists suggest that age groups are defined by the **capitalist system**. For example, **adults** are people of **working age**, and the **elderly** are people who are **too old to work**.

2) **Phillipson (1982)** argues that capitalism views the **elderly** as a **burden on society**. This is because their **working life** has **ended**, and they usually have **less spending power**. Old age is a **stigmatised** identity.

Life Expectancy is Increasing in the UK

1) The UK has an **ageing population**. The **Social Trends 33 (2003)** report said that between 1970 and 2001, the **number of people over 65** rose from **13%** to **16%**.

2) This is partly because people are **living longer**. According to **Social Trends 33 (2003)**, between 1971 and 2001, **life expectancy** in the UK **increased** from 69 years to 75 years for men, and from 75 years to 80 years for women.

3) **Giddens (1986)** argues that **longer life expectancy** has an **effect on family life**. For example, people are more likely to know their grandparents or great-grandparents. Families continue for much longer after the children have left home.

4) **Postmodernists** say that **attitudes** to old age are **changing**. **Featherstone and Hepworth (1993)** found that magazines aimed at older people portray an image of "youthful" old age — enjoying holidays and sports, wearing fashionable clothes etc. They also argue that people can **mask their age** more than ever before, e.g. through cosmetic surgery.

5) On the other hand, **Ginn and Arber (1993)** suggest that the **ageing population** has led to an increase in **ageism**. This is because younger people are concerned about the **cost to taxpayers** of the ageing population. **Negative news articles** suggest that the **NHS and welfare services** will be put under **strain** by the increasing number of elderly people.

Disability and Identity

Society puts Disabled People into a **Separate Category**

1) **Tom Shakespeare (1994)** argued that 'disability' is a label that society uses to **categorise people**. Being in the category of 'disabled' is often **more of a problem** than the disability itself. In this way, 'disability' can be seen as a **social construct**.

2) He argues that it is more useful to talk about disabilities as **impairments** — they don't make it **impossible** for people to do some tasks, they just make it **harder**. Since everyone's abilities are different, **everyone has some sort of impairment** — not just people traditionally defined as 'disabled'.

3) He also says that society should adapt so that **everyone** has access to the same services, regardless of how severe their impairments are.

There is sometimes **Prejudice** against Disabled People

1) There are **negative stereotypes** of disabled people as **weak** and **dependent on others**.

2) **Scott (1969)** studied the way that **blind people** were treated by **medical professionals**. He concluded that the blind people sometimes **learned helplessness** — they relied on sighted people for support because this was what the medical professionals **expected** them to do. Because they were **labelled** as dependent, it became a **self-fulfilling prophecy**.

3) Some people have challenged the idea that disabled people are unusual in being reliant on others. For example, **Marsh and Keating (2006)** argue that everyone is dependent on other people to some extent.

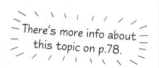
There's more info about this topic on p.78.

Disabled People are Under-represented in the Media

1) There's very **little representation** of **disabled people** in the **media**. **Roles** for disabled people are **limited**. Research by **Cumberbatch and Negrine (1992)** looking at British television over six weeks found the roles for disabled people were based on **pity** or **comedy**. They found that **disabled actors** never appeared **just as actors** playing a person who **just happened to have a disability**, only in roles **particularly about disability**. However, there are some positive portrayals of disabled people in films and TV — e.g. *Four Weddings and a Funeral*.

2) They also found that how people **interpreted** media messages about disability depended on their **personal experiences**. Those with real-life experience of disability were more likely to **reject unrealistic portrayals**, or to **reinterpret** them according to their own knowledge. This suggests that the media can only create **negative perceptions** amongst people who haven't already **formed their own ideas**.

Practice Questions

Q1   What characteristics have TV soap operas often given to teenage characters?

Q2   Give two examples of stereotypes about age groups that are sometimes presented by the media.

Q3   How do Marxists think that capitalism defines who society views as elderly?

Q4   What is Tom Shakespeare's view about how society should view disability?

Q5   How are disabled people usually portrayed in the media according to Cumberbatch and Negrine?

Exam Questions

Q1   Suggest two ways in which attitudes towards old age have changed.   (4 marks)

Q2   Explain and briefly evaluate how the media influences society's perception of disability.   (24 marks)

You want to retire with a pension at 17? — Oh, act your age...

Age is a flexible part of identity — everyone grows older and society's views of age change, often according to changes in the population within a single person's lifetime. On the other hand, disability is much more rigid — a person is unlikely to stop being disabled and society often unfairly views it as the most important attribute of an individual.

Leisure, Consumption and Identity

In a postmodern world, identity is all about shopping... ***These pages are for AQA only.***

Identity *is influenced by* Popular Culture

1) Many theorists and researchers have looked at the ways in which **individual identity** is influenced by **popular culture**.

2) According to **Blumler and Katz (1974)**, people use the media to meet their needs. They called this the "**uses and gratifications model**". Individuals **decide** which media to use, based on what they **want** to experience.

3) They classified people's use of the media into categories. "Personal identity" and "social interaction" were two of their categories. For example, they found that some viewers of TV quizzes liked to **compare themselves** with the contestants (personal identity) and would **talk about** the shows **afterwards** (social interaction).

Morley (1980) studied reactions of different social groups to media

Morley showed the same episodes of the current affairs programme *Nationwide* to different social groups. He demonstrated that different social groups created **different semiotic readings** of the same product:

- **black** viewers were likely to see the programmes as **racist**.
- **union** organisers were likely to see them as **anti-union**.
- **management** trainees were likely to see them as **pro-union**.
- **university** students drew attention to the way the programmes were **constructed**.

The uses and gratifications model suggests that **popular culture** is **involved** in personal **identity**, but doesn't create it. Morley's *Nationwide* study points to the influence of a **range of factors** such as class and ethnicity on the way individuals **engage** with **popular culture**.

Some argue that Identity *is increasingly linked to* Leisure

1) **Traditional patterns of employment** helped create a strong sense of identity through **work**, **family** and **location**. When people were often expected to stay in the same skilled or semi-skilled job for a lifetime, and when work was closely linked to family and community traditions, it was easier to build your sense of **identity** around your **job**.

2) People have become more **geographically** and **socially mobile**, jobs are **less secure**, and families (traditional, extended and nuclear) are **less stable**.

3) **Willis (1990)** suggests that work is now **less satisfying** because it often requires little **skill**. All of this leads to people using their **leisure time** to gain **satisfaction** and build their **identity**.

Postmodern *sociology says* Class, Gender *and* Ethnicity Don't Mean *so much*

1) Traditional sociology has looked at the way patterns of leisure and identity are linked to **social class**, or **gender**, or **ethnic** background.

2) In recent years, sociologists have suggested that people do not feel constrained by these social determinants, and are now much more likely to build their identities through **symbolic consumption** (see p.5).

3) Some examples of this include the "new man" (caring, sensitive, does the housework), "ladettes" (young women who take on some features of traditional masculine identity) and "wiggers" (white people adopting aspects of black identity). In all of these cases, individuals use **leisure time** and **products** from the **culture industries** to build **identities** for themselves.

4) Some sociologists, such as **Chris Rojek (1995)**, have concluded that **culture**, rather than social class, is the best way to understand patterns in leisure.

Leisure, Consumption and Identity

As *Leisure* expands, the *Culture Industries* also *Expand*

1) The **classic Marxist explanation** of this is that the cultural industries exist just to **make profits**. They **control** and **exploit** consumers in their free time, making them **think** that they need **expensive leisure pursuits and entertainment**. Workers keep working in order to buy cultural commodities and spend money on leisure.

2) The **cultural decline explanation** (see p.6) says that people are encouraged by popular culture to waste their time on **vulgar worthless activities** when they could be improving themselves with **education** and **high culture**. According to this view, greedy companies are making easy money by providing cheap, trashy entertainment.

3) **Willis (1990)** says that these two views are actually quite similar and **equally wrong**.

Willis suggests that capitalism has acted exactly as you would expect — of course it's tried to **profit** from the increased desire for leisure in modern audiences. However, the audience **wants** all this material because it **needs to be creative**. Now that work is often **less creative** than it used to be, people find ways of being creative and finding identity through leisure. Willis refers to **"symbolic creativity"** — a pick and mix approach to the cultural industries that allows people to **construct their identity** from little bits of high culture and little bits of mass culture.

Symbolic Communities are constructed through Culture and Leisure

1) **Cohen (1985)** suggests that communities are now **"symbolic communities"**. Instead of the traditional idea of a group of people **living near each other** and providing mutual support, a community can now be any group of people who are **connected** to each other. For example, supporters of a football team, work colleagues, users of a website.

2) **Jenkins (1996)** argues that groups such as **football supporters** use the symbols and rituals of the group to **define themselves** as people. He said that there are **three important elements** to this:

- Defining yourself and others as belonging to the group.
- Defining who is not a member of the group (the "other").
- Being defined by other people in the group as "one of us".

3) The idea of symbolic communities is closely connected to Willis's idea of **symbolic creativity**.

1) **Lifestyle shopping** makes us feel like **individuals** — because we choose the products that we buy to express our identity. For example, you might feel that your limited edition Hello Kitty® bag really says something about **you**.

2) **Lifestyle shopping** also helps us to belong to **symbolic communities** — because we choose products that have symbolic meanings which other people share. When you see another person in town with a limited edition Hello Kitty bag, you might feel a sense of **kinship** with them.

Practice Questions

Q1 What is the "uses and gratifications" model?

Q2 What reason does Willis give for leisure becoming a more important factor in identity?

Q3 What are symbolic communities?

Exam Question

Q1 Assess the view that individuals now build their identities through their leisure time. (24 marks)

It says it's about leisure but it looks like work to me...

Phew... It's the end of the section. There's been a lot of heavy theory in this section — but if you've managed to get your head around it, you'll find the sections that follow much easier. The usual suspects — Marxists, functionalists, postmodernists, feminists and interpretivists — have an opinion about everything and turn up throughout the book...

The Nature and Role of Family in Society

The family is one of the most important social groups for Sociology because almost all people experience living in a family for some of their life. **These pages are for OCR and AQA.**

Families *and* Households *are* **Not** *Necessarily the* **Same Thing**

A **household** is a group of people who **live together** who may or may not have family or kinship ties. The 2001 UK census recorded **24.4 million households** in the UK. **Families** make up the **majority** of households, but there are other types, e.g. **students** or **friends** sharing a house or flat. A recent **social trend** in Britain is the **increase** in the number of people **living alone**. (This information is from **Social Trends 33 (2003)** — a report by the Office for National Statistics).

A **family** is a type of household where the people living together are **related**. Most commonly, a family is also a **kinship** group. Kinship means being related by **birth** or **blood** — parents, children, grandparents, cousins. Families also include non-kinship relationships — foster children, guardians, step-parents and stepchildren, mother-in-law etc.

Here are the main types of family:

1) **Nuclear family**: Two generations living together (mother and father and dependent children).

2) **Traditional extended family**: Three or more generations of the same family living together or close by, with frequent contact between grandparents, grandchildren, aunts, cousins etc.

3) **Attenuated extended family**: Nuclear families that live apart from their extended family, but keep in regular contact, e.g. via phone or e-mail.

4) **Single-parent families:** A single parent and their dependent children.

5) **Reconstituted families:** New stepfamilies created when parts of two previous families are brought together. E.g. a reconstituted family may comprise of two new partners who bring children from former partners together to create a new family group.

Functionalists *Emphasise the* **Positive Role** *of the Family*

Functionalists see **every institution** in society as **essential** to the **smooth running** of society. A **key functionalist study** by **Murdock (1949)** concluded that the family is **so useful** to society that it is **inevitable** and **universal** — in other words you **can't avoid** having family units in a society, and societies **everywhere** have family units.

> "No society … has succeeded in finding an adequate substitute for the nuclear family … it is highly doubtful whether any society will succeed in such an attempt." Murdock, G.P. (1949) *Social Structure*, Macmillan, New York

Murdock (1949) looked at 250 societies in different cultures

Murdock argued that some form of the nuclear family existed in all of the 250 different societies he looked at. He argued the family performed 4 basic functions – sexual, reproductive, economic and educational (social).

Sexual   Provides a **stable sexual relationship** for **adults**, and **controls** the sexual relationships of its members.

Reproductive Provides new babies — **new members of society**.

Economic   The family **pools resources** and **provides** for all its members, adults and children.

Educational The family **teaches children** the **norms** and **values** of society, which keeps the values of society going.

In the 1950s, American sociologist **Talcott Parsons** argued that the family always has **two basic and irreducible** (vital) **functions**. These are the **primary socialisation of children** and the **stabilisation of adult personalities**.

1) **Primary socialisation** is the process by which children **learn** and **accept** the **values** and **norms** of society. Parsons described families as **"factories"** where the next citizens are produced.

Remember: functionalists see the positive nature of the family as 2-way — it's equally useful and beneficial to individuals and society.

2) For adults, the family **stabilises personalities** through the **emotional** relationship between the parents. The emotional relationship gives the **support** and **security** needed to cope in the wider society. It's a **sanctuary** from the **stress** of everyday life.

Some Say **Functionalists Ignore** *the* **Negative Aspects** *of Family Life*

The functionalist perspective has been **criticised** for **idealising** the family — focusing on the good bits and blanking out the bad bits. **Morgan (1975)** points out that Murdock makes no reference to **alternative households** to the family or to **disharmony** and **problems** in **family relationships**.

The **functionalist** view of the family was **dominant** in sociology into the 1960s. Since then there's been **widespread criticism** that neither Murdock nor Parsons look at issues of **conflict**, **class** or **violence** in relation to the family. Some feminists argue that they also ignored the issue of **exploitation of women**.

The fact that functionalists **overlook negative aspects** of family life **makes their position look weak**.

The Nature and Role of Family in Society

Marxists See the Family as Meeting the Needs of the Capitalist System

Like functionalists, Marxists view the family as performing **essential functions** for modern industrial society. The key difference is that **Marxists** argue that the family **benefits** the minority **in power** (called the "**bourgeoisie**") and the economy, but **disadvantages** the **working class** majority (called the "**proletariat**").

1) **Engels (1884)** said the family had an **economic function** of keeping wealth within the **bourgeoisie** by passing it on to the next generation as **inheritance**. In other words, when a **rich person dies**, their **kids get their money**.

2) **Zaretsky (1976)** focused on how the family helped the capitalist economy. He argued that the family is one place in society where the **proletariat** can have **power** and **control**. When the **working man** gets home, he's **king of his own castle**. This relieves some of the **frustration** workers feel about their low status, which helps them to **accept** their **oppression** and exploitation as workers.

3) The role of women in the family in capitalist society as "**housewife**" means workers are **cared for** and **healthy**. This makes them **more productive** — a great benefit that the capitalist class (the employers) get for **free**.

4) The **family household** is a unit with the **desire** to buy the **goods** produced by capitalist industry, e.g. washing machines, cars, fridges. The family is a **unit of consumption**. The family buys the goods for more than they cost to produce and the **bourgeoisie get the profit**.

All in all, Marxists argue the family is a **very useful tool of capitalism**.

The Marxist View is Criticised for being too Negative

The Marxist view of the family is all about it being a **tool of capitalist oppression**, and **never mentions nice things**, like bedtime stories for the kids, or trips to the zoo.

Criticisms of the Marxist view of the family

1) Marxist sociology is entirely focused on **benefits to the economy**, and benefits to the working man's **boss**. It **ignores other benefits** to individuals and society.

2) Traditional Marxist sociology **assumes** that the worker is **male**, and that women are **housewives**.

3) There is **no Marxist explanation** for why the family flourishes as an institution in **non-capitalist** or **communist** societies and there is little Marxist research on **alternatives** to the family.

Functionalists and Marxists both see the family as having a **key role** in society in **reproducing social structure and order**. The **key sociological debate** between them is whether this is **positive** or **negative** and **who benefits**.

Practice Questions

Q1 What do sociologists define as a household?
Q2 What are the key functions of the family according to Parsons?
Q3 Explain the ways in which functionalist and Marxist perspectives on the role of the family are similar.
Q4 Explain the ways in which functionalist and Marxist perspectives on the role of the family are different.

Exam Questions

Q1 Suggest four functions that nuclear families might perform. (8 marks)

Q2 Examine the view that the family performs the vital function of maintaining the 'status quo' in society. (24 marks)

Cog in society's machine or tool of capitalist oppression — you decide...

If you're comparing functionalist and Marxist perspectives about the role of the family, make sure you cover the pros and cons of each view — and most importantly, make sure you answer the question. Remember, functionalists believe that the family is there to keep society chugging along smoothly, and Marxists believe it's there to help exploit the common worker.

The Nature and Role of Family in Society

There's a lot of different feminist theory about the family — it's generally left-wing and anti-traditional. But it's worth looking at recent right-wing pro-traditional ideas as well. And at the postmodernists — who say everyone can do what they like. Hooray. **These pages are for OCR and AQA.**

Most Feminists Believe the Family Exploits and Oppresses Women

1) From a **feminist perspective**, the **family** helps to **maintain the existing social order**. (If that sounds familiar, it's because functionalists and Marxists also talk about keeping up the existing social order.)

2) Feminists call the existing social order **patriarchy**. Patriarchy is the **combination of systems, ideologies and cultural practices** which make sure that **men** have power.

3) Feminist theory argues that the family **supports** and reproduces **inequalities** between men and women.

4) The idea is that women are **oppressed** because they're **socialised** to be **dependent** on men — and to put themselves in second place to men. The **family** has a central role in this socialisation — **male and female roles** and **expectations** are **formed in the family** and then **carried on into wider society**.

5) Feminist sociologists say that there's an **ideology** about men's **roles** and women's **roles** in the family.

An ideology is a set of ideas about the way things are and the way things ought to be.

There are Three Main Strands of Feminist Thought on the Family

The three strands of feminist thought are **radical feminism**, **Marxist feminism** and **liberal feminism**.

The distinction between the three theories comes from what they see as the **root cause of patriarchy**. For radical feminists it's the **power dominance of men**, for Marxist feminists it's the **capitalist system** and for liberal feminists it's **cultural attitudes** and laws that allow **discrimination**.

All these theories generalise quite a bit.

Marxist feminism — key points

Marxist feminism sees the **exploitation of women** as essential to the success of **capitalism**. The family produces and cares for the next generation of workers for society at almost **no cost** to the capitalist system. It's cost-free because society accepts that **housework** should be **unpaid**. Men are paid for work outside the home, but **women aren't paid** for work **inside** the home. If this sounds outdated, remember evidence shows that even when women work outside the home they still do **most** of the domestic labour (see p.38-39). **Benston (1969)** points out that if housework were paid even at **minimum wage** levels it would **damage capitalist profits** hugely. **Ansley (1972)** thinks that men take out their frustration and stress from work on women, instead of challenging the capitalist system.

Radical feminism — key points

Radical feminist theory also highlights **housework** as an area of **exploitation of women**, but... and it's a big but... radical feminists don't see this as the fault of the capitalist system. Radical feminists see exploitation of women as being down to the **domination of men in society**. Radical feminism believes that **men will always oppress women**. **Delphy and Leonard (1992)** are radical feminists who see the family as a patriarchal institution in which **women do most of the work** and **men get most of the benefit**.

Liberal feminism — key points

Liberal feminists emphasise the **cultural norms** and **values** which are reinforced by the family and by other institutions in society. The family is only sexist because it **supports mainstream culture** which is sexist. Liberal feminists believe **social change is possible**. They try to put pressure on institutions such as the **legal system** and **government** to change laws and social policies which discriminate against women.

Feminist Theory has been Criticised

1) All strands of feminist theory have been **criticised** for portraying women as **too passive**. It plays down the ability of individual women to **make changes** and **improve** their situation.

2) Feminist sociology **doesn't acknowledge** that **power might be shared** within a family.

3) Some feminist theory has been criticised for **not considering** the households in society which **don't** feature a **man and woman partnership**, e.g. **lesbian** and **gay** relationships and **single-parent** households. The power structures in those families **don't get looked at**.

4) Some **black feminists** have pointed out that a lot of feminist theory doesn't address the fact that women from different **ethnic backgrounds** have different **life experiences**.

The Nature and Role of Family in Society

The New Right Believe the Nuclear Family is the Bedrock of Society

1) **New Right theory** developed in sociology in the **1980s**. It's based on the idea that the **traditional nuclear family** and its **values** (mum, dad and kids, parents married, dad in paid employment) are best for society.

2) New Right theorists reckon that **social policies** on family, children, divorce and welfare have **undermined** the **family**.

There's more about the New Right on page 52.

3) **Charles Murray** is a New Right sociologist who says the traditional family is under threat. **Murray (1989)** says that **welfare benefits** are **too high** and create a "**culture of dependency**" where an individual finds it easy and acceptable to take benefits rather than work.

4) New Right theorists are particularly concerned about giving lots of **welfare benefits** to **single mothers**. They also think that it's a very **bad idea** to have children brought up in families where adults aren't working.

5) New Right sociologists believe that the increase in **lone-parent** and **reconstituted** (step) families and the easier access to **divorce** have led to a **breakdown in traditional values**. They say that this causes social problems such as **crime** to increase.

6) Some politicians have made use of the new right theory. It's had an influence on **social policy** — making it **harder** for people to **get benefits**.

Pine cladding — that's the real bedrock of society

New Right theory has been **criticised** for "**blaming the victim**" for their problems.

Postmodernists Say Diversity in Family Structures is a Good Thing

1) The **central idea** of **postmodern views of the family** is that there's a much **wider range** of **living options** available these days — because of social and cultural changes. There are traditional nuclear families, stepfamilies, cohabiting unmarried couples, single people flatsharing, more divorced people etc.

2) Postmodern sociologist **Judith Stacey (1990)** reckons there's **such a diversity** of family types, relationships and lifestyles that there'll **never** be **one dominant type** of family in Western culture again. She says that "Western family arrangements are **diverse**, **fluid** and **unresolved**". This means a person can move from one family structure into another, and not get stuck with one fixed family structure.

3) Postmodernists say the **key thing** is the idea that contemporary living is so **flexible** that one individual can experience lots of different types of family in their lifetime. Postmodernists see this **diversity** and **flexibility** as **positive** — because it means individuals can always **choose** from several options depending on what suits their **personal needs** and lifestyle. People aren't hemmed in by tradition.

4) Sociological **criticism** of postmodern theory **questions** whether this "journey through many family types" is really all that typical. **O'Brien and Jones (1996)** concluded from their UK research that there was **less variety** in family types than Stacey reported, and that **most** individuals actually experienced **only one or two** different types of family in their lifetime.

Practice Questions

Q1 Identify three different strands of feminist thought about the family.

Q2 Give two characteristics of patriarchy.

Q3 What does Murray mean by a "culture of dependency"?

Q4 Why do postmodernists think there will never be one dominant type of family in Western culture again?

Exam Questions

Q1	Outline and evaluate the view that men benefit from existing family structures while women suffer.	(33 marks)
Q2	Outline and evaluate the view that the traditional nuclear family is under threat from a culture of dependency.	(33 marks)

If this is too difficult to learn, blame your family. Or blame society...

Another couple of pages all about different views of the family. Feminist theory is complicated because there are different varieties of feminism. Which one you go for depends on exactly how unfair you think family life is on women, and exactly whose fault you think it is. Don't forget to learn the reasons why sociologists say each theory might be wrong, or flawed.

Changes in Family Structure

The average family today doesn't have the same structure as the average family 300 years ago.
Sociologists suggest various reasons for this, mostly to do with people moving to cities to work in factories.
These two pages are only for AQA.

Industrialisation *Changed* Family Structure

1) There are **two basic types of family structure** you need to know: **extended** and **nuclear** (see p. 26).

2) There are **two basic types of society** you need to know:

> **Pre-industrial society:** This means society before industrialisation. It is largely **agricultural** and work centres on home, **farm**, village and **market**.
>
> **Industrial society:** This means society during and after **industrialisation**. Work centres on **factories** and production of goods in **cities**.

Industrialisation is the process by which production becomes more mechanical and based outside the home in factories. People travel outside the home to work and urban centres (cities) are formed. Industrialisation in the UK started in the 18th century.

3) What you really, really need to know is **how these two affect each other**.

> In **pre-industrial** society the **extended** family is most common. Families **live and work together** producing goods and crops to live from, taking the surplus to market. This is where the term **cottage industry** comes from.
>
> In **industrial** society the **nuclear family** becomes dominant. There is a huge increase in individuals leaving the home to work for a wage. The key social change is that industrialisation **separates home and work**.

Remember — **industrialisation is historical fact** but the **nature** of the **social change** it created is **a subject of sociological debate**.

Functionalists *Say Industrialisation Changed the* Function *of the Family*

American sociologist **Talcott Parsons** studied the **impact of industrialisation** on **family structure** in American and British society. Parsons thought that the dominant family structure changed from extended to nuclear because it was **more useful** for industrial society — i.e. the **nuclear family** is the **best fit** for **industrial society**.

1) Lots of **functions** of the family in **pre-industrial** society are **taken over by the state** in **industrial** society — e.g. policing, healthcare, education.

2) The nuclear family can focus on its function of **socialisation**. The family socialises children into the roles, values and norms of industrialised society.

3) Parsons said the industrial nuclear family is "**isolated**" — meaning it has **few ties** with local **kinship** and economic systems. This means the family can up sticks and **move easily** — ideal for moving to where the work is.

> In short, **family structure adapts** to the **needs of society**.

Most functions of extended family taken over by state

Specialised for socialising children

Mobile

Nuclear family

Functionalists *Say Industrialisation Changed* Roles *and* Status *in the Family*

Status for an individual in **pre-industrial society** was **ascribed** — decided at birth by the family they were born into. Parsons reckoned that in industrial society an individual's status is **achieved** by their success in society **outside their family**.

The idea here is that the **nuclear family** is the **best** for allowing individuals to **achieve status** and position without **conflict**. It's OK for an individual to achieve higher or lower status than previous generations. This allows for greater **social mobility** in society. People can **better themselves**.

Parsons says that **specialised roles** for men and women develop within the family. He thought that men are **instrumental** (practical / planning) leaders and women are **expressive** (emotional) leaders in a family. As a **functionalist**, Parsons said these roles come about because they're **most effective** for society. **Feminists** and **conflict theorists** disagree — they say these roles come from **ideology** and **power**.

Other Sociologists *say it's all* More Complicated

Functionalists are **criticised** for seeing the modern nuclear family as **superior** — something that societies have to evolve into. They're also criticised for putting forward an **idealised** picture of history. **Historical evidence** suggests there was actually a **variety** of family forms in the past.

Sociologist **Peter Laslett (1972)** reckons that the **nuclear family** was the **most common** structure in Britain even before industrialisation. His evidence comes from **parish records**. Also, **Laslett and Anderson (1971)** say that the **extended family** actually was **significant** in industrial society. Anderson used the **1851 census** for evidence. He said that when people moved to the cities for industrial jobs, they lived with relatives from their extended family.

Changes in Family Structure

Willmott and Young Said Families Have Developed Through Three Stages

British sociologists **Willmott and Young (1960, 1973)** did two important studies looking at family structures in British society from the 1950s to the 1970s. They mainly studied families in different parts of London and Essex. Their work tested the theory that the nuclear family is the dominant form in modern industrial society.

You need to remember their conclusion, which was that **British families have developed through three stages**. (Initially, they set out four stages, but there wasn't a lot of evidence for the last stage, so they dropped it.)

Stage One: Pre-Industrial	Family works together as **economic production unit**. Work and home are combined.
Stage Two: Early Industrial	Extended family is broken up as individuals (mostly men) leave home to work. Women at home have strong **extended kinship** networks.
Stage Three: Privatised Nuclear	Family based on **consumption**, not **production** — buying things, not making things. Nuclear family is focused on its **personal relationships and lifestyle**. Called "**the symmetrical family**" — husband and wife have joint roles.
Stage Four: Asymmetrical	Husband and wife roles become **asymmetrical** as men spend more leisure time **away from home** — in the pub, for example. *this stage got dropped*

Husband and wife roles are called "conjugal roles" by sociologists.

Other Sociologists have Criticised Willmott and Young

1) Willmott and Young (and other functionalists) have been criticised for **assuming** that family life has got **better and better** as structure adapts to modern society. They're described as "**march of progress**" theorists, which, I believe, is a bit of an insult in the world of sociology.

2) Wilmott and Young **ignore** the **negative** aspects of the modern nuclear family. Domestic violence, child abuse and lack of care for the elderly and vulnerable are all problems in society today.

3) **Feminist** research suggests **equal roles** in the "symmetrical family" don't really exist (see pages 38 and 39).

Different Classes Might Have Different Family Structures

Willmott and Young's work in the **1960s** and **1970s** supported the **theory** that **working class** families had **closer extended kinship networks** than middle class families.

To get up to date, the British Social Attitude Surveys of **1986** and **1995** showed that **working class** families have **more frequent contact** and ties outside of their nuclear family.

Recent work by **Willmott (1988)** suggests that **extended family ties** are **still important** to the modern nuclear family but they're **held in reserve** for times of **crisis** rather than being part of everyday life. For example, if your house floods, you might go and stay with your sister, even if you don't usually spend loads of time with her. In Parsons' terminology this makes the modern family "**partially isolated nuclear**".

Practice Questions

Q1 Give an example of social change caused by industrialisation.
Q2 What roles did Parsons believe men and women had within the nuclear family?
Q3 What is meant by the term "symmetrical family"?
Q4 Outline one criticism of Willmott and Young's "march of progress" theory.

Exam Questions

Q1 Examine the ways in which industrialisation changed the function of the family. (24 marks)

Q2 Examine the view that the extended family remains an important aspect of modern industrial society. (24 marks)

My mum works at Sellafield — we're a real nuclear family...

OK — here's something where it helps to have a vague idea about history, and about what this "industrialisation" business was. The idea is that when people went to live in cities and work in factories, society changed. Of course, it'd be far too much to expect sociologists to agree about it. Oh no. So you have another couple of pages of sociological debate...

The Family and Social Policy

Politicians sometimes try to promote certain family structures through their policies. ***These pages are only for AQA.***

Governments *try to Influence Family Structure through* Social Policy

1) The UK government often makes **laws** that are designed to influence family life or family structure. These laws are part of **social policy**.

2) Social policy laws cover areas such as **divorce**, changes to the **benefit system** which affect family income, reforms to the **education** system, **adoption/fostering** and **employment**.

Social Policy *has Changed* Over Time

1) The way that governments tackle social policy has **changed** quite a lot in the period since the Second World War.

2) In the 1945–1979 period, the state's social policy was quite **interventionist**.

3) **The Welfare State** (see p.54), which was set up by a Labour government in 1948, supported families through benefits, public housing, family allowances and free health care.

4) People paid into a **national insurance** scheme to pay for the welfare state. It was **universal** — everyone had the same benefits and services.

The NHS even covered floating baby syndrome...

The 1979 *Conservative Government Believed in* Reduced State Intervention

The Conservative Party was elected in 1979 with **Margaret Thatcher** as their leader. Reacting to several years of political instability, they set about **reforming** the relationship between society and the state.

1) The Conservatives were influenced by **New Right** ideology. They believed that nuclear families were the cornerstone of society, but also thought that society as a whole should be **freed from interference** by the state as much as possible. They thought the UK had become a "nanny state" with too much government control over individual lives.

2) They set out to make individuals more **responsible** for their own lives and decisions — the state would **intervene much less** in private matters. So benefits were cut and **taxes lowered**. **Means testing** was introduced for some benefits with the aim of helping only those in **genuine need**. (Means testing is when you only get a benefit if your household income is below a set level.)

3) Mothers were encouraged to **stay at home** through preferential tax allowances. Families were pushed to take on more responsibility for **the elderly** through benefit cuts.

Mrs Thatcher's Conservatives echoed the concerns of Charles Murray, who first coined the phrase 'culture of dependency' (see page 29).

The Conservatives Legislated *to Protect People in a* Traditional Family

The Conservatives valued **traditional**, **nuclear families**. In 1988, Thatcher described the family as "the building block of society. It's a nursery, a school, a hospital, a leisure place, a place of refuge and a place of rest."

The Conservatives created several laws that enforced the **rights** and **responsibilities** of individuals in families.

1) The **Child Support Agency** was established in **1993** to force absent fathers and mothers to **pay** a fair amount towards the upkeep of their children.

2) The **Children Act 1989** outlined for the first time the rights of the child.

3) The Conservatives also considered a law to make **divorce more difficult** — a compulsory **cooling off** period of one year was proposed before a couple could divorce. In the end they abandoned this idea because they couldn't find a way to make it work in practice.

The Family and Social Policy

New Labour Promised a Compromise between the Old Ideologies

New Labour came to power in **1997** led by Tony Blair.

1) They based their ideology on 'The Third Way' — a middle ground between left-wing and right-wing politics. Their policies were designed to be more pragmatic and less ideological than either the 1979 Conservative government or previous Labour governments.

2) In their 1998 consultation paper 'Supporting Families', they made it clear that marriage is their preferred basis for family life.

3) However they have shown an awareness of, and concern for, diversity of family life.

4) In 2005 they introduced civil partnerships, a union a lot like marriage that is available to gay couples.

5) They've also introduced laws allowing any type of cohabiting couple to adopt children.

6) They have adopted some New Right ideas when it comes to family policy — e.g. they've cut lone parent family benefits, supported means-tested benefits and are opposed to universal benefits.

Feminists Believe that Social Policy is Designed to Protect Patriarchy

1) Feminists believe that the New Right want to reinforce a sexist and exploitative model of the family by keeping women in the home and making them the main support for their children.

2) They also think that social policies continue to support a patriarchal society even under New Labour — for example the differences in maternity and paternity leave reinforce the idea that the mother is the primary carer and the father is the earner and provider.

Marxists Argue that Social Policy is Designed to Protect Capitalism

1) Marxists also oppose the policies of the New Right. They argue that reducing benefits to the poor only makes them poorer, and that means testing for benefits is degrading for the claimant and likely to dissuade worthy applicants.

2) They believe that social policies tend to be designed to maintain the capitalist system. By reinforcing traditional gender roles, social policy moulds women into a reserve army of labour which can be drawn on in times of crisis.

Practice Questions

Q1 What is social policy?

Q2 Give two examples of Conservative policies in the 1980s that affected family life.

Q3 What has been New Labour's attitude towards family diversity?

Q4 Give two criticisms of the New Right's attitude towards social policy.

Exam Questions

Q1 Suggest two ways that social policy has influenced family life in the UK since 1997. (4 marks)

Q2 Examine the view that social policies in the UK have sustained inequality both inside and outside the family. (24 marks)

My social policy — Thursday is the new Friday...

Politicians usually want to support the traditional nuclear family, but since 1979 they've generally also wanted to reduce state intervention in people's private lives. Marxists think that New Right ideas about the family prop up capitalism while feminists think they help exploit women. Think of a way to remember that if you can.

Family Diversity — Changing Family Patterns

These pages are about which family types are getting more common, and which are getting less common.
These pages are for AQA and OCR.

Social Trends Indicate More Variety of Families and Households

Official **Social Trends** statistics clearly show that the **variety** of family types has **increased** in Britain since the **mid 20th century**. There's now no such thing as "the British family" — there are several kinds of family structure out there.

Look at the evidence:

1) There were **24.4 million** households in the UK in 2002 — up by a third since 1971.

The stats in points 1–5 are from "Social Trends 33 (2003)"

2) The **average size** of households is getting **smaller**. The number of households made up of **5 or more** people has **fallen** from **14%** in **1971** to **7%** in **2002**.

3) You might think that more small households means more nuclear families. However, the percentage of households which are **nuclear families** has **fallen** from **33%** in **1971** to **25%** in **2002**.

4) Two of the biggest **increases** have been in **single person** households and **lone parent family** households. This explains why the average size of households has got smaller.

5) There's been an increase in the **proportion** of families which are **reconstituted** families — also known as **stepfamilies**. There are **more stepfamilies** now that there's **more divorce**. In 2001-2, **8%** of all households were **reconstituted families**.

6) **Weeks, Donovan et al (1999)** found that there had been an increase in the number of **gay** or **lesbian** households since the 1980s. This is due to changes in attitudes and legislation.

7) There has been a rise in the number of people **cohabiting** without marrying — it is estimated this will reach **3 million** couples by 2020.

8) The number of children born **outside marriage** has increased to **40%** of all births.

The two **overall patterns** are:

1) There's been an **increase** in the **diversity** of families in the UK. There are more **different kinds** of family.

2) The **nuclear family** is still the most **common** type of family, even though the **proportion** of nuclear families is going down. In 2002, **78%** of children lived in nuclear families.

Rapoport and Rapoport (1982) Identified Five Types of Family Diversity

Organisational diversity	Differences in the way families are **structured**, e.g. whether they're nuclear, extended, reconstituted or any other form.
Cultural diversity	Differences that arise from the different norms and values of **different cultures.**
Class diversity	Different views are often held by **different parts of society** concerning families. For example, more affluent families are more likely to send their children to boarding school than poorer families, leading to a different relationship between the parents and children.
Life-course diversity	Diversity caused by the **different stages** people have reached in their lives. E.g. family relationships tend to be different for childless couples, newly-weds with children and people with grown-up children.
Cohort diversity	Differences created by the **historical periods** the family have lived through. For example, children who reached maturity in the 1980s may have remained dependent on their parents for longer due to high unemployment.

Class, Ethnicity and Sexuality Affect Which Types of Family You Experience

Eversley and Bonnerjea (1982) found **middle class** areas in the UK have a **higher** than average proportion of **nuclear families**. Inner-city **working class areas** are more likely to have a higher proportion of **lone parent households**.

Lesbian and **gay** families have been hidden from the statistics. The **official definition** of a couple has only included **same-sex couples** since 1998.

The study of **ethnic minorities** by **Modood et al (1997)** found that:

1) Whites and Afro-Caribbeans were most likely to be **divorced**. Indians, Pakistanis, Bangladeshis and African Asians were most likely to be **married**.

2) Afro-Caribbean households were the most likely to be **single parent families**.

3) **South Asian** families are traditionally **extended** families, but there are more **nuclear family** households than in the past. **Extended kinship links** stay strong and often reach back to India, Pakistan or Bangladesh.

4) There's **diversity** within each ethnic group though.

Family Diversity — Changing Family Patterns

Fewer People Marry and More People Live Together Instead

In 2001 the **lowest** number of **marriages** took place in the UK since records began.

This does NOT mean a decline in family life, though:

1) Over the same period of time there was an **increase** in the number of adults living with a partner (**cohabiting**). In 2001-2 a **quarter** of all non-married adults aged 16-59 were **cohabiting**.

2) **Social trends statistics** show that living with a partner doesn't mean you **won't** get married — it often just means a **delay** in tying the knot. A **third** of people who cohabited with a partner went on to **marry** them.

3) The **majority** of people in the UK do marry, but the **proportion** who are **married at any one time** has **fallen**.

4) **Men** tend to **die** before women. **Elderly widows** make up a lot of **single person households**. There are **more old people** these days, so this helps explain why there are so many single person households.

The UK has one of the Highest Divorce Rates in Europe

1) There's been a **steady rise** in the **divorce rate** in most **modern industrial societies**.

2) The **divorce rate** is defined as the **number of people per 1000 of the population** who get **divorced** per year. In 2000, Britain's divorce rate was **2.6** compared to the European average of **1.9**.

3) **Actual divorces** in the UK rose from **25,000** in **1961** to **146,000** in **1997**.

4) The **proportion** of the population who were **divorced** at any one time was **1%** in **1971** and **9%** in **2000**.

5) The average **length** of a marriage before it ends in divorce has remained **about the same** — **12 years** in **1963**, **11 years** in **2000** (source — Census 2001 report).

6) Although the divorce rate is increasing, divorced people are **marrying again**. In 2001, **40%** of all marriages were **re-marriages**.

You don't have to learn all of these statistics, but if you can learn some of them off by heart and quote them in your essays, you'll look very bright and shiny.

There are several **social**, **cultural** and **political** factors you **need to know about** when you're explaining why divorce is increasing in the UK.

1) Divorce has become **easier to obtain**.
2) Divorce is more **socially acceptable**.
3) Women may have **higher expectations** of marriage, and **better employment opportunities** may make them less financially dependent on their husbands.
4) Marriages are increasingly focused on **individual emotional fulfilment**.
5) The New Right believe that marriage is **less supported by the state** these days.

Availability and acceptability are the buzz words in the debate on divorce.

Remember — the **link** between divorce and marriage breakdown isn't completely straightforward. Some couples separate but never actually go through with the divorce procedure.

You **can't assume** marriage was **happier** in the past because there were **fewer divorces**. A marriage can break down but the couple still **stays married** and living together. This is called an **empty-shell marriage**.

Practice Questions

Q1 Which household types have increased in the UK in recent years?
Q2 Give five types of family diversity.
Q3 What evidence is there that divorce has increased in the UK in recent times?

Exam Question

Q1 Outline and evaluate the view that divorce rates have risen because divorces are now easier to obtain. (33 marks)

86% of people get bored of reading about divorce statistics...

Sometimes I wonder what sociologists would do without the Office for National Statistics, and their Social Trends reports. Anyway, jot down your own list of trends in the size of the family, the number of single person households, the number of divorces and the number of people cohabiting. You have to know which are going up and which are going down.

Family Diversity — Changing Family Patterns

There have been some trends in family diversity that almost everyone agrees on. But not everyone agrees on their causes.
These pages are for AQA and OCR.

People are Having *Fewer Children* and Having them *Later in Life*

One very clear change in British family life is the **decrease** in the **average number of children** people have.

1) People are having **fewer children**. The average number of children per family was **2.4** in **1971** compared to **1.6** in **2001** (the lowest ever recorded).

2) Women are having children **later**. The average age of women at the birth of their first child was **24** in **1971**, compared to **27** in **2001**.

3) More people are **not having children at all** — 9% of women born in **1945** were childless at age 45, compared to **15%** of women born in **1955**.

1971 2.4

2001 1.6

Social changes have influenced these trends. **Contraception** is more readily available and **women's roles are changing**. The emphasis on the **individual in post-industrial society** is a key factor. Children are expensive and time-consuming, and couples may choose to spend their time and money in other ways. The **conflict** between wanting a **successful working life** and being a **mum** has made many women **put off having kids until later**.

Families with many generations of only children are called **beanpole families** because their family tree can be arranged in a single vertical line, so it looks a bit like a beanpole.

New Technologies have Created New Family Structures

1) **Macionis and Plummer (1997)** highlighted the ability of new fertility treatments to allow family structures that were previously impossible.

2) Treatments such as **in vitro fertilisation** allow an egg to be fertilised in a **test tube** and then medically implanted into the womb of a surrogate mother who may not have been the original egg donor.

3) In 1991, **Arlette Schweitzer** acted as a surrogate mother using a fertilised egg originally taken from her own daughter. So it's arguable that the child is both her **daughter** and her **granddaughter**.

4) Fertility treatments have allowed **gay and lesbian** couples, and **single and older women** to have children when they wouldn't have been able to before. This means that family structures exist that were **impossible** in the past.

Eversley and Bonnerjea (1982) found Regional Variations in Family Structure

Eversley and Bonnerjea (1982) found that some types of family structure were more likely to be found in certain types of area.

Inner cities have higher concentrations of **single parent** and **ethnic minority** families.

Southern England has a high number of **two-parent**, upwardly-mobile families.

Coastal areas are home to a large number of **retired couples** without dependent children.

Rural areas tend to be characterised by extended families and strong external patterns of kinship.

Declining industrial areas have a large number of traditional families, but also show a high amount of diversity.

The New Right think that Family Diversity is Caused by Falling Moral Standards

1) **New Right** theorists believe that family diversity is the result of a **decline** in traditional values. They see it as a **threat** to the traditional nuclear family and blame it for **antisocial behaviour** and **crime**.

2) **Murray (1989)** suggests that **single-mother** families are a principle cause of crime and social decay, because of the **lack** of a **male role model** and authority figure in the home.

3) The New Right believe that state benefits should be cut and social policy targeted to **discourage** family diversity and **promote** marriage and the nuclear family.

The New Right have been criticised for their 'blame the victim' approach.

Family Diversity — Changing Family Patterns

Functionalists *Think that the Growth in Diversity has been* **Exaggerated**

1) The functionalist **Robert Chester (1985)** admits that there has been **some growth** in family diversity, but believes that the **nuclear family** remains the dominant family structure.

2) He argues that statistics show a **greater increase** in diversity than is actually happening. This is because **UK society** has an **ageing population**. The **distribution of ages** in society is changing so that the proportion of older people is **increasing**. This increases the number of people who are at a stage in their life when they're **temporarily** not in a nuclear family.

3) Chester has also suggested that nuclear families are becoming **less traditional** and **more symmetrical** (see page 31) to better fit modern living.

Postmodernists *see Diversity and Fragmentation as the New* **Norm**

1) Postmodernists claim that there is no longer a single dominant family structure — postmodern society is **highly diverse** and its diversity is **increasing**.

2) Improvements in **women's rights** and the availability of **contraception** have resulted in people having far more **choice** in their type of relationship.

3) People now tend to create their relationships to **suit their own needs** rather than following the traditional values of religion or the government.

4) Their relationships only last as long as their needs are **met** — creating even greater **diversity** and **instability**.

Postmodernists emphasise the rise of individualism as a crucial feature of postmodern society.

Beck (1992) identified the "negotiated family"

1) The postmodernist Beck believes that many people now live in **"negotiated families"** — family units that vary according to the changing needs of the people in them.

2) Negotiated families are **more equal** than traditional nuclear families, but are **less stable**.

3) **Weeks, Donovan et al (1999)** suggested that family commitment is now viewed as a matter of **ongoing negotiation** rather than something that lasts forever once entered into.

Jeffrey Weeks (2000) *says there's Increased* **Choice** *in* **Morality**

1) **Jeffrey Weeks (2000)** believes that personal **morality** has become an **individual choice** — rather than a set of values influenced by **religion** or dictated by **society**.

2) He sees modern **liberal attitudes** towards marriage, divorce, cohabitation and homosexuality as a major cause of **irreversible** diversity.

Practice Questions

Q1 Give two reasons for the decrease in the average number of children people have.

Q2 Explain why family structures are now possible that were impossible in the past.

Q3 Outline how region can affect family diversity.

Q4 On what grounds do New Right theorists oppose family diversity?

Q5 Give two reasons that postmodernists give for the growth of family diversity.

Q6 Explain how the decline in the influence of religion may have affected family diversity.

Exam Questions

Q1 Identify and explain two of the reasons given for increasing family diversity. (17 marks)

Q2 Outline and evaluate the view that people have become less idealistic in their attitudes towards family structure. (33 marks)

Have you met the nuclear family? They make you feel right at-om...

Postmodernists think family diversity is the new rule, the New Right think it's the result of falling standards and Jeffrey Weeks thinks that everyone just makes their own mind up. At least everyone agrees that diversity is increasing. Well, except functionalists.

Roles and Relationships Within the Family

As well as studying the place of the family unit in wider society, sociologists also research what happens within the family. The key focus is on the different roles and expectations of men, women and children within the family.
These pages are for AQA and OCR.

The **Rise** of the **Nuclear Family** led to **Joint Conjugal Roles**

Conjugal roles are the roles of **husband and wife** (or partner and partner) within the home. **Elizabeth Bott (1957)** studied how **jobs and roles within the family** were **allocated** to **men and women** in modern industrial Britain.
Sure, her study is **old**, but it's a **good foundation** for the debate, so don't dismiss it — **learn it**.

Bott (1957) identified two ways household jobs can be shared

Segregated roles	Husbands and wives lead separate lives with clear and **distinct responsibilities** within the family. The man goes out to work and does DIY. The woman stays home, looks after the kids and does all the emotional stuff.
Joint roles	Husband and wife roles are **more flexible** and shared with less defined tasks for each. Usually leisure time is shared. Responsibility for making decisions is also shared.

Willmott and Young (1973) studied the changing structure of the British family from extended to nuclear (see p.30-31). They reckoned that the increase in the nuclear family meant that **joint conjugal roles** would develop. They predicted that **equal** and **shared responsibilities** would be the **future norm** in British families.

Willmott and Young's picture of **widespread equality** in marriage was **criticised** as soon as it was published.

Oakley (1974) pointed out that their study only required men to do a **few things round the house** to qualify as having joint roles. Their **methodology** overlooked the **amount of time** spent on housework — making 10 minutes' washing up equivalent to an hour's hoovering, an hour's ironing and all the rest of the housework too. Oakley's research found it was **pretty rare** for men to do a lot of housework.

Conjugal Roles are **Still Unequal** Although Most **Women** have **Paid Jobs**

Since the early studies by Bott, Willmott and Young, **new family structures** have developed. There are now lots **more families** where **both partners work outside the home**. Sociological evidence shows that an **equal share** of **paid employment** hasn't led to an **equal share** of **domestic labour**.

1)   Edgell (1980) tested Willmott and Young's theory and found none of his sample families had joint conjugal roles in relation to housework. However, he did find increased sharing of childcare between men and women.

2)   Oakley (1974) found that women took on a double burden — taking on paid jobs and still keeping the traditional responsibilities for home and children.

3)   Boulton (1983) concluded that men may help out with specific bits of childcare like nappy-changing, but women are still primarily responsible for children.

4)   Ferri and Smith (1996) found that two thirds of full-time working mothers said they were responsible for cooking and cleaning. Four fifths of the same group said they were responsible for laundry.

These are all **small-scale studies** — it's important to look at research of a much **larger sample**. The **British Social Attitudes Survey 1991** was a **large-scale study** that questioned about **1,000 people** about housework. It showed a very **clear division of labour** — **women** did **most of the housework**. For example, washing and ironing was mainly done by women in 84% of households, shared equally in 12%, and mainly done by men in 3%.

Industrialisation led to the **Creation** of the **"Housewife"**

1)   **Oakley** thinks that the role of the **housewife** was **socially constructed** by the **social changes** of the **Industrial Revolution**, when people started **going to work in factories** instead of working at home.

2)   **Married women** were often **not allowed** to work in factories. A new role of **housewife** was created for married women.

3)   Middle class households had female **servants** to do domestic work. Working class women did it themselves.

4)   The **cultural values** that said women should be in charge of housework were **so dominant** that domestic work came to be seen as **"naturally"** (biologically) the role of women.

Roles and Relationships Within the Family

Decision-Making and Sharing of Resources can be Unequal

As well as looking at the **division of labour** and tasks in the home, sociologists have researched how **power is shared** in the home. The traditional role of the **man** holding **power to make decisions** was **so widespread** that the phrase "**who wears the trousers**" is often used to mean who's in charge.

Edgell (1980) interviewed middle class couples

He found that **men** had **decision-making control** over things both husband and wife saw as important, whilst women had control over minor decisions. Half of husbands and two thirds of wives expressed a view that sexual **equality** was a **bad thing**.

Alas, no one knows who was wearing these trousers. It's a mystery.

Pahl (1989, 1993) researched money management by 100 dual income couples

She concluded that the most common form of financial management was "**husband controlled pooling**", which she defined as: the money is shared but the husband has the dominant role in how it's spent.

Explanations for Inequality are based on Theories About Power in Society

Guess what? There are **functionalist**, **Marxist** and **feminist** theories on power in society.

1) For **functionalists**, men and women still largely perform **different tasks** and **roles** within the family because it's the **most effective way** of keeping society **running smoothly**.

2) **Marxist** sociologists interpret the fact that men and women have different roles as evidence of the **power of capitalism** to **control** family life. They say women and men have unequal roles because **capitalism works best that way**. Even with more women working outside the home in equal hours to men, the capitalist class needs to **promote women** as "naturally" **caring** and **nurturing** to ensure workers are kept fit, healthy and happy. This role for women is maintained **ideologically** through the **media**, e.g. in adverts.

3) From a **feminist** perspective, inequality in household roles demonstrates **inequality in power** between men and women. A **patriarchal** society will produce **unequal conjugal relationships** because society's **systems** and **values** will **inevitably** benefit men at the expense of women.

So, all explanations of conjugal roles lead back to **different theories** about **power in society**.

These explanations all agree that different roles for men and women in the family help to **maintain the status quo** (keep things the way they are at the moment) in society — the disagreement between them is over **who benefits**.

Practice Questions

Q1 Define the term "conjugal roles".

Q2 Describe the differences between joint and segregated conjugal roles.

Q3 What is meant by the "double burden" of women in modern society?

Q4 How was the role of "housewife" socially constructed?

Q5 Identify two areas of inequality in conjugal relationships other than household chores.

Exam Questions

Q1 Outline and evaluate the evidence that conjugal roles are still unequal in modern British society. (33 marks)

Q2 Outline and evaluate the view that power is the key to understanding relationships within the family. (33 marks)

I'll have a cup of tea while you're on your feet, love....

This is mainly about inequality in the family. You know, who does the housework, that sort of thing. Some sociologists look on the bright side and say that things are getting more equal. Others say they still aren't equal enough. Remember to look at the possible causes and social construction of inequality. And learn some of the statistics — it gets you more marks.

Roles and Relationships Within the Family

This page examines emotional work within families and the dark side of family life — domestic violence and child abuse.
These pages are for AQA and OCR.

Women *in Families can be Responsible for all the* Emotional Work

Doing **emotional work** in a family means **reacting** and **responding** to other family members' emotions, **alleviating** pain and distress, and **responding** to and **managing** anger and frustration.

1) **Diane Bell (1990)** suggested that there is an **"economy of emotion"** within all families and that running the economy is the responsibility of women.

2) She says managing family emotions is a bit like **bookkeeping** — the woman's role being to balance the family's **emotional budget**.

1) **Duncombe and Marsden (1995)** found that women in families are often required to do **housework and childcare**, **paid employment** and **emotional work** — amounting to a **"triple shift"** of work.

2) They found that married women were **happier** when their husbands **shared** some of the burden of emotional work.

3) But they also found that emotional work is predominantly **gendered** — women have the **main responsibility** for managing the whole family's emotions.

1) **Gillian Dunne (1999)** studied **lesbian households**. She found that the **distribution** of **responsibilities** such as childcare and housework tended to be **equal** between the partners. The couples were **flexible** and fair in the way they **shared work**.

2) Dunne thought that in **heterosexual relationships**, the division of work in the household was usually **less fair** because of traditional ideas about **masculinity** and **femininity**.

Some Sociologists See Child Abuse *in Terms of* Power

Sociologists study the issue of **child abuse** by parents and carers in terms of **power relationships**. You need to be able to **explain abuse** as a **form of power** rather than explore **details** of abuse itself.

A parent or carer is able to abuse a child by **manipulating** the **responsibilities and trust** which go along with the role of parent or carer. Families are **private** and separate from the rest of society. This makes it less likely for children to report abuse.

Social policies have been **adapted** to give some **protection** to children. The **Children Act 1989** was set up so the state can **intervene** in families if social workers are **concerned** about children's safety.

Domestic Violence *Affects Many Families in the UK*

Research by Professor **Elizabeth Stanko (2000)** found that:

1) A woman is **killed** by her current or former partner **every three days** in England and Wales.

2) There are 570,000 cases of **domestic violence** reported in the UK every year.

3) An incident of domestic violence occurs in the UK every **6 - 20 seconds.**

The Home Office estimates that **16% of all violent crime** in the **UK** is domestic violence.

The fourth **United Nations Women's Conference in 1995** reported that **25%** of women worldwide experience domestic violence.

Roles and Relationships Within the Family

Radical Feminists See Domestic Violence as a Form of Patriarchal Control

Radical feminist theory says **violence against women** is treated **differently** to **other violent crime**.

1) Dobash and Dobash's first UK study (1979) found the **police usually didn't record** violent crime by husbands against their wives.

2) Since 1979 the police have set up **specialist domestic violence units**, but still the **conviction rate is low** compared to other forms of assault.

3) **Before 1991**, British law said a husband was **entitled** to have **sex** with his wife **against her will**. In 1991 **the rape law changed** to say that a husband could be charged with raping his wife.

4) Evidence like that above is used by **radical feminists** to support their argument that **laws** and **social policies** in society have traditionally worked to **control women** and keep men's power in society going.

Radical feminists believe that **violence against women** within the **family** is a form of **power and control**.

> "Violence was used by the men they lived with to silence them, to 'win' arguments, to express dissatisfaction, to deter future behaviour and to merely demonstrate dominance."
> — Family Violence Professional Education Taskforce 1991, *Family Violence: Everybody's Business, Somebody's Life*, Page 116, Federation Press, Sydney, By permission of the Publisher.

The **social climate** helps to **maintain this situation** by making women feel **ashamed** and **stigmatised** if they talk about the violence. The shame and stigma are part of the **ideology of patriarchy** — the school of thought that says women should know their place.

Shame also comes from the idea that women **should know better** — not get involved with violent men in the first place. There's a tendency to **blame the victim**.

Dobash and Dobash found that most women who left violent partners returned in the end. This was because of **fear of being stigmatised** — and because they were **financially dependent** on their partner.

Abusive partners often **condition** their victim into thinking that nobody cares and there's nowhere to go. The pressure not to leave an abusive partner comes from **the relationship** as well as from society.

Remember, not all feminists agree with the radical feminist view

Radical Feminism is Criticised for Overemphasising the Power of Men

There are **two main criticisms** of **radical feminist** theory of the family.

1) It **overemphasises** the **place** of **domestic violence** in family life. **Functionalists** argue that most families operate **harmoniously** and **postmodern theory** argues that individuals have much more **choice** and **control** to avoid, leave or reshape their family relationships.

2) It presents men as **all-powerful** and women as **powerless** when in reality women often hold some power over men. The journalist **Melanie Phillips (2003)** highlights the fact that **women abuse men too** and **male victims** are often **ignored** by society and the police. The pressure group **Families Need Fathers** campaigns for men to have **equal rights** in **family** and child law.

Practice Questions

Q1 What is meant by 'emotional work' in families?
Q2 What proportion of women worldwide experience domestic violence?
Q3 What do radical feminists think is the cause of domestic violence?
Q4 Give two criticisms of the radical feminist view of domestic violence.

Exam Questions

Q1 Outline and evaluate the view that domestic violence is part of the ideology and practice of patriarchy. (33 marks)

Q2 Identify and explain the ways in which feminist sociologists have contributed to our understanding of family roles and relationships. (17 marks)

Brrrr... not pleasant, is it...

You'd be forgiven for thinking that this stuff is all a bit depressing. But abuse does happen and you need to know how society deals with it and the different explanations people have for it, fair or unfair.

Childhood

These pages examine the social construction of childhood, the position of children in today's society, and the future of childhood. ***These pages are for AQA and OCR.***

Childhood is Partly a **Social Construct**

1) Sociologists say **childhood** is not only a **biological stage of development** but a **social construct** (see p. 69) as well. The idea of how children are **different** from adults in their **values**, **behaviour** and **attitudes** isn't the same everywhere in the world, and it hasn't been the same for all times. In other words, it's **not universal** — different societies, with different cultures and values, can view childhood in different ways.

2) An example of this is how the school leaving age in Britain has moved from 12 to 16 in the last century. It would now be not only **socially unacceptable**, but also **illegal**, to leave school and work full-time at the age of 12. Effectively, the age at which childhood ends and adulthood begins has moved in line with social attitudes.

3) **Jane Pilcher (1995)** highlighted the **separateness** of childhood from other life phases. Children have different rights and duties from adults, and are regulated and protected by special laws.

Ariès says a **Cult of Childhood** Developed After Industrialisation

Sociologist Philippe Ariès' work on the construction of childhood is a classic study.

Ariès (1962) looked at paintings

Ariès said that the concept of **childhood** in Western European society has only existed in the **last 300 years**. Before this, in medieval society a child took on the role of an adult as soon as it was physically able. Children in medieval paintings look like mini-adults.

With **industrialisation** social attitudes began to value children as needing specialised care and nurturing. The importance of the child reinforced the importance of the role of the **housewife** — it was the housewife's job to look after children.

This '**cult of the child**' as Ariès referred to it first developed in the middle classes and over time has become a part of working class values.

> You need to be aware that although Ariès' work is very important, it has been criticised. E.g. Pollack says that Ariès' work looks weak because it uses paintings for its main evidence.

Children are Protected by **Special Laws**

1) Children are subject to laws that restrict their **sexual behaviour**, their **access to alcohol and tobacco**, and the amount of **paid work** they can perform. These laws act **in addition** to the laws that affect adults.

2) They are offered **additional protection** by the **Children Act 1989**, which allows them to be **taken away from their parents** by the state if it judges the parents to be **incapable** or **unsuitable**.

3) They are given **price reductions** on many **goods and services**, e.g. they pay less on **public transport** and don't have to pay **VAT on clothing**.

4) But organisations such as the **National Society for the Prevention of Cruelty to Children** (the **NSPCC**) argue that they need greater protection. An NSPCC report by **Cawson et al (2000)** said that **16%** of children aged under 16 have experienced **sexual abuse** during childhood, and **25%** of children have experienced **physical violence**.

British Society in the 21st century is More Child Focused than Ever

1) There's now lots of **social policy** related to childhood. Children are recognised as having unique **human rights**. The **United Nations Convention on the Rights of the Child** was ratified (agreed to) in 1990 by all the UN members (except the USA and Somalia).

2) In Britain the Child Support Act 1991 established the **Child Support Agency**. This gave children the legal right to be **financially supported** by their parents, whether the parents are **living with the child or not**. This Act also made courts have to ask for the **child's point of view** in custody cases and take the child's view into consideration.

3) Children also hold more **power** in modern British society than at any other time in history. This has been identified by advertisers who recognise the **financial power** of children — this is often referred to as "**pester power**". Advertisers advertise a product to children because they know the children will **pester** their parents to buy the product.

Childhood

Functionalists *See the Position of Children in Society as a* Sign of Progress

Some functionalist sociologists, including **Shorter**, make the **"march of progress"** argument:

1) Society has a functional need for **better**-educated citizens and **lower** infant mortality rates.
2) So school leaving ages have **gone up** and child protection has **improved**.
3) That means that the current position of children is the result of **positive progression** from the past.

Childhood Varies *according to* Class, Gender *and* Ethnicity

Some sociologists suggest that the experience of childhood varies depending on class, gender and ethnicity.

1) Children living in **poverty** tend to suffer poorer health, a lack of basic necessities, lower achievement in school, poorer life chances, and higher incidences of neglect and abuse.
2) **June Statham and Charlie Owens (2007)** found that black and dual-heritage children were more likely to end up in care than white or Asian children.
3) **Julia Brannen (1994)** said that Asian families were much stricter with their daughters than their sons.
4) **Hillman (1993)** found that **boys** are generally given more **freedom** by their parents than girls.

Child Liberationists *Believe that Society* Oppresses *Children*

Diana Gittins (1985) argues that there is an "age patriarchy" — adults maintain authority over children. They achieve this using enforced dependency through 'protection' from paid employment, legal controls over what children can and can't do, and in extreme cases abuse and neglect.

Hockey and James (1993) noted that childhood was a stage that most children wished to escape from and which many resisted.

Sociologists Disagree *over the* Future *of Childhood*

1) **Neil Postman (1994)** believes that childhood is **disappearing**.
2) Children grow up **very quickly** and experience things only open to adults in the past.
3) He argues that our definitions of 'childhood' and 'adulthood' will need to be **changed** soon.

1) **Nick Lee (2005)** disagrees with Postman.
2) He agrees that childhood has become an **ambiguous** area, but argues that parents have **financial control** and children can only spend as much as their parents allow.
3) So the **paradox of childhood** is one of **dependence** and **independence** at the same time.

Practice Questions

Q1 Explain how the notion of childhood has been socially constructed.
Q2 Give two ways in which 21st century British society could be said to be more child focused than before.
Q3 Describe how functionalists see the role of children in society.
Q4 How do class, ethnicity and gender influence a person's experience of childhood? Give examples.
Q5 What arguments have been put forward to support the view that childhood is disappearing?

Exam Question

Q1 Outline and evaluate the reasons for the change in status of children since industrialisation. (33 marks)

Here's looking at you, kid...

The main idea on these pages is that childhood is socially constructed and that theories about it are not universally accepted.
Remember that it's not enough to say that something is a "social construct" — you need to say how and why.

Poverty and Welfare

The sociological questions here are: "Which groups have the most / least?", "Is inequality increasing or decreasing?", "How much should the State help the poor?" and "Why does poverty exist at all?" So, that's all pretty straightforward then.
This section is for AQA only.

Wealth *is the* Value *of a* Person's Possessions

Wealth is defined in official statistics as the **value of all the possessions** of an individual **minus** any **debt**. It includes houses, land, money in the bank, shares and personal goods.

Wealth can be divided into **marketable wealth** and **non-marketable wealth**. Marketable wealth means **things you can sell**. Non-marketable wealth means things like your **salary** or a **pension fund**.

Percentage of marketable wealth owned by:	
The richest **1%** of society	**22%**
The richest **5%** of society	**42%**
The richest **10%** of society	**54%**
The richest **25%** of society	**75%**
The richest **50%** of society	**94%**

These figures come from the Social Trends 33 (2003) report by the Office of National Statistics. The pattern's pretty consistent over the last 25 years, by the way.

1)   Every year government statistics on wealth in the UK are published in the Social Trends report.

2)   The table shows that over half of the country's wealth is owned by a small percentage of the population. The less well off 50% of the population share only 6% of the country's wealth. These dramatic patterns show a society where a few people are extremely wealthy.

3)   Wealth largely results from ownership of business and property. Most of this gets passed down to the next generation, so wealth stays in the same families for years. However, lots of the richest people in Britain have generated their own wealth (see below).

The *Sunday Times* publishes a list of the **1000 richest individuals** in the UK every year.

1)   The 2003 list revealed that the super-rich are mostly men. Only 77 out of 1000 were women.

2)   753 of them were self-made millionaires, 247 inherited their wealth. The ten richest individuals had money from business and land. The wealthiest individual in Britain in 2003 was the Duke of Westminster, but in 2007 it was Lakshmi Mittal, a self-made billionaire who trades in steel. (Sunday Times Rich List © The Times, London 2003, 2007).

Income *is the* Money *a Person Receives on a* Monthly / Yearly Basis

1)   The vast **majority** of the British population **doesn't have significant wealth**. For most individuals their money comes from an **income**. Income is defined as the **personal funds an individual receives** on a **monthly / yearly basis**. This is usually from a **job** but can be from **benefits**, or **interest** on a savings account.

2)   Household **disposable income per head** has **grown steadily** in the UK since the early 1980s. This reflects **overall growth in the economy**, and could be said to show that **everyone is getting richer** to some extent.

3)   On the other hand, the **gap** between **rich and poor** has **widened** in recent years (according to Social Trends 34, 2004). This means that the rich are getting richer whilst the poor are getting **relatively** poorer. Ahhh... the stuff sociology is made of...

£9.18 a month just doesn't go as far as it did in my day.

There are Patterns *of* Which Social Groups *are likely to* Earn *the* Least

The **Social Trends** report shows how many people have an income of **less than 60% of the median income** (the government measure of poverty). The **median** income is the **middle** income. **Half** the population **earn more** than the median, **half** of them **earn less**.

1)   Households where adults are **unemployed** are **most likely** to have an **income below 60%** of the median. Which makes sense — you don't earn a lot of money when you're unemployed.

2)   According to **Social Trends 34 (2004)**, in 1998, **21%** of pensioners lived in households with **incomes of less than 60%** of the median. Which makes sense — you don't earn a lot of money when you're **retired**, either.

Poverty and Welfare

Income Also Seems to be Related to Ethnicity

The Social Trends 33 (2003) report also includes statistics about how ethnicity and income are related.

1) Overall, people in ethnic minority households were more likely than people in white households to be in the lowest earning category.

2) White, Afro-Caribbean and Indian households were pretty much equally likely to be the highest earners.

3) 64% of Pakistani and Bangladeshi households were in the lowest earning category.

4) White and Afro-Caribbean households were fairly well spread across all income groups.

Absolute Poverty is a Lack of the Minimum Requirements for Survival

1) An individual is in absolute poverty if they don't have the income to afford the basic necessities — food, warmth and shelter. By this definition there are very few individuals in the UK in poverty.

2) Rowntree (1871-1956) set up the first major studies of poverty in the UK in 1899 and measured it in absolute terms. He made a list of essentials needed for life and recorded how many families could afford them. Those whose income was too low were classed as in poverty. He found 33% of the population in York were in poverty.

3) There are criticisms of Rowntree's study. His definition of poverty didn't allow for any wasted food and it assumed the cheapest options were always available. The lists of essentials were compiled by experts and didn't match the lifestyle of the folk he surveyed. He did listen to his critics though, and for two further studies, (published in 1941 and 1951), he added more items to the list of essentials. By this time, more people could afford the basics on the list. His conclusion was that poverty was disappearing fast in 20th century Britain.

4) Another study of poverty in absolute terms is Drewnowski and Scott (1966). They devised a "level of living index" which worked out the income needed for basic needs, adding cultural needs to the list. However, it's debatable whether cultural needs like TV should be included in a study of absolute poverty.

Bradshaw (1990) Devised the Budget Standard Measure of Poverty

1) Bradshaw (1990) used an approach similar to Rowntree's idea of absolute poverty. He studied the spending patterns of the least wealthy and used those patterns to calculate an adequate budget. Anyone earning less than the adequate budget was classed as "poor".

2) The main difference between Bradshaw's approach and Rowntree's was that Bradshaw studied how people actually spend their money whereas Rowntree assumed that if people earnt more than the usual total cost of essential items then they weren't poor.

3) Because Bradshaw's test isn't relative (see p. 46), it gives clear and unambiguous statistics that are easy to compare between different studies.

4) Critics have argued that Bradshaw set a very low 'adequate budget', so his conclusions are not a true reflection of deprivation in society.

Practice Questions

Q1 Give a one-sentence definition of each of the following: wealth, income and absolute poverty.

Q2 How much of marketable wealth is owned by the richest 1% in British society, according to Social Trends, 2003? And how much is owned by the poorest 50%?

Q3 How did Bradshaw's work differ from Rowntree's?

Exam Question

Q1 Explain the meaning of the term 'income'. (2 marks)

We can all dream of being rich...

Most rows between married couples are about money. It's troublesome stuff, but you can't live without it. Learn the basic pattern of wealth distribution — if you can learn a couple of figures as well, that'd be useful. And learn how Bradshaw advanced the methods of Rowntree — they both used absolute figures but Bradshaw factored spending patterns into his calculations.

Poverty and Welfare

Not all sociologists agree with the absolute definition of poverty — they prefer relative definitions of poverty.

Relative Poverty is a Comparison with the Average Standard of Living

Many sociologists (especially left-wing ones) favour the **relative** definition of poverty.
Relative poverty shows whether an individual is rich or poor **in relation to the other people** they **share** their **society** with, rather than whether people have the basics like food and shelter.

Townsend (1979) Introduced the Concept of Relative Deprivation

1)   **Townsend (1979)** devised a **"deprivation index"** — a list of 60 things **central to life** in the UK. The list included **social activities**, such as inviting other people over for meals, and **possessions**, such as owning a refrigerator.

2)   From his list of 60 things, he selected **12** that he thought were **equally essential to the whole population**.

3)   He then gave each household a **deprivation score** based on whether or not they had the items on his shortlist of 12 items.

4)   Looking at his statistics, he found that the deprivation score **went up rapidly** after wealth dropped **below a certain threshold**. The threshold was about 150% of the 1979 basic supplementary benefit levels (now called income support).

5)   So he classified all households that **earnt below the threshold** as **"suffering from poverty"**.

6)   Using his measure, Townsend calculated that **22.9%** of the population were suffering from relative poverty.

Barney was well stocked in all his essential life items.

1)   **Piachaud (1987)** has argued that Townsend's deprivation index is too **subjective** and **culturally biased**, citing shortlist items such as having **cooked breakfasts** and **Sunday joints**.

2)   **Wedderburn** also criticised Townsend's method for creating the deprivation index. She argued that he should have carried out **research** into the customary behaviour of people in society. It seemed to her as though he had just picked items based on his own **cultural opinions**.

Mack and Lansley (1985) Measured Poverty using a Consensual Approach

1)   **Mack and Lansley (1985)** measured poverty in a similar way to Townsend, but acted on some of the criticisms his work had received. They defined poverty to be "an **enforced lack** of **socially perceived necessities**".

2)   They used a **survey** to determine which items to include on their list of perceived necessities. They asked respondents what they considered to be the necessities. Any items that were classified as essential by **over 50%** of the respondents were added to their list. They ended up with a list of **22 items**.

3)   They then surveyed households to find out which necessities they lacked. Households could answer that they had the item, wanted but couldn't afford the item or didn't want the item. Only those that said they **wanted but couldn't afford the item** were considered to be **deprived**. Mack and Lansley therefore argued that their figures would only reflect **involuntary** deprivation.

4)   If a household involuntarily lacked **three or more items** from the list of necessities then they were classified as **poor**.

5)   They reported that **14%** of the population were living in poverty in **1983**. When they repeated the study in **1990**, they found that this figure had risen to **21%**.

6)   A more recent study by **Gordon et al (2000)** found that **24%** of the population were living in poverty in 1999 according to the test set by Mack and Lansley.

Poverty and Welfare

Mack and Lansley's Studies Have Been Criticised

1) Critics have argued that because the 1990 survey and the 1983 survey didn't produce **the same list of necessities**, their results are not **directly comparable**.

2) They also argue that as long as **some difference** exists between the richest and poorest, some of the poorest will be **relatively deprived**.

The Different Definitions of Poverty have Advantages and Disadvantages

	Advantages	Disadvantages
Defining poverty absolutely	1) Absolute poverty is always measured on the **same scale** — no matter what group you're looking at. That makes it easy to **compare** statistics between groups. 2) It gives a better idea of the standard of life in **developed countries**, where people who are relatively poor may still have more than enough wealth to **meet their basic needs**.	1) Measuring absolute poverty means making some assumptions about people's **basic needs**. 2) It also assumes that everyone has **the same** basic needs. It disregards information about occupation, gender, age and culture that might be relevant to deciding someone's **basic needs**.
Defining poverty relatively	1) Relative poverty takes into account **people's expectations** and the **subjective quality** of their lives. 2) So it gives a **more realistic** picture of the **relative** deprivation that is caused by **inequalities in society**.	1) As long as there is **any difference** between people in society, some of them will **appear to be "poor"** in a relative poverty study. 2) If the rich are getting richer **more quickly** than the poor are getting richer, then relative poverty will **increase** even though the lives of the poor are **improving**.

How much poverty there is out there really depends on how it's **defined** and **measured**.
With an **absolute** definition of poverty, Rowntree concluded **poverty** was soon to be a **thing of the past**.
Studies based on the **relative** definition of poverty suggest that poverty **persists** in the UK.

But then again, it always will because it's <u>relative</u>.

Practice Questions

Q1 Give two advantages of defining poverty absolutely.

Q2 What was Townsend's "deprivation index"?

Q3 How did Mack and Lansley's work differ from Townend's?

Q4 What is the difference between measuring absolute poverty and measuring relative poverty?

Exam Question

Q1 Assess the problems involved in defining and measuring poverty. (24 marks)

Poverty is a bad thing, no matter how you measure it...

Make sure you understand the difference between relative poverty and absolute poverty and between voluntary and involuntary deprivation. Townsend studied poverty by looking at what households lacked. Mack and Lansley's work was similar, but they used surveys to work out what society thinks a household should possess, and allowed for voluntary deprivation.

Explanations of Wealth Distribution

Evidence shows that wealth is distributed unequally, and that incomes vary from small to huge. To sociologists, a pattern like this needs explanation — and of course there are lots of different explanations for the way that wealth is shared out.

Early Theories **Blamed the Poor** for Being Poor

1) The first theories of poverty **blamed the individual** for the poverty they were in.

2) The **19th century** sociologist **Herbert Spencer** said the **poor** were those in society who had **failed** to do the best for themselves. He suggested that they were immoral, lazy and more interested in booze than an honest day's work.

3) Spencer said the **state shouldn't intervene** to help the poor because the poor are a useful **example to others** not to follow that way of life.

Functionalists Say **Unequal Distribution** of **Wealth** is **Good** for Society

Functionalism says some people are richer / poorer than others because **society functions that way**. **Functionalist theory** argues that as societies develop, they have to find a way of allocating people to suitable roles and jobs. The most **important jobs** need to be **rewarded more highly than others** to motivate **intelligent people** to **train** and **qualify** for them. The key study to know here is *Some Principles of Stratification* (**Davis and Moore 1949**). Don't worry that it's old — it's classical functionalism.

Functionalist arguments have been **criticised** — they assume the best jobs are allocated on the basis of **talent** when in reality **discrimination** by social class, age, ethnicity and gender often influences who gets the top jobs. **Tumin (1967)** reckons that Davis and Moore **ignore all the talent and ability in the working class** which society doesn't use.

Weberians Say Distribution of Wealth is Based on **Market Situation**

1) Weberian sociologists (followers of **Max Weber**) say that the distribution of wealth and income is based on what they call **market situation**.

2) An individual's market situation is how **valuable** their **skills** are for society and how **scarce** their skills are. It's about **supply and demand** of skills. High demand for your skills makes them worth more.

3) For example, currently **plumbers** can earn **higher wages** than other skilled manual workers, because there's a **shortage** of plumbers and people **need their skills**. So plumbers have a good market situation at the moment.

4) Weberians say **poor people** have a **poor market situation**.

5) There **isn't always the same demand** for the **same skills** — the same people don't always have the best market situation. This means there's always some **movement of wealth in society**.

6) Individuals **compete** to improve their market situation. **Powerful people** like judges, politicians and the directors of big companies can do the most to keep themselves in a good market situation.

Car mechanics are always in demand in the tiger economies.

Marxists Blame Capitalism for Inequalities in Wealth and Income

1) Marxists say that the social groups which have **low levels of wealth** and **income** are the ones which are **powerless** in society.

2) According to Marx and his followers, **capitalism thrives** on **inequality of income** — if there were equal distribution of wealth there wouldn't be any profit for the capitalists. The capitalist class **needs profit** to keep up its **power in society**.

3) Marxism says **exploitation** is an **essential part of capitalism** — and inequalities in wealth and income are a central part of that exploitation.

4) Marx predicted that as capitalism develops, **more oppression** of the proletariat (working class) is needed. Marxists say the current **widening gap between rich and poor** is evidence of this.

As you may have noticed, the Marxist explanations for most things are quite similar. Capitalism, exploitation, etc., etc...

Explanations of Wealth Distribution

Recent **Changes in Society** Have **Increased** the **Gap** between **Rich** and **Poor**

1) The gap between the income of the rich and the income of the poor **went down** in the **1970s**.
   Under the **Labour government (1974-1979)**, **benefits** given to the poor **went up** and taxes paid
   by the rich were **very high**.

2) In the **1980s**, under the Conservative government, the **gap widened**. The top rate of tax went down
   so the **rich kept more of their earnings**. Taxes that everyone pays like **VAT** and **fuel tax** went up.
   The economy did well, so rich people earned more money on their **investments**. **Benefits** went **down**.

3) **Adonis and Pollard (1997)** reported that the gap continued to widen into the 1990s. In addition to policies introduced
   during the 1980s, they identified the **increase in private education** as a factor affecting wealth distribution.

4) An **Office of National Statistics** report by **Penny Babb (2004)** based on the 2001 census suggested that the gap
   between rich and poor continued to grow under New Labour.

5) There has been an **increase** in the number of **single parent households**. Single parent households
   tend to have less money (see below) and this means the statistics show **more poorer households**.

6) There are also more **two earner households** — e.g. families where both parents work.
   Income is measured by household, so a **household with two people** in **good jobs** is
   relatively rich. This contributes to the statistics showing an **increase in rich households**.

Some Social Groups are **More Likely to be Poor** Than Others

For these statistics, poverty is defined as having an income that's less than 60% of the median income.

> **Women** — in 1992, there were **5.2 million women** living in **poverty** in the UK, compared to **4.2 million men**.
>
> **Older people** — in 1992, **32%** of households where the **main adult was over 60** were poor.
>
> **Single parents** — in 1992, **58%** of **single parents** had an income of less than half the average.
>
> **Disabled people** — in 1996, **47%** of **disabled** people had an income of less than half the average.
>
> **Ethnic minorities** — in 1997, the Policy Studies Institute said that overall UK ethnic minorities are **more likely**
> to be poor. **Pakistani** and **Bangladeshi** households are the most likely to have **low income**.

1) Women tend to be poorer than men **partly** because they're **more likely** to be **single parents** than men.
   Working mums are more likely to be in **part-time jobs** that fit in with childcare, but that pay less.

2) Older people tend to be poorer because they're **retired** — some retired people only get a **basic state pension**.

3) **Single parent** families tend to be poor because it's hard to get **good work** and **look after kids** at the same time.

4) **Disabled** people face **discrimination** in the job market. Disabled people, and people with long-term illnesses who
   can't work, live on **incapacity benefit** and **disability benefit**, which means they have a fixed, relatively low income.

5) **Some ethnic minorities** tend to be **richer / poorer** than others — and there's **variation** in the
   level of income within ethnic minority groups. It's not as clear-cut as the statistics suggests.

Practice Questions

Q1 Why did Spencer argue inequality of income is good for society?

Q2 How does an individual's market situation affect their wealth?

Q3 Did the gap between rich and poor decrease or increase in the 1980s?

Q4 Write down five groups in British society who are more likely to be poor than others.

Exam Questions

Q1 Examine the view that "Inequality in wealth is beneficial to society".   (24 marks)

Q2 Examine the social composition of the poor in British society.   (24 marks)

Ever seen how much plumbers charge...

Remember that the gap between rich and poor went down, then up again. It's mainly related to tax and benefits. Learn those functionalist, Weberian and Marxist explanations for the distribution of wealth. You can probably guess the functionalist one: "it's all for the best" and the Marxist: "it's cos of evil capitalism, grr". Watch out for those Weberians and their plumber though.

Why Does Poverty Exist?

Unsurprisingly, different schools of sociological thought have different explanations of why poverty exists.

Oscar Lewis said Culture was the Cause of Poverty

Lewis (1959, 1961, 1966) studied the poor in Mexico and Puerto Rico

Lewis thought that the **values**, **norms** and **behaviour** of the **poor** were **different** to the rest of society and these values were passed on from generation to generation.

He said individuals learn how to be poor and learn to expect to be poor through the subculture of poverty they're socialised into.

He reckoned that this **culture** of resignation, apathy and lack of participation in wider society initially starts as a response to poverty but then becomes a culture which keeps people in poverty. He called it a '**design for life**'.

1) Lewis's work was **controversial** and **criticised** from the start. Similar research done at the same time found **highly organised community facilities** and **political involvement**.

2) **Schwartz (1975)** concluded that the poor **weren't culturally different** from the well-off.

1) Situational Constraints theory says that the poor have the **same values and norms** as the **rest of society** and any difference in the **behaviour** of the poor is because they're **limited** by their **poverty**. For example, unemployment restricts lifestyle options.

2) **Coates and Silburn (1970)** studied poor areas of Nottingham. They found that **some people** in poor areas **did feel resigned to being poor**, and that it wasn't worth trying to get out of poverty. But... they said this was actually a **realistic assessment** of an individual's situation. It **wasn't proof** of some kind of **alternative value system**.

3) Coates and Silburn's research supported the idea that **poverty leads to other forms of deprivation** which can trap people into a **cycle of deprivation**. This means poverty is **practically hard to get out of**, not culturally hard to get out of.

Different Reasons have been Given for the Growth of Poverty

1) **Brewer and Gregg (2002)** argued that **changes in the economy** have caused a growth in poverty rates.

2) They identified an increase in the number of households with **no working adults** at one end of the scale and an increase in the number of households with **two working adults** at the other. These changes have led to an increase in the **gap** between **high earning households** and **low earning households**.

3) They also found that **reductions in income tax** for employed people had been **greater than raises in benefits** for unemployed people. This caused an **increase in relative poverty**.

1) **Smith, Smith and Wright (1997)** think that **modern educational policy** reinforces current trends in poverty.

2) They say that **market-driven educational reforms** (see p. 65) favour middle class children. So working-class children are more likely to end up in **failing schools**.

3) They also found that the **abolition of maintenance grants** in 1998 means that working class children are less likely to consider **going to university**.

4) They argue that a **poorer education** leads to **poorer work opportunities**, reinforcing the **gap in earnings** between rich and poor.

New Right Theorists Blame Dependency on Welfare for Poverty

1) **Charles Murray (1993)** described a sector of society which he thought had a **culture of dependency on the state** and an **unwillingness to work**. He called this group the **underclass**.

2) Murray identified the **rising number** of **single parent families**, **rising crime**, and **attitudes** of **resistance to work**. Murray accepts that not all poor people are work-shy but he thinks a significant group just don't want to work.

3) In Murray's opinion, **Welfare State benefits** are **too high**. He says this means there's not much encouragement to get off welfare and get a job.

4) Another right-wing sociologist, **Marsland (1989)**, thinks that the **level of poverty** is **exaggerated** by other writers. He says society should **keep a small level of poverty** to **motivate** others to work. Marsland agrees with Murray that the **Welfare State is too generous** and encourages a **culture of non-work** amongst some groups.

Sociological **criticism** of Murray says his **evidence** for the existence of an underclass is **too weak**. **Walker (1990)** found **very little evidence** of **different values** and **behaviour** among the poor. His opinion was that **blaming** the poor **distracts** from the **real causes** of poverty such as the **failure of social policy**.

Why Does Poverty Exist?

Weberian Sociologists Blame Inequalities in the Labour Market

1) **Max Weber** thought that an individual's **position in the labour market** was the key to their life chances, wealth and status. The people whose skills were most **valued** and **needed** would always be the **wealthiest**.

2) **Dean and Taylor-Gooby (1992)** think that **changes in the UK labour market** have led to increased poverty. There are more casual and temporary jobs, but less job security and far fewer "jobs for life". Dean and Taylor-Gooby say this means more people are likely to experience poverty at some point.

3) **Townsend (1970, 1979)** has the view that the key **explanation for poverty** is the **low status** of some workers, which doesn't give them much power to improve their labour market situation.

Marxists Blame the Capitalist System for Poverty

Marxists think that the working class tends to be poor because of capitalist exploitation. They say it's a mistake to focus on the poor as a **separate group** — poverty comes from **class structure**, so sociologists should focus on the **working class** instead.

They think that **poverty exists** because it **serves the needs of the capitalist class** in society. **Kincaid (1973)** explains it like this:

1) The low-paid provide a **cheap labour supply** for the **capitalist class**, which keeps **profits high**.

2) The varying pay levels within the working class keep individuals **competing** against each other to get the best jobs. This **divides the working class**. Marxism says that if the working class all **united together** they'd be a **threat** to capitalism — so it's in the **interests of capitalism** to keep the **working class divided**.

3) Kincaid believes poverty is **not an accident** — he thinks it's an **inbuilt part** of the capitalist system.

Marxists say welfare benefits don't do much good

1) Marxist sociologists **Westergaard and Resler (1976)** argue that state benefits only **blunt the extremes** of poverty.

2) They say that **welfare benefits stay low** so that people **still need to sell their labour** even if their wages are low.

3) They also argue that most of the **money paid out in welfare benefits** has been **paid in by the working class in tax** or **subsidised by their low wages**. The working class are getting their own money back, not money from the rich.

Marxist Explanations of Poverty Have Been Criticised

1) Marxist explanations of poverty **don't explain** why some groups in society are much more likely to experience poverty than others. Marxists treat poverty (and just about everything else) as a **characteristic of capitalism**, and as something that the **working class as a whole** suffers. They don't look for much **detail** about the experience of poverty for **individuals** or **groups**.

2) Marxism **ignores** the effects of **gender** and **ethnicity** on poverty. It doesn't explain why women are more likely to be poor than men, or why Bangladeshi households are more likely to be poor than Afro-Caribbean households.

3) **Townsend (1970, 1979) rejects** the argument that the Welfare State (e.g. state benefits) doesn't do much good. He believes that **social policy can and should improve standards of living** even within a capitalist system.

4) **Capitalism** creates **wealth** in the economy. This increase in wealth contributes to the **reduction of absolute poverty**.

Practice Questions

Q1 Give an example of an attitude and a behaviour which Lewis (1959, 1961, 1966) argues causes poverty.

Q2 What does Murray (1993) identify as the key processes which create an underclass?

Q3 Give an example of how poverty is helpful to the capitalist class, from a Marxist perspective.

Exam Question

Q1 Assess the view that the poor are to blame for their poverty. (24 marks)

Blame the victim or blame the system...

It's not as easy as you might think to explain why people get stuck in poverty. Each of these theories makes some sense, but they don't all look at the big picture. When you're answering an exam question that asks you to "critically examine the arguments" bear that in mind — remember the downsides of each theory. Use one theory to criticise another.

Social Policy and Poverty

You need to know what kind of things governments do to sort out poverty.

The **New Right** believes in the Reduction of the **Welfare State**

1) The **New Right** think that a **generous welfare state** actually **makes people poorer**.

2) British New Right thinker **Marsland (1989)** thinks all **universal benefits** (paid to everyone regardless of wealth) should be abolished because they **encourage dependency**. He says that benefits should only exist to support those in the most desperate need for the shortest possible time. He argues that this will encourage people to "stand on their own two feet".

3) **Right wing policy** encourages **business** so that **wealth will be created**. Right wing politicians would prefer everyone to make their own money and decide how to spend it, instead of paying lots of tax or getting benefits from the state.

4) American sociologist **Murray (1993)** recommended a "**moral**" benefits system to discourage people from forming **single parent families**. He thought that unmarried mums should get no benefit at all.

> In the UK, the most recent Conservative governments (1979-1997) were influenced by New Right theory. They **reduced spending** on welfare by removing some universal benefits and having benefits **only for the poorest**. They made it clear that they wanted to **get rid of the dependency culture** by **reducing benefits** and **allowances**.
>
> The idea was that people would be **better off working**.
>
> The idea was also that resources freed up by these welfare cuts would **boost the economy**, which would benefit society as a whole. Conservatives said the money at the top would "**trickle down**" to make **everyone** in society wealthier.

Examples of Conservative welfare reforms

1) **Stopped paying benefits** to **16-18** year olds.

2) **Replaced grants** for basic necessities with **loans**.

3) **Abolished** entitlement of **students** to **benefits** in the **academic holiday**.

4) Introduced the **Child Support Agency** — forcing **absent parents** to pay for the support of children, rather than the state.

People on low incomes used to be able to get a "social fund" grant to buy things like a new cooker. Nowadays they can get a loan, which they have to pay back.

So, some of the **New Right solutions to poverty** have **been tried** in the UK. They've been criticised by some sociologists for **increasing** relative poverty.

Social Democrats Believe Social Policy Reforms Could Solve Poverty

Social Democrats see **institutions** in society as the cause of poverty. They believe **inequality** in **wealth and income** is the root cause of poverty, so they want government policy to **redistribute wealth** and resources from **rich** to **poor**.

The big idea is that the state **should** work to stamp out poverty — and that the state **can** work to stamp out poverty.

1) Social democratic theory says **increasing welfare provision** will help to **solve poverty**.

2) **Mack and Lansley (1985)** suggest a big increase in benefits. They conducted a public opinion poll in which British people said they were **prepared to pay higher taxes** to get rid of poverty.

3) **Townsend** sees the solution to poverty in the **labour market**. He says **social policy** must have the job of **reducing inequalities** in the labour market.

4) The poor are most often unemployed or low-paid. This means **policies** are needed to **improve wages** and conditions and to **protect workers' rights**. The **National Minimum Wage** and **Working Families' Tax Credit** brought in under the New Labour government are examples of this kind of intervention.

5) British sociologists **Walker and Walker (1994)** argue for an "active employment strategy" where the government would actually **create work** for the unemployed.

> Social democratic theory has been **criticised** by people on the **right wing** and on the **left wing**.
>
> 1) **New Right** theorists say the social democratic policy of **strengthening the Welfare State** and increasing the power of social policy would be an **absolute disaster** in terms of solving poverty. The New Right say these things led to the increase in poverty in the first place.
>
> 2) Left wing **Marxists** say the **state** will always **serve the interests** of those in **power**, which means that nothing the government does can make a big difference to poverty in capitalist society.

Social Policy and Poverty

Since 1997, the New Labour Government has had a "Third Way" Approach

When New Labour took power in Britain in 1997, it claimed its social policies would reduce poverty significantly. Their philosophy **combines** both the **New Right** and the **social democratic** theories — so it was called "**the third way**".

The theme was that the poor need "**a hand up not a handout**". The "hand up" part means the state should have **social policies** which **help the poor** — rather like the social democratic theory. The "not a handout" part means people **shouldn't depend** on benefits — rather like **New Right theory**.

They say the state has a responsibility to **help people in real need**, and individuals have a **responsibility to help themselves**. The "**New Welfare Contract**" of 1998 says that the **government** has to **help people find work**, make **work pay**, help with **childcare**, help the **poorest** old people and help those who really **can't work**. It says that **individuals** have to look for work, be as **independent as possible**, support their own family, save for retirement and not defraud the taxpayer by claiming benefit when they shouldn't.

Don't worry — you don't need to know all the New Labour social reforms in detail. Here are some examples which help show the ideology behind them.

Reforms to remove dependency on benefits — so working pays more than benefits...

1) **Working Families' Tax Credit** — tax reductions for the **low-paid but working**.
2) **National Minimum Wage** — to ensure every employer **pays more than benefit levels**.
3) **New Deal** — a **training** and **support** package for people **returning to work** from benefits.
4) **Welfare to Work** — a series of opportunities for **young, unemployed people** paid for by tax on profits of privatised gas and electricity companies.
5) **Income Tax cuts** — they halved the **starter rate** (the lowest rate), meaning that poorer families **keep more** of what they **earn**.
6) **Educational Maintenance Allowance** — extra money for **students** from poorer backgrounds who stay in education after they're 16. By keeping people in education for longer, New Labour hope that they'll be less likely to need benefits later on.

Reforms to make the poor less socially excluded and isolated

1) **Social Exclusion Unit** — launched to provide support to **reintegrate excluded people** back into society.
2) The concept of **stakeholders** — individuals could own a stake in organisations which affect them, either in financial terms or voting power.
3) **Childcare costs** paid for or subsidised by the government.

> There is conflicting evidence as to whether the government has achieved a reduction in poverty since 1997. The Social Trends 33 (2003) report showed that the distribution of wealth had changed little over the past 28 years. The number of people classed as unemployed had fallen though.

Marxists say Nothing Will Work Except the Overthrow of Capitalism

1) Marxists believe that the root cause of poverty is the **inequality** central to the **capitalist system**. Therefore, the Marxist solution to poverty is the **removal** of the **capitalist system**.
2) Marxists say that while the capitalist system keeps on going, poverty will still be around — **no matter** what **social policy** you throw at it. **Westergaard and Resler (1976)** think no big **redistribution of wealth** can happen until capitalism is overthrown and replaced by a **socialist** society where **wealth is communally owned**.
3) The most **common criticism** of the Marxist approach is the **evidence** that **socialist** and **communist societies haven't eradicated poverty**. People were poor in Soviet Russia and there is poverty in Cuba.

Practice Questions

Q1 Why do the New Right think that the Welfare State can be too generous?
Q2 Give an example of a social policy which could be used to lessen poverty.
Q3 Explain how Marxist theory argues poverty could be eradicated in Britain.

Exam Question

Q1 Assess the view that ideology lies behind all solutions to poverty. (24 marks)

Sounds great on paper — but will it work in real life?

Although the four theories here are different, they all make some kind of sense on paper. It'd probably be great if everyone earned enough money to buy the best kind of private welfare. It'd probably be great if the state provided really good public welfare for everybody. In real life it's hard to make things work. At the moment, the jury's still out on the Third Way idea.

Welfare Provision

Welfare means all the institutions that look after people — whether they're state-provided or not.

Four Sectors provide Welfare — Public, Private, Voluntary and Informal

Public Sector

These are **state services** which are **funded**, **regulated** and **run by the state**. Examples — the NHS, the free **education system** and the **benefits system**. Most services are **free at the point of delivery** and are **funded by taxes** and **national insurance**.

Private Sector

These services are **run by companies for profit**. They often offer **alternatives** to state services — e.g. **private hospitals**, **schools** and **nurseries**. There's no state funding but they have to **meet state regulations**. The individual **pays for these services directly**.

Voluntary Sector

These services are provided by **charity**. They often provide **extra** facilities and services beyond what the state provides. E.g. the **hospice** movement and **Help the Aged**. They have to **conform to state regulations**. Voluntary services **may get some state funding**. The individual receives these services **free** or at a **subsidised low cost**.

Informal Sector

This means services and help provided by **friends and family** as and when needed. The informal sector often provides services **in addition to state services** or when there isn't **enough state provision**. Examples — **family carers**, **family childminders**. There's **little** or **no state funding** or **regulation**. It's usually **free** to the individual but **costs the provider money**.

1) The **combination** of all four types of welfare provision is known as **welfare pluralism**.

2) The British system is based on welfare pluralism. Since the 1979 Conservative government, there has been a **steady growth** in **private**, **voluntary** and **informal sector welfare** and a **relative decline** in **public sector welfare**.

The Welfare State — Health, Housing, Education, Social Work and Benefits

1) The British **Welfare State** was set up in the **1940s** after the **Beveridge Report** was published. The Welfare State was designed to wipe out the social problems of society. Beveridge defined these as the **"five evils"**.

Ignorance (poor education)	⟹ **1944 Education Act**
Disease (poor health)	⟹ **NHS set up in 1946**
Want (poverty)	⟹ **National Insurance Act**
Idleness (unemployment)	⟹ **National Assistance Act**
Squalor (poor housing)	⟹ **Council Housing Programme**

2) People in work would pay into a **national insurance scheme** which would **pay for the Welfare State**. The Welfare State was designed to be free at the point where you actually needed it. For example, going to the doctor = free.

3) The British Welfare State is **universal**. This means all benefits and services are given to **everyone** rather than **selectively** to the poorest. **Checking** that people are **poor enough** to get a selective benefit is called **means testing**.

4) The **cost of the Welfare State** has **risen a lot**. (This graph is based on information from the **Centre for Analysis of Social Exclusion**, CASEbrief 5, April **1998**).

Welfare spending in billions of pounds measured at 1996 prices

Year	Spending
73-74	103.9
76-77	124.8
79-80	122.1
83-84	133.3
89-90	143.6
93-94	177.8
95-96	182.6

There have been a lot of **Conservative reforms** to **reduce the size** of the Welfare State and **cut costs**.

1) **Increase** in **selective benefits** — e.g. 1980 Housing Act, 1988 Social Security Act.

2) **Reduction** in **universal benefits** — e.g. general entitlement to free eye tests abolished.

3) **Privatisation** of welfare provision — e.g. local authority care homes closed, replaced by private care homes.

4) **Increase** in **voluntary** and **charitable** welfare provision — e.g. housing associations taking over council houses.

Under **New Labour** there's been an emphasis on trying to make the NHS and social security more **efficient** to **save money**. Most benefits and services cut by the Conservative governments **haven't been reintroduced**.

Welfare Provision

Social Democrats believe the Welfare State can Reduce Inequality

The founders of the Welfare State thought it'd **reduce inequality** because the rich and poor would all get the **same benefits** and **services**. Resources would be shared out more **equally**. Part of the vision of the Welfare State was that these policies would help create a society where all people had **equal opportunities**. But...

...There's research demonstrating **persistent hard-to-shift inequality** in all five areas of welfare — **health**, **education**, **housing**, **unemployment** and **poverty**. A good overall study by **Le Grand (1982)** found not much evidence of redistribution of resources. Le Grand found that **middle class** families were more likely to use the free services of the welfare state — not the working class, or the poor.

Marxist sociologists **Westergaard and Resler (1976)** argue that the welfare state has failed to reduce inequality between social classes in Britain. Their research focused on **tax** and **benefits**, and concluded that the **working class contributed most** as a **proportion** of their **income** and that the **middle class benefited the most**. However, the middle classes as a group pay most in terms of the total tax received by the government. Some sociologists have argued that by focusing on the contribution as a proportion of total income, **Westergaard and Resler** emphasised the inequality aspect.

The New Right Prefer Selective Benefits and Means Testing

1) Remember, the New Right theory blames poverty on an **overgenerous welfare state**.

2) So, from the New Right point of view, the ideal welfare state has a **small range** of **minimal benefits** which are only selectively available to the very **poorest**.

3) Selective benefits would be **means tested** the government would only provide them to people whose incomes were below a certain level.

4) The New Right say that governments must focus on creating a **strong economy**. In a strong economy **private welfare providers** can compete giving individuals **choice** and **value**. New Right thinkers reckon the **free market economy** is the **best way** to ensure services are provided at the **lowest prices** and the **best quality**.

5) The New Right think that a **strong market** will encourage individual endeavour, leading to an increase in standards of living for everybody. The Welfare State would only be needed as an **emergency back-up**.

For Marxists the Welfare State Reproduces and Legitimises Capitalism

1) According to Marxists, the Welfare State makes sure the capitalist class always has a **healthy workforce** through the NHS. For Marxists, they don't do this to be **nice** to the individual worker but to **keep them working**, which is essential to keep **making profits**.

2) The Welfare State helps to portray the image of a **caring society** where the state **cares** for the individual. Marxists say this is **useful** to the capitalist class because it **hides** the real **oppressive** nature of capitalism and **keeps the working class quiet** — which prevents a revolution.

3) Not all Marxists agree, mind you. An **alternative Marxist view** is that the **Welfare State exists** because it was **fought for** by **workers' struggle** and the capitalist class wouldn't have provided it otherwise.

Practice Questions

Q1 Name four sectors which provide welfare.
Q2 What were the key social problems the Welfare State was founded to address?
Q3 List four Conservative reforms of welfare provision.
Q4 Outline the findings of Le Grand (1982).

Exam Questions

Q1 Explain the difference between public sector and private sector welfare. (4 marks)

Q2 Examine the Marxist theory of the Welfare State. (24 marks)

Shall we give the poor some money, or shall we not bother...

You might think that the New Right theorists are all mean old grumpyboots with no heart, or that Marxists are just dreamers with no grip on reality. The thing is, they both genuinely believe they're doing the best for everyone. With these social policies, it's hard to tell who's wrong and who's right, but you can look at real-life examples — most of these ideas have been tried somewhere.

The Role of the Education System

Section Four is for AQA only. Different theories try to explain the role or function of education in society. Some of them look at the positive functions. Some look at how education oppresses pupils and maintains inequality. Some look at pupil interaction in the classroom. Some say we should get rid of school altogether... Yay.

Functionalism *Says Education Has* **Three Functions** *that Help Society*

1)   Education teaches the **skills** needed in **work** and by the **economy**.

2)   Education **sifts and sorts people** for the **appropriate jobs**. This is called the **allocation** function.

3)   Education plays a part in **secondary socialisation**, passing on **core values**.

1)   **Durkheim** said that education passes on **norms** and **values** in order to **integrate** individuals into society. Education helps to **create social order** based on cohesion and value **consensus**.

2)   **Parsons** describes school as a bridge between the family and adult roles of society. Schools pass on a **universal value** of **achievement**. Parsons says that education **selects** children into **appropriate roles** because it's **meritocratic** (meaning that the best students rise to the top). He agrees with Durkheim that education helps to make people agree about norms and values.

3)   **Davis and Moore (1945)** say that every society sorts its members into different positions. They think that there are **rules** for how education does this — called "**principles of stratification**". They believe that there has to be a system of **unequal rewards** (more money or status) to **motivate** people to train for the top positions.

> The **functionalist** perspective says that education is **meritocratic**. A **meritocracy** is when social **rewards** are allocated by **talent** and **effort** rather than because of a position someone was **born** into.
>
> **Talent + motivation + equal opportunity = qualifications and a high position in society**

Marxism *Says* **Education Legitimises Inequality** *through* **Ideology**

1)   Education **prepares children** for the **world of work** by giving them **skills** and **values** they'll need.

2)   Education **justifies inequality**.

3)   Education passes on **ruling class ideology** that **supports capitalism**.

1)   The neo-Marxist **Althusser** sees education as part of the "ideological state apparatus". In other words, it's a tool of capitalism which is used to pass on the belief that society is fair. Althusser thinks education produces a **docile and obedient workforce**.

2)   **Bowles and Gintis (1976)** say that there is a close link between school and work. They say that there's a **correspondence** between **pupil experiences of school** and **adult work**:
- Pupils are taught to accept the **hierarchy** at school. Work also has a hierarchy.
- Pupils are **motivated by grades** to do **boring work**. Workers are **rewarded with pay** to do **boring work**.
- The **school day** is broken into **small units**. So is the **work day**.
- At school and work **subservience** (following the rules) is **rewarded**.

    Bowles and Gintis say that the '**hidden curriculum**' (things like being on time for lessons, and doing your homework) **prepares people for work**. They also say that meritocracy is a **myth** used to **blame individuals** for not succeeding.

3)   **Willis (1977)** says that education **doesn't turn out** an **obedient workforce**. Some kids form an **anti-school subculture** and cope with school and then adult work by mucking about.

4)   **Bourdieu** used the concept of **cultural capital** (language, skills, knowledge and attitudes) to explain how the middle class get into the top positions. There's **plenty** on this on pages 58–59.

Radicals *like* **Illich** *Want to* **Get Rid Of School Completely**

Illich (1971) believes that education has four functions:

Illich agrees with functionalists about the functions of school — but he thinks the functions aren't good enough. So we should give up school as a bad idea.

1)   Education **looks after kids** during the day.

2)   Education **sorts pupils into job roles**.

3)   Education **passes on dominant values**.

4)   Education helps people learn **skills and knowledge**.

The problem for Illich is that schools **don't create equality** or **develop creativity**. Illich wants to "**deschool society**". He wants everyone to have **access to education throughout their lives** according to what they need.

The Role of the Education System

There are **Problems** with **Functionalist** and **Marxist Views**

Criticisms of Functionalism

1) Evidence of **differential achievement** in terms of class, gender and ethnicity suggests that education is **not meritocratic**.

2) **"Who you know"** is still more important than "what you know" in some parts of society. So the allocation function isn't working properly.

3) It can be argued that the education system **doesn't prepare people** adequately for **work**. For example, the lack of engineering graduates indicates education is failing to produce what **employers** and the **economy** needs.

4) Functionalism doesn't look at how education may serve the interests of particular groups in terms of **ideology** and **values**. It **doesn't explain conflict**.

Criticisms of Marxism

1) Marxism assumes people are **passive victims**. It **exaggerates** how much working class students are **socialised** into **obedience**. Willis showed how students actually resist authority.

2) Most people are **aware of the inequality** in education. Most people don't believe that society is fair.

The problem with both approaches is that they don't look at interaction and social processes within the school.

There are **Similarities** and **Differences** Between **Functionalist** and **Marxist Views**

1) Both functionalism and Marxism look at the **big picture** — institutions and the whole structure of society. They tend to **ignore social interaction** — with the exception of Willis. Both say education has a **huge impact** on the individual and that there's a **close link** with the **economy** and **work**.

2) The biggest **difference** is how they see **inequality**. Marxists say education helps to **maintain inequality** and **make people accept inequality**. Functionalists say education passes on the value of **meritocracy** and lets people **better themselves**.

Feminists say that the Education System is **Patriarchal**

1) Some feminists argue that the hidden curriculum unofficially **reinforces gender differences**.

2) There are still **gender differences** in **subject choice** in schools. Gender stereotyping may still exist.

3) Girls are now outperforming boys at school — but **boys** still **demand more attention** from the teacher.

4) **Men** seem to dominate the top positions in schools (**head teacher**, **deputy head**) and even more so in universities.

Liberal feminists want **equal access to education for both sexes**.
Radical feminists believe men are a bad influence, and want **female-centred education** for girls.
Marxist feminists want to consider gender inequalities **combined with inequalities** of **class** and **ethnicity**.

Practice Questions

Q1 Name three functions that the education system performs according to functionalists.
Q2 What is meant by meritocracy?
Q3 Name two functionalist studies of education.
Q4 What did Bowles and Gintis say pupils' experience of education had a close correspondence with?
Q5 Give two problems with the Marxist theory of education.
Q6 What is the difference between Marxist and functionalist approaches to education?

Exam Questions

Q1 Identify two ways in which schooling in capitalist societies mirrors the working world. (4 marks)

Q2 Examine the Marxist view that the function of the education system is to pass on ideology and reproduce the existing class structure. (20 marks)

Getting rid of school sounds good, but what'd you have instead?

*Mmm, there's lots of theory here. If you know what Marxism, functionalism and feminism are, then their views of school **shouldn't come as a big shock**. Functionalists think education brings social harmony. Marxists say school is there to produce an obedient workforce. Feminists think school reinforces gender inequality and difference. They're so predictable.*

Class and Differential Achievement in Education

Sociologists have investigated how social class affects how well people do at school.
Financial and cultural factors are studied, as well as in-school factors like streaming.

Social Class tends to Affect Educational Achievement

1) Pupils from **professional** backgrounds are significantly **more likely** to enter **higher education** than those from unskilled backgrounds.

2) Pupils from **middle class** backgrounds are more likely to study for **A-Levels**, whereas **working class** pupils are more likely to take **vocational** subjects.

3) Pupils from disadvantaged backgrounds are **more likely** to **leave school at 16** and **less likely** to start school being able to **read**.

4) Pupils from **unskilled backgrounds** on average achieve **lower scores** on SATs and in GCSEs and are more likely to be placed in **lower streams** or **bands**.

I wonder if class affects how well you do in a school of fish...

Some sociologists have suggested that the relative intelligence levels of different socio-economic and ethnic groups account for discrepancies in educational attainment (**Eysenck (1971)** and others). But it is difficult to determine whether IQ or social factors are more important to educational achievement.

Processes Inside School — Labelling, Streaming and Subcultures are Factors

1) **Negative labelling** of students can lead to a **self-fulfilling prophecy of failure**. **Becker (1971)** and **Keddie (1971)** say that teachers tend to evaluate pupils in terms of an **ideal student**, by looking at appearance, personality, speech and social class.

2) Negative labelling can mean students get put into **lower streams or bands**. **Ball (1981)** found that the pupils in the top bands were from **higher social classes**. Teachers had **higher expectations** of them and they were **taught in different ways**. Keddie found that teachers allowed pupils in the top streams access to higher levels of knowledge. Working class students didn't get this knowledge.

3) As a response to negative labelling and frustration with low status, pupils may form **anti-school subcultures**. **Hargreaves (1975)** found that those in the **bottom streams** were more likely to be non-conformist. **Woods (1983)** responded by saying that there are lots of different reactions to school, but **non-conformist** reactions were more likely to come from **working class** students.

These explanations are useful when looking at day-to-day experiences in schools. The problem is that they don't explain how **factors outside of school** (e.g. poverty, cultural deprivation) can influence achievement.

Labelling theory is also too **deterministic** — it says that once you're negatively labelled that's it, you're more likely to fail. This isn't always the case.

Material Deprivation Outside School Can Affect Achievement

The theory of **material deprivation** says that **economic poverty** is a big factor in low achievement at school.

1) In 1997, the **Joseph Rowntree Foundation** classified **one in ten** children as **poor** — which was defined as being in a family that couldn't afford at least three things other families took for granted.

2) **Halsey (1980)** found that the **most important factor** preventing working class students staying on at school was a **lack of financial support**.

3) **Douglas (1964)** found that children in **unsatisfactory living conditions** (poor housing, lack of nutritious food, overcrowding) didn't do very well in ability tests compared to kids from comfortable backgrounds.

4) **Unemployment** or **low income** means less money for books, internet access and school trips. Low income families can't afford **nurseries** and **private schools** and they can't afford to support their kids through **uni**.

5) Poverty and unsatisfactory living standards may cause **health problems** and **absence from school**.

Cultural Deprivation Outside School Can Affect Achievement

The theory of **cultural deprivation** says that **working class culture** and **parenting** aren't aimed at educational success.

1) **Douglas (1964)** thought the **level of parental interest** was the most important factor in affecting achievement. For example, middle class parents are more likely to visit schools for open evenings. Bear in mind though that **working class parents** may not go to open evenings because they work **inconvenient shifts** — not because they aren't interested.

2) Some sociologists say that working class kids don't have the **knowledge** and **values** that help achievement. **Museum visits**, **books** and **parental knowledge of education** may help middle class pupils to succeed.

3) Some **styles of parenting** emphasise the importance of education more than others.

Class and Differential Achievement in Education

Some Sociologists say **Class Affects Attitudes** to **Education**

1) **Sugarman (1970)** said that pupils from non-manual backgrounds and manual backgrounds have **different outlooks**. The pupils from **manual** backgrounds lived for **immediate gratification**. The pupils from **non-manual backgrounds** were **ambitious** and **deferred their gratification** — they invested time in studying and planned for the future.

2) **Hyman (1967)** said that the **values** of the working class are a **self-imposed barrier** to improving their position. He said that the working class tend to place a **low value** on education.

ethnocentric = believing your group/nation/culture is superior to others.

But...

Material and cultural deprivation theories **don't** explain how **factors inside school** affect achievement.

Cultural deprivation theory **generalises a lot** about differences between middle class and working class life. It **ignores** working class families who **do** place a high value on education, and tends to **assume** that working class families have **no culture** at all, or that working class culture can't be **relevant** to school. This is **ethnocentric**.

The **method** may be **unsound**, e.g. attending parents' evenings might not be a good measure of parental interest.

The two Bs (**Bernstein** and **Bourdieu**) — Investigated **Differences** in **Achievement**

1) **Bernstein (1970)** found that working class pupils in the East End of London weren't comfortable with the style of language required by school. They used a **restricted code** — short forms of speech.

2) **Middle class students** knew how to use the same **elaborated code** as the **teachers** — a much more wordy style of speech with everything made very explicit.

3) In terms of **language**, the working class kids were at a disadvantage.

1) **Bourdieu (1971, 1974)** reckons middle class students are at an advantage because they have the right kind of "**cultural capital**" — the right **language**, **skills**, **knowledge** and **attitudes**.

2) He thought that the **more cultural capital** you have, the **more successful** you'll be in education — and he believed that working class pupils don't have **access** to cultural capital.

3) **Middle class** families **pass on cultural capital** and **expectations** from parents to children. This is called **cultural reproduction**.

Problems with Bernstein's theory	Problems with Bourdieu's theory
There are **variations within** the middle class and working class. Different sections of these groups **vary** in how they use the **elaborate code** — the "posh language" of teachers.	**Halsey (1980)** found that **material factors** are important. **Lack of money** may **stop kids staying on at school** or **getting to university**.
Some sociologists have developed his ideas to say working class speech patterns are inferior or somehow "wrong" — controversial... **Labov (1973)** thinks the elaborated speech code is just **different**.	**Not all working class students fail**, even if they don't have cultural capital.

Recent Studies Suggest that Social Class **Remains a Factor** in Achievement

1) **Willmott and Hutchinson (1992)** studied inner-city schools in Manchester and Liverpool and identified an increase in the number of students leaving school with **no GCSE passes**. They linked the increase to **deprived social backgrounds**.

2) **Leon Feinstein (2003)** found that social class continued to have a **significant impact** on educational achievement. He argued that **redistributive policies** like Sure Start (see p. 66) should carry on throughout a **student's entire education**, rather than being restricted to their pre-school years.

Practice Questions

Q1 Give two facts about the links between social class and educational achievement.

Q2 Explain how processes outside school can cause underachievement by children from working class backgrounds.

Q3 What is cultural capital and who does it help in education?

Exam Question

Q1 Outline some of the sociological explanations for the underachievement of children from lower social classes. (12 marks)

Immediate gratification sounds good to me...

A warning — the exam might ask something like "Assess how factors inside and outside school affect achievement". To answer, you'd need to look at home and school factors for ethnicity, gender AND class. So revise pages 60–63 as well as these ones.

Ethnicity and Differential Achievement in Education

Ethnicity is another factor that can influence how well people do at school.
Quick reminder — ethnicity means the shared cultural traditions and history which are distinct from other groups
in society. Modern Britain is said to be a multicultural society made up of many different ethnic groups.

Some *Ethnic Groups* Do *Better* Than *Others*

These figures are from **Modood et al (1997)** — the Policy Studies Institute's fourth survey of ethnic minorities in Britain.

All these statistics are averages. If you look at someone and say "she does well cos she's Chinese" you might be wrong.

Higher levels of achievement

1) The survey found that **Chinese**, **African Asians** and **Indian** groups were more qualified than whites. **Afro-Caribbean women** were more likely to have **A-levels** than white women.

2) Ethnic minorities were **more likely than white pupils** to continue into **further education** (from ages 16-19).

3) People from ethnic minorities who were **born in the UK** had much **higher qualifications** than people who moved to the UK from abroad.

Lower levels of achievement

1) **Bangladeshi** and **Pakistani women** were least well qualified. **Afro-Caribbean**, **Pakistani** and **Bangladeshi men** were least qualified.

2) **Pakistani** and **Afro-Caribbean** groups were **less likely** to get onto **university** courses, and **more likely** to get into **less prestigious universities**.

3) **Afro-Caribbean boys** are **more likely** to be **excluded from school**, more likely to be put in **lower streams** and more likely to do **vocational** courses.

African Asians means people of Indian origin who lived in Kenya and Uganda and then moved to Britain in the 1970s.

There are big **variations** between the **average achievement level** of different ethnic minority groups. There must be something behind it all — probably more than one factor, and probably some **social** and **economic** factors.

Some people say that **intelligence is inherited** — i.e. people underachieve because they've inherited low IQ.

HOWEVER... **IQ tests** can be **biased**. Sometimes they ask things that aren't really a test of brains, but really a test of **cultural knowledge**. The **Swann Report (1985)** found that if you took into account social and economic factors there were **no significant differences in IQ** whatsoever between different **ethnic groups**.

Processes Inside School — *Labelling*, *Curriculum* and *Prejudice* are Factors

Labelling theory says that teachers have **different expectations** of **different ethnic minority groups**. **Gillborn (1990)** found that teachers sometimes **negatively label black students**. Afro-Caribbean students were seen as a **challenge** to school **authority** — and were more likely to be excluded from school. Gillborn calls this the "myth of the black challenge". Teachers had high expectations of Asian students, which could lead to a self-fulfilling prophecy of **success**. In contrast, negative labelling could result in a **self-fulfilling prophecy of failure**.

There's also an issue about whether the school curriculum is **ethnocentric** — i.e. that it might fit the mainstream, white, middle class culture better than other ethnicities. It could be **Europe-centred** too. Languages in the National Curriculum are mainly **European** — kids usually learn French and German, not Gujarati or Chinese. **Assemblies, school holidays** and even **history lessons** may not fit with the culture and history of particular groups.

Some sociologists see British education as "**institutionally racist**". This is where **policies** and **attitudes** unintentionally discriminate against ethnic minority groups. **Wright (1992)** found that even though members of staff said they were **committed to equal opportunities**, Asian girls got **less attention** from teachers and felt their cultural traditions were disapproved of (e.g. they might get told off for wearing a headscarf if it isn't part of the school uniform). **Afro-Caribbean boys** were more likely to be punished and **sent out of class**.

Some sociologists say that these factors may lead to **low self-esteem** for ethnic minorities. **Coard (1971)** said that black students are made to feel inferior in British schools.

Low Self-Esteem Exists — But it *Isn't Really All That Widespread*

1) **Mirza (1992)** found that black girls had **positive self-esteem** and **high aspirations**. The girls experienced discrimination but had **strategies** to minimise the effects of racism. It **wasn't low self esteem** that affected their achievement — it was being **unwilling to ask for help**, or unwilling to **choose certain subjects**.

2) **Fuller (1980)** found Afro-Caribbean girls in London **resisted negative labelling** and **worked hard** to gain **success**.

3) Negative labelling and racism can affect pupils' reactions to school. Pupils may use either a **pro-school subculture** or an **anti-school subculture** to maintain their self-esteem.

Ethnicity and Differential Achievement in Education

Factors Outside School — *Language Difference* Affects Achievement

1) **Language** was a barrier for kids from **Asian** and **Afro-Caribbean immigrant families** when they **first arrived** in the UK.

2) The **Swann Report** found that **language didn't affect progress** for **later generations**.

3) **Driver and Ballard (1981)** also found Asian children whose **first language** was **not English** were **as good at English** as their **classmates** by the age of 16.

4) **Labelling theorists** would say that language might not be a barrier, but **dialects** or having an **accent** might **influence teacher expectations** and lead to **negative labelling**. For example, a teacher might **assume** that a child isn't good at English because they have a foreign accent and put them in a lower set.

Factors Outside School — *Family Difference* Affects Achievement

1) Some studies say that **family life varies** for different groups and this can influence achievement.

2) **Driver and Ballard (1981)** say that the **close-knit extended families** and **high parental expectations** increase levels of achievement in **Asian communities**.

3) Some sociologists say the relatively high levels of **divorce** and **single-parenthood** in Afro-Caribbean households could result in **material deprivation**. On the other hand, the **independence of Afro-Caribbean women** can mean that girls get **positive role models**.

Ethnicity Combines with *Social Class* to Affect Achievement

On their own, the factors inside and outside of school may not seem all that convincing. If you bring **social class** and **material factors** into the equation you get a more complex picture.

1) The **Swann Report** found that **socio-economic** status was a factor in the lower levels of achievement of **Afro-Caribbean** pupils.

2) **Pakistani**, **Bangladeshi** and **Afro-Caribbean** groups are more likely to be in **lower class positions** such as routine occupations (assembly line workers, factory workers) and elementary occupations (cleaners, labourers). This may result in poor housing, periods of unemployment, poverty and **material deprivation**.

3) **Chinese**, **African Asian** and **Indian** groups are more likely to be in **higher class** positions and **less likely** to experience material deprivation.

Leon Tikly (2005) Says That *Dual Heritage* Children Face *Unique Problems*

1) **Dual heritage** children are children whose parents are from **different ethnicities**. Around **7.3%** of London school pupils and **3.3%** of all UK school pupils are dual heritage.

2) **Tikly (2005)** observed that the **level of achievement** for dual heritage children is **below average** and that they are **more likely** to be **excluded from school** — especially if they're **male**.

3) He suggested that the problems might stem from the facts that dual heritage children often live in families with **lower income levels**, are more likely to come from **single parent families** and face **more racism** from other students.

4) He also found that teachers often classified dual heritage children as "black" and did not consider their **unique needs**.

Practice Questions

Q1 Give two facts about the links between ethnicity and educational achievement.

Q2 Why do sociologists dislike genetic explanations of intelligence and educational success?

Q3 Name one factor inside school that explains the underachievement of some ethnic minority groups.

Q4 Give an example of how social class combines with ethnicity to affect achievement.

Exam Question

Q1 Assess the significance of factors inside school in explaining the educational achievement of different ethnic minority groups. (20 marks)

It's more complicated than you might have thought...

Remember that not all ethnic minorities underachieve — so don't go storming into your exam answer with a pre-prepared rant that it's all about white / black racism. There are always several different factors that affect each ethnic group.

Gender and Differential Achievement in Education

Gender is another factor that can influence how well people do at school.
Since the 1980s, things have changed. Sociologists used to talk about female underachievement.
Now there are worries that boys are falling behind. Geez Louise, make your minds up...

Here are **Six Facts** about **Gender** and **Differential Educational Achievement**

1) Girls get **better results** at all levels in National Curriculum tests.
2) Girls get **better results** in **most subjects** at **GCSE**.
3) Girls are **more likely** to **pass** their **A-levels**.
4) Women are more likely to go on to **university**.
5) **Men** seem to have most success at the **highest levels** of university.
   A higher proportion of male students get **first class degrees** and **PhDs**.
6) **Girls** tend to go for **communication based subjects** like English and sociology
   and **boys** tend to go for **technical** ones like maths and physics.

Don't be tricked by these facts into thinking that boys are doomed.
You could say that there's been a bit of a '**moral panic**' about males underperforming (see p. 131).

Factors Inside School *Explain Why* Females Now Do Better

1) **Mitsos and Browne (1998)** say teaching has been **feminised**. Women are **more likely to be classroom teachers**, especially in primary schools. This gives girls **positive role models**.
2) **Textbooks** and **teaching resources** have changed and are less likely to **stereotype girls** into passive roles.
3) The National Curriculum **forced** girls to do **traditionally "male"** subjects. For example, more girls started to do **science**. Other Local Education Authority and government initiatives tried to encourage girls to do these subjects, e.g WISE (Women In Science and Engineering) and GIST (Girls Into Science and Technology).
4) **GCSEs** include more **coursework** than earlier qualifications. Some people argue that coursework suits girls better because they put in **more effort**, are **better organised** and can **concentrate** for longer than boys (that's quite a sweeping generalisation though...)
5) **Swann and Graddol (1993)** think that high female achievement is a result of the **quality of interaction** they have with their **teachers**. Most of the time teachers spend with girls is used to **help them with their work** but most teacher time spent with boys is focused on **behaviour management**.
6) **Jackson (1998)** says that schools label boys **negatively**. Boys are associated with poor behaviour, which gives the school a bad name, and with **low achievement**, which lowers the school's **league table position**. This negative label becomes a **self-fulfilling prophecy**.

Factors Outside School *Explain Why* Females Now Do Better

1) Policies such as the **Equal Pay Act** and **Sex Discrimination Act** have helped to create **more equal opportunities** in the wider society. This has **changed the values** of society and attitudes in school.
2) **Sue Sharpe (1994)** found that girls' priorities have changed. They now want **careers** — and qualifications. More women go out to work, so girls see lots of **positive role models** in work. Girls nowadays often want to be **financially independent** — they don't just want to marry a rich man any more.
3) **Boys** tend to spend their leisure time being **physically active**. **Girls** are more likely to spend their leisure time **reading** and **communicating**. This means girls develop **language skills** that are useful for most subjects.
4) The **feminist** movement caused a **change in female expectations**, and made more people **aware of inequality**. People are now more careful about negative stereotyping, sex discrimination and patriarchy.

> The Equal Pay Act (1971) makes it illegal to pay men and women different wages for the same work. The Sex Discrimination Act 1975 means employers can't discriminate on the basis of gender.

Archer (2006) *says that Females Still Face* Problems at School

1) **Archer (2006)** argues that the current **underachievement** by boys in education masks the **continuing problems** that girls still face.
2) She claims that **high-achieving Asian** and **Chinese** girls get negatively labelled by teachers as **robots** who are **incapable of independent thought**.
3) She also argues that **high-achieving black working class girls** get negatively labelled by teachers as **loud and aggressive**.
4) She concludes that the ongoing achievement of girls is "**fragile and problematic**".

Gender and Differential Achievement in Education

Here are Some *Reasons* Why *Boys Underachieve*

1) Boys may be having an **identity crisis**. The rise of **female independence**, the decline of the **breadwinner** role for men and the rise in **male unemployment** might mean that boys don't see the point of education. This may lead to anti-school subcultures.

2) **Interpretivists** say that teachers have **lower expectations of boys**. Teacher expectations may lead to a **self-fulfilling prophecy** of poor behaviour. **Negative labelling** may explain why they're more disruptive. Boys are more likely to be **excluded** from school.

3) The **feminisation** of **teaching** means that boys don't have as many **role models** in school.

4) **Reading** is often seen as "uncool" or "girly". Boys who **avoid books** like the plague won't develop important **communication skills**.

Burly men in Santa hats can read books, too.

Subcultures help to Explain *Gender* and *Achievement*

Negative labelling and putting students into different **streams** or bands can cause some pupils to rebel against school's values. They form **subcultures**. These can be either **pro-** or **anti-school** subcultures.

1) In the 1970s **Willis** looked at why working class kids get working class jobs. He studied a group of boys later called "Willis's lads". The lads **rejected school** and formed an **anti-school subculture**. They **coped** with their own underachievement by having a **subculture where education didn't matter**, and where having a laugh was more important.

2) **Mac an Ghaill (1994)** says that **subcultures are complicated**. There are lots of different types. Boys may join a **macho lad subculture** because of a crisis of masculinity. But boys could also join **pro-school subcultures** and be proud of academic achievement.

3) **Fuller (1980)** found that **Afro-Caribbean girls** in **London** formed a **subculture** that worked hard to prove negative labelling wrong.

There are Different Ways to Explain Gender and Subject Choice

Girls tend to go for **arts and humanities**. Boys tend to go for **science and technology**.

1) **Subject choice** may still be influenced by **gender socialisation**. The ideas of **femininity** and **masculinity** create different **expectations** and **stereotypes** of what to study. Kids often see biology as "the science that it's OK for girls to do" and girls who do physics as "super hardcore science chicks" (or "geeky girls who do physics").

2) **Kelly (1987)** found that **science** is seen as a **masculine subject**. Boys dominate the science classroom.

3) **Parental expectations** and **teacher expectations** may encourage girls to follow what they see as the traditional "**normal**" choice for their gender. There's a pressure to **conform** to a social norm.

Practice Questions

Q1 Give two facts about the links between gender and educational achievement.
Q2 Name one factor inside school that helps explain why girls now do better than boys.
Q3 Give two reasons why subcultures are formed by some school pupils.
Q4 Give one reason why boys and girls choose different subjects.

Exam Questions

Q1 Explain what is meant by the 'feminisation of teaching'. (2 marks)

Q2 Identify three educational policies that have led to improvements in girls' performance. (6 marks)

Girls are DOOMED... no wait, boys are DOOMED... no wait... ah, forget it...

*Once again, you can't look at gender without looking at class and ethnicity. Working class girls don't do as well as middle class girls. Also remember that there's a **lot of generalisation** with these sociological theories. Of course not all girls prefer coursework to exams. I bet they prefer lounging around on the beach to doing exams though. Pity they don't test that.*

State Policy and Education

All governments are interested in education. The 1870 Forster Education Act introduced elementary schooling for 5–10 year olds in England and Wales. Since then there have been some major changes. Place your votes, please.

The **1944 Education Act** Introduced the **Tripartite System** and the **11+**

By the time of the Second World War, the main problem in education was that there was a **huge divide** between the types of secondary education available for the rich and poor. The **1944** Act (often called the **Butler Act** after the man who introduced it) tried to create education for all — secondary schools were made free for all and the school leaving age was raised to 15. You took the **11+ exam** (like an IQ test) at the end of primary school and then went to one of three types of school:

1) **Grammar schools** were for the able kids who passed the 11+. Pupils were taught traditional subjects ready for **university**. About **20% of kids** got in to grammar school.

2) **Secondary modern schools** were for the **75-80%** of pupils **who failed** the 11+. Secondary moderns offered **basic education**.

3) **Technical schools** were meant to provide a more **vocationally-minded** education for those pupils with aptitude for **practical subjects**.

This **tripartite system** aimed to improve the education of all children, but several problems remained:

1) The **11+ didn't necessarily measure your intelligence**. It was **culturally biased**, and suited the middle class more than the working class.

2) **Few technical schools were built**, so the vocational part of the plan didn't work especially well.

3) Most children ended up either at grammar or secondary modern schools. These schools were supposed to have "**parity of esteem**" — they were supposed to be considered as having **equal value**. The problem was that grammar schools were seen as the best. Not a surprise since which school you went to was decided by how well you did in an exam.

4) Kids who failed the 11+ were **labelled as failures**, which sometimes turned them off education.

5) If well-off middle class pupils failed, their parents could still afford to send them to **private schools**.

In **1965** the Labour Government made Schools **Comprehensive**

The Labour government insisted that Local Education Authorities (LEAs) **reorganised most schools** so that everyone had equality of opportunity. "**Comprehensive school**" means it's universal — everyone's meant to get the same deal.

Positive aspects of the comprehensive system	**Criticisms** of the comprehensive education system
There's no 11+, so 80% of the school population don't get labelled as **failures.**	Comprehensive schools still **stream** pupils into sets depending on test scores. (So it's still possible to feel like a failure without the 11+.)
High-ability pupils generally still do well with this system. Lower ability pupils do better in comprehensive schools than in the old secondary moderns.	Schools in **working class** areas have **lower pass rates** than those in middle class areas.

The comprehensive system has not achieved equality of opportunity. Schools tend to be 'single-class', depending on the local area. Where people can afford to live (and whether there are good schools nearby) is important in educational attainment.

In **1976** the Push for **Vocational Education** Started

Labour Prime Minister James Callaghan thought British education and industry was in decline because schools didn't teach people the **skills they needed in work**. All governments since then have had policies to create a closer link between school and work. This is called **vocationalism**.

1) **Youth Training Schemes (YTS)** started in 1983.

2) In 1993, **GNVQs** and **NVQs** were introduced — **practical qualifications**.   *YTS were job training schemes for 16-17 year old kids leaving school.*

3) The introduction of the **New Deal** in 1997 means people on benefits must attend courses if they don't accept work.

4) Recently, **key skills** qualifications have started. These are supposed to be useful for all jobs.

5) **Curriculum 2000**, a reform of post-16 education, included the introduction of the **vocational A-Level** — a qualification intended to be of equal worth to a traditional, academic A-Level.

There are some **problems** with vocational education:

1) Some sociologists argue that vocational education aims to teach **good work discipline**, not skills.

2) Some Marxist sociologists say that vocational training provides **cheap labour** and that governments encourage people into training schemes to **lower unemployment statistics**.

3) Lots of **young people** have **part-time jobs**, so they **already have work skills**.

4) Vocational qualifications often aren't regarded as highly as academic qualifications by universities and employers.

State Policy and Education

The *1988 Education Reform Act* — *Choice, Inspections and More Tests*

In the late 1980s, the **Conservative** government introduced some **major reforms** in education.

Education should link to the economy

The government introduced **more vocational courses** and more **work placement schemes**.

There should be better standards in education

1) The government introduced a **National Curriculum** of **compulsory subjects** for all **5 to 16 year olds**.

2) **OFSTED** (Office for Standards in Education) was set up to **inspect** schools and make sure they were doing a **decent job**. You might have seen **teachers** getting somewhat **frantic** before an inspection.

3) Schools could **opt out** of their local education authority and become **grant-maintained schools**. This means that they got money **straight from the government** and could **spend it how they liked**. The government believed this would **improve standards**.

There should be a system of choice and competition

1) Parents could **choose** which school to send their child to — if the school had **space**.

2) Parents could use **league tables** to help them choose. **League tables** show **how many** kids at each school **pass their exams**, and how many get **good grades**.

3) Schools worked like **businesses** and **advertised** for students.

There should be more testing and more exams

Pupils had to sit **SATs** at **7, 11 and 14**, and **GCSEs** at **16**.

New Labour Try to *Mix* Some of the *Old Ideas Together*

In 1997, New Labour took over. They wanted to do something about **inequality**, but they also said there should be **choice** and **diversity** in education. It's a bit like the old Labour policies and the Conservative policies **mixed up together** — it's called "**third way politics**".

The government has made some changes since 1997:

1) They've **reduced infant class sizes** to a maximum of **30**.
2) They've introduced **numeracy hour** and **literacy hour** in **primary schools**.
3) New Labour have allowed **faith schools** and **specialist status schools**.
4) They've set up **Education Action Zones** to help in areas of deprivation.
5) They've tried to **increase** the **number of people going to university**.

A big change in 16-18 year olds' education came in 2000. Policy changed to make A-level education broader. Students now have to do **AS/A2s** and **key skills**, and there are more **vocational courses**.

The government are also keen on **citizenship education** to make pupils more **aware of politics**.

Practice Questions

Q1 What was the aim of the 1944 Education Act?
Q2 Name the three types of school in the tripartite system.
Q3 Briefly explain two problems with comprehensive schools.
Q4 Briefly describe two changes brought about by the 1988 Education Reform Act.
Q5 Name two changes in schools brought about by New Labour.

Exam Questions

Q1 Outline some of the ways in which state policies have influenced educational attainment. (12 marks)

Q2 Examine the ways in which social policies in education may reproduce and legitimise social class inequalities. (20 marks)

They'll never make their minds up...

Governments have been trying to "Sort Out Education Once And For All" and "Shake Up Britain's Failing Schools" for ages. But whatever happens, kids go to school, teachers teach 'em things, and there are exams at the end of it all...

State Policy and Education

These pages examine and evaluate the motivation behind recent state policies in education.

Some Policies Aim to **Reduce Class Inequality**

Compensatory education tries to make up for **material** and **cultural deprivation**, by giving **extra help** to those who need it.

> 1) **Sure Start** began in 1999. It's a government programme to improve early education and childcare in England. It now offers up to two years of **free childcare** and **early education** to all three and four year olds.
>
> 2) The **Educational Maintenance Allowance (EMA)** gives up to £30 per week to students who stay on in education after they're 16. A series of **bonuses** are available for good attendance and progress. EMA is **means-tested** so only children from poorer families benefit from it.
>
> 3) Other education policies designed to reduce class inequality include **free school meals**, **breakfast clubs** and **bursaries** for university places.

Some people have criticised the **methods** by which compensatory education is **implemented**.

> 1) They claim that the policies are **unfair** to students just **outside of the criteria for inclusion** — e.g. if their parents earn just over the limit that makes them eligible for EMA.
>
> 2) They also say that the policies are only **token gestures** towards solving the issues they identify — they rarely address **underlying problems**.

Some Policies Aim to **Promote Gender Equality**

Female underachievement used to be a problem

> 1) The **1988 National Curriculum** gave all pupils equal entitlement to all subjects for the first time. This has been credited with the increased achievement of girls in the last 20 years.
>
> 2) Initiatives such as the **Computer Club for Girls** (CC4G) and **Women Into Science and Engineering** (WISE) encourage girls to get involved with subjects they have **traditionally avoided**.

Recent policies have focused on boys' underachievement

> 1) In 1999 the government gave **grants** to primary schools to hold **extra writing classes** for boys to help push up their **SATs scores**.
>
> 2) In 2005 the **Breakthrough Programme** introduced **mentoring, after-school classes** and **e-tutorials** for teenage boys in an attempt to improve their exam performance.

The **New Right** has Influenced Many Modern Policies

1) The **New Right** believe in the introduction of **market principles** to all aspects of social and economic life. This includes **less central control** from the government, and encouraging **more competition**. They argue that this makes services **more efficient** while **reducing dependence** on the state.

2) Policies such as the introduction of school **league tables**, **Ofsted** inspections and **performance-related pay** have tried to create a '**market**' in schools — by creating incentives for schools and teachers to try to **outperform** each other.

3) Ideas such as **local management of school budgets**, **grant-maintained schools** and **academies** are attempts to reduce the amount of **centralised control** over education.

State Policy and Education

Chubb and Moe (1990) Proposed a Voucher System

1) **Chubb and Moe (1990)** suggested a scheme under which parents would be given a voucher to pay for the education of their children.

2) They'd have **free choice** over where to spend their vouchers — including deciding between the **private sector** or **existing state schools**.

3) Schools which provide **poor value for money** would lose customers and **close**. Schools which provide **good value for money** would attract customers and **grow**.

4) So competition would **drive up standards** in education.

Even the New Right Wants Some State Involvement in Education

1) **New Right** thinkers value the importance of education in **socialisation** — the process by which children learn the norms and values of society.

2) They believe education can help socialise children through **religious assemblies** and the **National Curriculum**, e.g. **citizenship lessons**.

The New Right has been Criticised for Distorting Educational Practices

1) Opponents of the New Right's market reforms argue that schools have become **more concerned with league tables** than the individual needs of pupils.

2) They also argue that the New Right's preferred "norms and values" are **enthnocentric** and **aren't representative** of the diversity of values and beliefs in society.

New Labour Policies Follow Third Way ideas

1) The 'Third Way' is a **middle ground** between New Right ideas on **marketisation** and the left wing policies of **government intervention**.

2) New Labour have continued the process of **market reforms** begun by the previous Conservative government. For example, they've allowed schools to **specialise** in certain subjects — e.g. by becoming Music Colleges or Science Colleges — to try to **create diversity** and **increase choice for parents**.

3) They've also pursued some interventionist policies, such as setting up **Educational Action Zones** in areas of high deprivation.

> **New Labour have been criticised**
>
> 1) **New Right** thinkers have **criticised** New Labour for not giving parents **greater choice** in which schools they send their children to.
>
> 2) **Left wing** sociologists such as **Geoff Whitty** have argued that market-oriented educational reforms **create greater social divisions** by benefiting middle class families more than working class families.

Practice Questions

Q1 Give three examples of social policies designed to reduce educational inequalities.

Q2 Give four examples of social policies influenced by New Right thinking.

Q3 Give three criticisms of New Right educational policies.

Q4 Describe and evaluate two New Labour educational social policies.

Exam Questions

Q1 Identify **three** policies which have attempted to introduce market forces into schools. (6 marks)

Q2 Assess the ways in which social policies may reproduce and legitimise social class inequalities in education. (20 marks)

My educational policy is to revise everything...

Girls used to underachieve compared to boys, but now it's the other way round. That seems to be evidence that policies can affect equality, if nothing else. The New Right want policies that give everyone choice and give the market a chance to drive up standards, the left want the state to intervene and directly correct problems where they arise. And New Labour want both.

Definitions of Health

Most people believe they're unwell if they don't feel like they normally do. Sociologists see health as more than just not feeling poorly. **Pages 68-77 are for AQA and OCR.**

There are *Three* main *Perspectives* on *Health*

1) The **biomedical model** (favoured by **scientists**) says that health and illness are caused by factors **within** the body.
2) **Lay definitions** are **ordinary people**'s explanations for health and illness.
3) The **social model** (favoured by **sociologists**) says that health and illness are caused by factors **outside** the body.

The Biomedical Model says Health and Disease are *Natural, Physical Things*

Health professionals generally follow the **biomedical model of health**. This model has three key characteristics:

Key characteristics of the biomedical model

1) Health is seen as the **absence of biological abnormality**.
2) The human body is likened to a **machine** in that it needs to be **repaired** by treatment when it breaks down.
3) The health of society is regarded as dependent on the **state of medical knowledge**.

Nicky Hart (1985) identifies **five features** of the **biomedical model**:

1)	Disease is **physical**	The **biomedical model** concentrates on **physical symptoms** of disease, not social and environmental factors. Disease happens in an **individual's body**, not as part of society.
2)	**Doctors** are an **elite**	The **medical elite** (doctors) are the only people sufficiently **qualified** and **skilled** to **identify** and **treat** illness.
3)	Medicine is **curative**	The body can be **repaired** with drugs and surgery.
4)	Illness is **temporary**	Illness can be cured by the medical elite. **Wellness** is the **normal** state of affairs.
5)	**Treatment** is special	Treatment of disease takes place in **recognised healthcare environments** (e.g. doctors surgeries, hospitals), which are **distinct** from the environment where the patient got ill.

Example: A **biomedical view of disability**.

The biomedical model **looks in** at the patient and tries to **fix** the disability through medical practice.

Medical practice is **interventionist** — it's something that's **done to** the patient.

The *Biomedical* Model has been *Criticised*

1) Some sociologists, e.g. **McKeown (1976)**, say that **improved nutrition and hygiene** have been more important in improving health — starting with 19th and 20th century public health reform.
2) **Ivan Illich (1975)** and others have argued that modern medicine actually **creates disease** (see p. 76).
3) **Marxist sociologists** in the 1970s accused biomedicine of distracting attention away from what they see as the real causes of illness — the **social causes**.
4) The biomedical approach can be viewed as **stigmatising** people who have an illness or disability — it views illness or disability as something **abnormal** that should be **fixed**.
5) **Tom Shakespeare (2000)** said that traditional approaches **medicalise** and **individualise** disability. They deal with the symptoms of each case separately and **ignore** social patterns.

Lay Definitions of health *Vary* between *Social Groups*

1) **Lay definitions** are ones you get from **non-specialists**, in this case, definitions of health and illness from people who are neither scientists nor sociologists.
2) According to research carried out by **Mildred Blaxter** in 1990, the way you define health depends on which **social group** you belong to. For example, she found that **younger men's** idea of health was being **physically fit** and strong, while the **older women** she studied thought health included **good social relationships**. She also found that **non-scientists** were influenced by the **biomedical model**. Most people saw health as the **absence of illness**.

Definitions of Health

The **Social Model** says that health and disease are **Social Constructs**

A "social construct" is an **idea that's created by a society** — as opposed to an idea that's based on objective and testable **facts**. It's specific to the **values and behaviour** of that society — it's not universal. *But* people living in that society will usually accept it as **natural** and **"common sense."**

1) **The medical elite** (doctors) **haven't always dominated** the definition and treatment of illness and disease — it's a modern phenomenon. For example, in the 1700s, mental illness was often thought to be caused by evil spirits — a religious thing, not a medical thing.

2) In modern society illness is only recognised as serious if it has been **diagnosed** by the medical elite. The **social model** says **definitions of health and illness** are "social constructs" — not actually always related to real physical symptoms.

3) A **social model of health** would look to see which **environmental, social and behavioural factors** have contributed to make an individual person ill.

Example: A **social view of disability**.

The social model looks outwards from the individual to the **environmental** and **social** factors which disable an individual, e.g. lack of access, rights, and opportunities.

A person using a **wheelchair** might feel more disabled by the **lack of a wheelchair ramp** than the fact that they can't use their legs to walk.

Equal opportunities at work

Accessibility (wheelchair ramps, disabled toilets etc.)

Negative attitudes and prejudice in society

The social model of health **challenges** the idea that **wellness** is the normal state of affairs. Individuals with an illness are seen as **"living with"** their condition instead of having something **"wrong"** with them.

Senior and Viveash (1998) say there is a **Social Process** of becoming **Ill**

Senior and Viveash (1998) argue that the **six stages** of getting ill are:

1) **Social factors** (such as diet, housing or stress) make some people more likely to become ill than others.

2) An individual develops **symptoms** — these can be **physical** (for example, throwing up), **psychological** (for example, feeling depressed) or **social** (for example, feeling that your marriage is collapsing).

3) The individual interprets their symptoms as an **illness**. Whether you **decide** you have an illness or not will depend on many influences, such as past experience, the mass media, family, culture and gender.

4) The individual decides to visit a **doctor**. This stage **differs** from one **social group** to another. For example, research by **Pui-Ling and Logan (1999)** showed that British Chinese people were less likely to report mental health problems because of social stigma.

5) The patient is **labelled** as **ill**. Although the doctor is powerful at this stage, patients can also be influential in persuading the doctor to label them.

6) **Statistics** are created based on information from doctors. These morbidity statistics are used to form **government policies** for **healthcare**. However, a very large amount of illness goes unreported. According to **Last (1963)** as much as 94% of illness is not reported to doctors. This phenomenon is known as the **clinical iceberg**.

Practice Questions

Q1 Why are doctors seen as part of a "medical elite"?
Q2 List the five features of the biomedical model of health and illness identified by Hart.
Q3 According to Senior and Viveash (1998), what are the six stages of the social process of becoming ill?

Exam Questions

Q1	Identify and explain two features of the social process of becoming ill.	(17 marks)
Q2	Outline and evaluate the view that the biomedical model can completely explain health and illness.	(33 marks)

All I care about is why I feel ill...

Hmm... the social model of illness seems a bit odd at first — how can it be society's fault that I've got a sore throat... But when you look into it, you have to admit that things like clean water, proper sewers and a good diet are at least relevant to health. As always, you're expected to know the key points of each theory, as well as their faults and pitfalls.

Inequalities in Health

*Your chances of staying healthy, and of recovering if you do get ill, depend on which social group you belong to. Sociologists have given various explanations for this. These pages are for **AQA and OCR**.*

Health has an Uneven Social Distribution

1) The **working class** have a **higher infant mortality rate** than the national average. The **wealthiest social groups** have **lower infant mortality rates** than the national average.

2) **Working class** people are statistically **more likely** to suffer from **serious medical conditions** such as heart disease, strokes and cancer.

3) **Working class** people are more likely to **die before retirement** age than the national average.

4) According to government statistics, people born in **social class 1** (professional) can expect to live for **seven years longer** than people born in **social class 5** (manual workers).

5) **Morbidity** and **mortality** rates vary between different **regions** of Britain. E.g. people in **Scotland** are more likely to die of lung cancer than people in **England**.

6) There is a **correlation** between **ethnicity** and **certain illnesses**. Some ethnic groups are genetically prone to particular illnesses — for example, **sickle-cell anaemia** is most common in people of **African** origin.

7) There are **gender** differences — women live **five years** longer than men on average. But they also **go to the doctor** more often.

8) **Age** affects health. Older people are more likely to develop **long-term illnesses**, while younger people are more likely to be involved in **accidents** or other **violent incidents**.

9) There are large variations in health **internationally**. **Developing** countries tend to have higher morbidity rates than **developed** countries. And there are differences between the developed countries too — in **2005** the **British Medical Journal** reported research showing that the traditional diet in **Greece** and other Mediterranean countries was linked to **longer life expectancy**.

> *Morbidity is another word for sickness. Mortality is another word for death.*

> *Points 1–8 are based on statistics from the Social Trends 33 (2003) report produced by the Office of National Statistics.*

Cultural Explanations Blame Bad Health on Variations in Attitude

Some sociologists attribute **differences in health** to the **values** held and choices made by **different social groups**. These are called cultural explanations. **Cultural deprivation theory** is a cultural explanation that looks at differences between social classes.

1) **Cultural deprivation theory** says that the **working class** lead **relatively unhealthy lifestyles** with relatively poor diets, more smoking, less exercise and more drinking.

2) It also says that the working class are less likely to take advantage of NHS **public health measures** such as **vaccinations**, **health screening** and **antenatal care**.

3) **Howlett and Ashley (1991)** found that **middle class** people are better **informed** about health, with more **understanding** of health issues. Therefore, they tend to follow **healthier lifestyles**.

Cultural deprivation theory suggests that society needs better **health education** to make people more **aware** of health issues. It's resulted in lots of **government initiatives** through the **Health Education Authority** — trying to get people to give up smoking, eat less fatty food, etc.

Structural Approaches link Health Inequalities to Material Deprivation

Many sociologists **disagree** with cultural explanations. Instead they believe that differences in health and illness are caused by the way **society is structured**. The **middle class** is healthier than the **working class** because society gives the poor **less access** to things that could keep them healthy.

1) **Healthier diets** can **cost more**, and **gyms** are often **very expensive**.

2) **Smoking and drinking** may be related to **stressful lives**, not **cultural values**.

3) Working class people are **less likely** to be able to afford **private health care**.

4) The fact that working class people often **don't take advantage** of **public health facilities** has also been blamed on feeling **intimidated** by health care and **health care professionals**. Health care professionals are **mostly middle class** and health care in general can seem like it's set up to suit middle class people.

Work it, baybee, work it.

Inequalities in Health

Health Inequalities are Strongly Linked to Social Class

Most sociologists **agree** that **economic deprivation** is probably the **major factor** causing health inequalities, even if they don't agree exactly **why**.

A major government survey, '**Inequalities in Health Working Group Report (1980)**' (also known as the **Black Report**) confirmed that the poorer you are, the less healthy you're likely to be. It also found that those with the **most** need for health care get **least**, and those with the **least** need get **most**. This is called the **Inverse Care Law**.

> The Inverse Care Law was first defined by **Julian Tudor Hart (1971)**.
>
> He wrote that "The availability of good medical care tends to **vary inversely** with the **need** for it in the population served".

The Artefact Explanation Argues that Patterns of Inequality Don't Exist

1) Different people belong to different **social classes**, have different **ethnic backgrounds**, live in different **regions of the country**, have different **ages** and can be either **male or female**. The factors affecting health could be any combination of these variables.

2) The **artefact explanation** argues that the **patterns of inequality** in health are an **illusion** created by statistics, and don't really exist. There are so many variables involved that it would be impossible to prove that one factor was **causing** health inequalities.

3) The Black Report (see above) **tested** this explanation, and concluded that it **isn't true**.

Social Selection Explanations have a different approach

According to the **social selection** model, poor health **causes** low social status. People who suffer from physical or mental illnesses **sink to the bottom** classes of society, while those who are physically and mentally strong **rise to the top**.

> Social selection explanations have been criticised
>
> **Senior and Viveash (1998)** say that there is some truth in the idea that being healthy can **help individuals achieve status** and that being unhealthy can be a **barrier to success**. But they also point out that a lot of healthy people **fail to move upwards** in society and a lot of people with health problems **do not move downwards**. In many cases other factors, such as **family background**, are more important in determining social status.

Practice Questions

Q1 According to research, why are people from Mediterranean countries often healthier?

Q2 What is meant by the Inverse Care Law?

Q3 How do social selection explanations account for the link between illness and poverty?

Exam Questions

Q1 Identify and explain two ways in which social class can affect health. (17 marks)

Q2 Outline and evaluate the view that inequalities in health are caused by cultural factors. (33 marks)

Everyone blames someone...

An awful lot of this sociology business is about blaming some system or other for the World's problems. Usual scapegoats are "working class values" and "unequal health provision". And some people just blame the statisticians for making everyone else blame each other. Make sure you know what the Inverse Care Law is — it's important for this whole module.

Access to Health Care

*The National Health Service was set up to give free and equal health care for all. It was mostly a success. Mostly. These pages are for **AQA and OCR**.*

There are **Inequalities** in the Health Care **Provided** by the **NHS**

The **NHS** was set up in 1948. It aimed to provide **free** and **equal** health care for **everyone** in the country. Unfortunately, although the NHS was **generally a success**, it **doesn't give 100% equal health care** to all.

1) NHS **money** is **shared out unequally** between different areas of the country.
2) NHS money is **spent differently** in different areas of the country.
3) **Specialist** hospitals, e.g. heart hospitals, **aren't spread out equally** across the country.
4) There's a **north-south divide** in the **supply of health care**, as well as in people's health.

Sociologists and politicians often claim that there's a **two-tier system** in the NHS — which means that it provides a **lower level of care** to some, and a **higher level of care** to others.

Politicians have introduced **lots of reforms** to try to **make the NHS work better** and **make it cost less money**.

The **Internal Market** in the NHS had **Good** and **Bad Consequences**

In the **1980s**, Mrs Thatcher's Conservative government tried to **reform** the NHS to make it **more efficient** and **less expensive** (a lot of taxpayers' money is spent on the NHS). They introduced an **internal market**.

This meant that **health care providers** would **compete** with each other to provide services, and **GPs** would be **responsible for their own budgets**. The idea is that **competition drives prices down**. It's an **economics** thing. More **hospital management** was brought in to manage and supervise these changes.

The government **encouraged private hospitals** and **private health insurance schemes**. This was to take some of the **pressure** off the NHS by getting people who could afford private care to go private.

Like most things in sociology, there are pros and cons, and lots of different opinions.

Positive Consequences

1) There's **more choice** for some "health care consumers" (patients).
2) **Competition** tends to **drive down costs**.
3) In some cases, health care became **more responsive to local needs**.

Negative consequences

1) **Inner city GPs** look after **more people** and **sicker people** than GPs in **middle class** areas. **Money has to go further**, so inner city GPs can't afford the same quality of treatment — it's a **two-tier system**.
2) Increased numbers of **NHS managers** and **accountants** could be a big **waste** of money.
3) **Competition** between health care providers means that **two hospitals very close together** might offer almost exactly the **same services**. This can also be seen as a **waste** of money.

Foundation Trusts Have Been Criticised for Increasing Inequality

1) In 2003, **New Labour** introduced **Foundation Trusts** to the NHS. Hospitals run by a Foundation Trust are often called **Foundation Hospitals**.
2) The government's target is that all NHS Trusts will have foundation status as soon as possible.
3) Unlike traditional NHS Trusts, Foundation Trusts are **independent legal entities** owned by their members. They can **opt out** of **government guidelines**, **raise their own money**, and **set their own priorities** for how to **treat patients**.
4) Critics point out that the **top hospitals** are better at **attracting investment**, so they have more money and **attract better staff**. They argue that this creates a **two-tier system** — the **best hospitals** collect more money to **get even better**.

Most Health Care in the UK is Provided by Women

1) Around **75%** of all **NHS workers** are **women**.
2) However, only **25% of doctors** and **13% of consultants** are **women**.
3) **Over 90%** of **nurses** are **women**.
4) Studies have also discovered that the vast majority of **informal care** of **children** and **elderly relatives** is carried out by women.

Radical feminists think the NHS is a **patriarchal institution** — in other words, one where men dominate.

Access to Health Care

The Inverse Care Law can be Applied Today to Inequalities in Health

Remember the Inverse Care Law from page 71.

The **Inverse Care Law (Tudor Hart 1971)** states that people whose **need** for health care is **greatest** are actually **least likely** to get it.

Julian Le Grand's survey (2003)

Le Grand's conclusion was that the **middle class** get far **more benefit** from the **NHS** than the working class. The benefit the middle classes got wasn't in proportion to their actual health needs.

Le Grand found that the middle class were 40% more likely to get a **heart bypass** operation than the working class. Also, the working class were 20% less likely to get a hip replacement despite being 30% more likely to need one.

Even with something as simple as **consultation times** in GPs' surgeries, Le Grand found that professionals were likely to get on average two minutes more of a doctor's time than working class patients.

Working class areas tend to have the worst health facilities, the **fewest doctors** and the **fewest hospitals**.

This evidence supports the idea that the health care system is biased towards middle class people.

Research by **Cartwright and O'Brien (1976)** suggests that **middle class patients** tend to have a **better relationship** with their **doctor** than working class patients. Working class patients said they **felt** like the **doctor doesn't listen**.

The Inverse Care Law Could Also Apply to Ethnic Minority Groups

Ethnic minority health needs were identified as **relatively high** in a report published by the **Department of Health in 1992**. Remember, "**relatively high**" doesn't mean "shockingly sky-high" or "loads higher than the white population". It means anything from a **tiny bit more** to a **lot more** than the **average population**.

1) The rate of **heart disease** is significantly more common in men and women of **Indian** origin.

2) **Afro-Caribbean** people have a higher incidence of **stroke**, **HIV/AIDS infection** and **schizophrenia**.

3) **Suicide** rates are **relatively high** amongst **Asian** women.

Some sociologists think that **ethnic minorities** have **relatively poor health** because they're **less likely** to get the **full benefit** from NHS services. **Various possible reasons** have been suggested for this:

1) The **cultural values** of the NHS might be **different** from those of some ethnic minority groups. Some advisers say the NHS **needs to adapt** to **fit** the **cultural values** of ethnic groups.

2) Some people from ethnic minorities, especially the elderly, **might not speak enough English** to communicate well with health care staff.

3) There's some evidence that **discrimination** and **racism** affect access to health care. E.g. research in the 1980s found that **Asian women** in family planning clinics experienced racism.

4) **Some ethnic minority groups** tend to see illness and disease as a part of life you can't do much about — and **don't bother** to go to the doctor.

Practice Questions

Q1 List the advantages and disadvantages of an internal market in health care.

Q2 What are foundation trusts?

Q3 Give three ways in which it can be said that the Inverse Care Law operates in today's NHS.

Exam Question

Q1 Assess the view that the people who need health care the most are least likely to get it. (20 marks)

In the great drought of 1811 they introduced a two-tear system...

See, there's that Inverse Care Law again. There's still inequality in people's access to health care. Some think it's getting better, others think it's not. Sociologists are most concerned about a two-tier NHS, and about discrimination within the NHS. Governments keep trying to tweak NHS policy to make the NHS work better, or to make it cost less, or both.

Mental Health

*These pages cover different perspectives on mental health in the UK. For **AQA and OCR**.*

Mental Illness in UK Society is Unequally Distributed

Sociologists and psychiatrists can't agree whether mental disorders have **physical causes** or **social causes**.

Sociologists have tended to favour the view that there is a **social basis** for mental illness. Given the **social inequality** in who has good or bad mental health, maybe the sociologists have a point. For example:

1) **Afro-Caribbean individuals** in the UK are **more likely** to be **admitted to a psychiatric hospital** than other ethnic groups. They're more likely to be "**sectioned**" under the Mental Health Act — **admitted against their will**. Afro-Caribbean men are more likely to be diagnosed with **schizophrenia**.

2) Women are statistically more likely to be diagnosed with **depression** or **acute stress** than men. They're also much more likely to be on **drug treatments** for **mental illness** — antidepressants etc.

3) **Working class** men and women are statistically **more likely** to be diagnosed with mental illness than **middle class** people.

4) **Single women** have **better mental health** than **married women**.

There are **different perspectives** on these trends, including **medical**, **feminist** and **interpretivist** approaches.

The Medical Approach is to Treat Mental Health as a Biomedical Condition

1) The medical approach to mental illness focuses on the **abnormal individual** rather than the **environment** that the individual lives in. It concentrates on the **physical symptoms** of mental illness. For example, a **medical approach to schizophrenia** would say it's caused by a **chemical imbalance in the brain**.

2) The medical approach is **cure-orientated**. It emphasises the importance of treatments involving **drugs or surgery** for depression.

3) The medical approach suggests that treatment is best carried out in the **medical environment** (e.g. a hospital rather than the community) and should always be carried out by the **qualified elite** (e.g. doctors).

Compare this with the key features of the biomedical model of illness on page 68.

1) In the 1930s, mental disturbance was sometimes treated surgically. Doctors actually severed neural connections between certain parts of the brain. This is called a lobotomy. It often had unwanted side effects, such as adverse effects on the patient's intellect. Lobotomies aren't done any more, although more refined brain surgery is sometimes used in extremely severe cases.

2) In the 1940s, electroconvulsive therapy (ECT) was used to treat depression. It's still sometimes used to treat very severe depression. In ECT, an electric current is passed through the patient's brain, to create a seizure a bit like an epileptic fit.

3) Drugs are used to treat all sorts of mental illness. Some drugs have severe side effects.

4) Mental illness is also treated by psychotherapy, where the patient talks to a therapist who tries to get them thinking in a more healthy way.

Feminists see Women's Mental Illness as a Result of Patriarchy

Joan Busfield (2001) thinks that women might be diagnosed with more than their fair share of mental health problems because of **sexism** in the **male dominated medical elite**. She thinks that doctors **label** and **interpret** behaviour differently depending on whether it's a man or a woman doing it. For instance, an **angry, stressed, upset woman** might be labelled **mentally ill** but an **angry, stressed, upset man** might just be "**overworked**".

Psychologist **Paula Nicolson (1998)** thinks that **postnatal depression** is more a **social thing** than a **physical thing**. She disagrees with the standard medical view that postnatal depression is a **mental disorder**, and that it's **normal** to be a **happy new mum**. Nicolson argues that it's **natural** for women to get **depressed** after having a baby.

Marxist feminists think that women's mental illness is caused by their "**dual oppression**" as **housewife** and **worker**.
Radical feminists suggest mental illness in women is a consequence of **patriarchal society** in which women have **low social status**, the **stress** of **housework** and **childcare**, and the stress of **social isolation**.

Mental Health

Inequalities *in* Ethnicity *and* Mental Health *have Different Explanations*

1) Some sociologists use **interpretivist thinking** to explain inequalities in **ethnicity and mental health**. **Littlewood and Lipsedge (1982)** found that psychiatric doctors and nurses were more likely to use sedatives with **black** patients. They suggested that this was because the medical staff were **mostly white** and did not understand how to speak to patients who were **culturally different**. They looked to drugs as an **easy solution**.

2) Others have offered structural explanations. **James Nazroo (1997)** found that ill health in ethnic minorities in general was linked to **poor housing**, **stress**, **low status** and **poverty**. Mental health differences could be part of the **same pattern**.

The *Interpretivist Approach* Sees Mental Health as a *Social Construct*

Thomas Szasz (1971) reckoned that **mental illness doesn't really exist**.

1) He thought that what we call "mental illness" is really just another **"social construct"** — a **label** society uses to **control non-conformist behaviours**. He said that people who behave in a way that the rest of society sees as **unacceptable** or **dangerous** are defined as "mentally ill".

2) People who are labelled as "mentally ill" can be admitted into psychiatric hospitals against their will. Szasz compared **forced treatment in mental hospitals** to the **persecution of witches** in the Middle Ages.

3) Szasz prefers a **system** where individuals are **free** to get psychotherapy **if they want to**. He says it's important that there's **no threat of force**, coercion or **loss of liberty**.

R.D. Laing was a psychiatrist who wrote in the late 1960s. He believed that "mental illness" is really a natural response to being in an unbearable situation. He also thought that mental illness needn't always be a negative thing. He had an idea that **mental breakdowns** could turn into **mental breakthroughs**.

1) **Erving Goffman (1961, 1970)** saw mental illness as a **stigma** caused by **negative labelling**.

2) Goffman was particularly **harsh** on the **role of mental institutions** in **reinforcing these labels**.

3) He thought that individuals in psychiatric institutions have to learn to **conform** to their label as "mentally ill". He said they **lose their old identities** in the process. Goffman calls this process a **"deviant career"**.

Goffman (1961) studied patients and staff in psychiatric institutions

Goffman described how patients respond to being labelled "mentally ill".

Withdrawal — Patient doesn't communicate with other patients — doesn't believe he / she belongs with them.

Rebellion — Patient refuses to cooperate with staff.

Cooperation — Patient plays along with the staff idea of how a mental patient behaves. Patient starts to act crazy.

The staff respond to the patient's "crazy" behaviour by **punishing** the patient — they take away the patient's liberty and privacy and they don't let the patient make choices. This is called **"mortification of the self"**. It ends up with the patient losing their personality.

The patient becomes **institutionalised**, which means they can't manage on their own outside the institution. After this, the staff can start from scratch, building up a "sane" conformist personality.

If a patient said, "I don't belong here — I'm not mad", the staff might think, "that's just what a mad person would say — you must be mad".

This is what happens to Jack Nicholson's character in the film One Flew over the Cuckoo's Nest.

Practice Questions

Q1 Which social groups are statistically most vulnerable to mental illness?

Q2 How would a "medical approach" define and treat disorders such as depression or schizophrenia?

Q3 According to Szasz, what is mental illness?

Exam Questions

Q1	Identify and explain two features of the medical approach to mental illness.	(17 marks)
Q2	Outline and evaluate the view that mental health is a social construct.	(33 marks)

If you say you're sane, it's proof you're not...

Mental illness is particularly interesting for some sociologists because it can be as much about social deviance as it is about mental health. In Stalinist Russia, you could get locked up as insane just for saying something the authorities didn't like. It's scary to think of. Learn about the medical treatments for mental health, the gender inequalities, and the negative labelling bit.

The Role of Medicine and Health Care Professionals

*There are sociologists who dispute the role of the medical elite in improving public health in modern times. Some even say doctors are the cause of much illness and disease. Blimey. For **AQA and OCR**.*

Medical Intervention Hasn't Done a Lot of Good — According to *McKeown*

1) **McKeown (1976)** claims that **medical intervention** by the biomedical elite **hasn't had much impact** on improvements in health over the last 200 years.

2) McKeown thinks that the big health improvements have been mainly down to **social factors** — things like **sewage disposal**, supply of **clean water** and **improved diets.**

3) The **social changes** that McKeown says changed people's health all happened in the **19th century** — before the medical elite came to dominate health.

4) McKeown uses evidence like **life expectancy** and **infant mortality statistics**. He points out that life expectancy went up and infant mortality went down **before** biomedical techniques came in. For instance, mass immunisation for TB (a biomedical approach) only happened after the death rate for the disease had already gone down.

The bathroom — where social health <u>really happens</u>.

Illich Says the *Medical Elite* Actually *Cause Bad Health*

1) **Illich (1975)** defines **health** as the **capacity** to cope with the **human reality** of **death**, **pain** and **sickness**. This is a very different definition to the mainstream biomedical definition.

2) Illich believes that medicine has **gone too far**, and started to "**play God**" — trying to **wipe out** death, pain and sickness. OK so far... he then says that **trying to control death and illness** is a bad move which **turns people into consumers** or even objects. In his opinion, this messes up people's natural capacity for health and **makes people ill**.

3) Illich uses the word **iatrogenesis** to mean this kind of illness that's caused by modern medicine. He says there are **three types of iatrogenesis**:

> 1) **Clinical iatrogenesis** — the **harm** done to patients by **ineffective** treatments, **unsafe** treatments or getting the **wrong diagnosis.**
>
> 2) **Social iatrogenesis** — the idea that **doctors** have **taken over control** of people's lives, and individuals can't make decisions about their problems. More and more of people's problems are seen as **suitable** for **medical intervention**. This is called the **medicalisation of social life.**
>
> 3) **Cultural iatrogenesis** — the **destruction** of **traditional** ways of **dealing** with and making sense of **death**, **pain** and **sickness.**

Illich thinks the **worst** is **cultural iatrogenesis**. He puts it like this:

> "A society's image of death reveals the level of independence of its people, their personal relatedness, self-reliance, and aliveness."
> Illich (1975) *Medical Nemesis*

According to Illich's view, dying has become the ultimate form of **consumer resistance** (when you're dead, you can't buy any more NIKE trainers, I'd imagine). **Death** isn't seen as something normal. It's become a **taboo**.

Functionalists See Illness as *Deviant* — Doctors *Control* this Deviance

1) According to **functionalists** like **Talcott Parsons (1951)**, doctors have an **important function in society** — they control the amount of time people take off **work** and **family duties**.

2) Illness is "**deviant behaviour**" which **disrupts** work and home life — you're not supposed to take time off sick.

3) Parsons said that sick people take on a "**sick role**". While a person is sick, they're allowed to stop functioning in their **normal role**. They don't have responsibility for making themselves better — but they are **expected** to **want to get better**, and to do whatever the doctor tells them.

4) Doctors are in charge of **confirming** that the patient is **actually ill**. Doctors **allow** the sick person to take limited time off, and **make them better** by using their **expert medical knowledge**. Parsons thought that doctors always put the patient's needs before their own needs.

Critics of Parsons say the medical profession don't always put patients first — they say private medicine is proof that doctors are self-interested. However, it **can't be denied** that doctors really do give people **sick notes** so they can take sick leave.

The Role of Medicine and Health Care Professionals

Marxists see Medicine as an Institution which Supports Capitalism

Marxists believe that the medical profession only do good for the **capitalist** class — they **keep class inequalities going**. Marxists say that the medical profession have a **conservative** role in society.

1) Doctors keep the workforce **healthy** and **productive**. **Healthy** workers can **work harder** and won't have to take **time off sick**. This means **more profits** for the capitalist class.

2) Doctors **check** that **workers** aren't spending **too much time on sick leave**. They say **how long** a worker can **stay off work**.

3) Marxists believe that doctors **hide the real social causes of illness** (poverty, class inequality etc.) by focusing on the individual and their physical symptoms.

Some Marxists think that **doctors** are **agents** of **large drugs corporations** — they believe that health care exists mainly to produce **profits** for drugs companies.

Weberians see the Medical Profession as Self-Serving

Weberians think that doctors **arrange** things so that they **keep** their **high status** in society.

They suggest that the medical profession is **self-serving**.

A Weberian is a follower of German sociologist, historian and economist Max Weber (1864-1920).

They argue that the medical profession has managed to **shut out** other forms of healing such as homeopathy, aromatherapy, faith healing and other types of **alternative medicine**. This gives modern medicine a monopoly.

Feminists see the Medical Profession as serving Patriarchal Interests

1) Some feminists say that most **contraceptive methods** (e.g. the pill and IUDs) are designed for men rather than women. This doesn't mean men are supposed to use them — it means they have **significant health risks** for women that **men would never put up with**.

2) **Oakley (1984)** has said that the process of childbirth has been "**medicalised**". In other words, women giving birth are treated like there's **something wrong with them**. **Control** over giving birth is taken away from women and given to **men**. Male doctors are often in charge, not midwives or the women who are actually giving birth.

3) Women tend to have **subordinate** roles in medicine — **nurses** and **auxiliaries** tend to be **women**, **consultants** tend to be **men**. Some feminists think that the role of being a nurse has been made to look like being a "doctor's handmaid" — a female servant obeying the male doctor.

4) **Cosmetic surgery** is criticised by some feminists as the "medicalisation of beauty", and also as a **social control** over women.

5) Feminists see the diagnosis and treatment of **depression** in women as another kind of **social control**.

Of course, not everyone agrees that drugs for depression are prescribed to make women shut up and stop whingeing. It depends on your ideological viewpoint...

Practice Questions

Q1 What does McKeown claim is responsible for improvements in health in the last 200 years?
Q2 What does iatrogenesis mean?
Q3 What three types of iatrogenesis does Illich identify?

Exam Questions

Q1 Identify and explain two ways in which the medical profession can be seen as patriarchal. (17 marks)

Q2 Outline and evaluate the view that health and sickness are defined by the powerful. (33 marks)

If doctors make you ill, do teachers make you thick...

Blimey, this iatrogenesis idea is a bit radical — it's actually the doctors' fault that we're ill... Still, you can kind of see some reasoning behind it. Oh, and as ever, you need to be able to compare and contrast functionalist (all for the best), Marxist (all set up for the benefit of the bosses), Weberian (all for the benefit of doctors) and feminist (all unfair to women) views. It's a right laugh.

Disability

There are two key viewpoints on disability that you need to learn: the biomedical model and the social model.
This page is for OCR only.

The **Biomedical Model** views Disability as a **Strictly Physical** Thing

1) In the 19th and early 20th centuries, the dominant view of disability was **biomedical** — a person with disabilities was seen as faulty and in need of **medical attention**.

2) Individuals had almost **no choice** over the medical attention they received — doctors did whatever they thought was necessary to '**fix**' the disability.

3) People with disabilities were not seen as part of **mainstream society**. Their access to the benefits of society, such as **jobs**, **education** and **relationships**, was often heavily **restricted**.

> **Tom Shakespeare (2000)** said that traditional approaches **medicalise** and **individualise** disability. They deal with the symptoms of each case separately and **ignore** social patterns.

> **Oliver (1990)** suggested that disability is usually treated as a **personal tragedy** — an **individual** problem rather than a **social** one. He felt that this led to a lack of useful action.

The **Social Model** views Disability as a **Product of Society**

The **social model of disability** rejects the biomedical model and says that it's **society** that's **at fault** — if a wheelchair user can't attend a school because it **lacks wheelchair access** then it's the school that needs to be fixed.

1) This view first became **influential** in the second half of the 20th century, as people with disabilities began to resist the **limitations** placed on them by society.

2) The **United Kingdom's Disabled People's Council** was established in 1981 to promote full **equality** and **participation** in UK society for people with disabilities.

3) The social model has prompted many changes in social policy. The most important of these is the **Disability Discrimination Act (DDA) 1995**.

> The Disability Discrimination Act 1995 makes equal opportunities for people with disabilities a legal requirement for employers, shops, educational and public bodies, landlords, transport companies and many other bodies.

People with **Disabilities** are Often **Portrayed Negatively** by Society

1) Many of the words traditionally used to describe disability are very **negative**, such as 'cripple', 'spastic' and 'Mongol'. 'Handicapped' is considered offensive because it implies **helplessness** and some people trace the origin of the word to 'cap in hand' **begging**.

2) Most people now prefer the purely descriptive phrase '**person with a disability**'.

3) Despite changes in language, many disability activists still feel that popular culture is '**disableist**' — prejudiced **against** disabled people.

> **Tom Shakespeare (2000)** found that the media representations of disabled people still relied on old **stereotypes** of **twisted villains**, **plucky heroes** and **weak victims**. He argued that the **mass media** encourages the able-bodied population to view people with disabilities as 'other' — an **abnormal** group that is not part of **mainstream society**.

Alternative Medicine

Some people disagree with the biomedical tradition of health care and seek alternative treatments.
This page is for OCR only.

CAM is short for 'Complementary and Alternative Medicine'

1)   CAM is any form of medicine that doesn't fit into the **biomedical tradition** of health care.

2)   Some forms of CAM, such as herbalism, are **traditional** in origin. Others, such as homeopathy, are more **recent** inventions.

3)   Some forms of CAM are more acceptable to professional doctors than others:

Complementary medicines

Complementary medicines are used **alongside** traditional health care. Some of them — such as hypnotherapy — are **available on the NHS**, and some conventional doctors even have training in complementary medicines.

Alternative medicines

Alternative medicines are used **instead** of traditional health care. They often have a 'spiritual basis' — e.g. treatments like crystal healing — and are **not available on the NHS**.

After a nasty kick to the groin, Barry had to spend months having his chakras re-aligned.

There is some **overlap** between complementary and alternative medicines. Some treatments, e.g. **acupuncture**, will sometimes be used to complement traditional healthcare and sometimes be used as an alternative.

CAM is Increasing in Popularity

1)   According to a **House of Lords** report (the **Select Committee on Science and Technology's Sixth Report, 2000**) complementary and alternative medicines are finding **increasing popularity** in the UK. **20%** of people asked had used some form of CAM during the previous **12 months**.

2)   The report argues that the growth in CAM can be explained by **negative experiences** with conventional medicine.

> 1)   **Chronic** illnesses, such as **arthritis**, **back pain** and **asthma** can't always be treated successfully by conventional medicine. Some CAM medicines claim to be able to **help** with these illnesses.
>
> 2)   Modern GPs are under a lot of **time pressure** and often don't have time to build **good relationships** with their patients — unlike many CAM practitioners.
>
> 3)   Many GPs work in group practices where the patient may see a **different doctor** every time they go.
>
> 4)   Prescription drugs often have **unwanted** or **unpleasant side-effects**.

3)   Some doctors believe that CAM only works because of the **placebo effect** — i.e. it works because the patient **believes** that it is going to. But some CAM practitioners have said the **same thing** about conventional medicine.

Practice Questions

Q1   How does the biomedical model view disabilities?

Q2   How does the Disability Discrimination Act help people with disabilities?

Q3   What is the difference between complementary medicine and alternative medicine?

Exam Questions

Q1   Identify and assess the reasons why people turn to complementary and alternative medicines.   (17 marks)

Q2   Outline and evaluate the view that the problems faced by people with disabilities are caused by society.   (33 marks)

CAM — proof that we're living in a society that's open to new ideas...

... even if the way the media represents people with disabilities suggests that some people are happier sticking to very old ideas. Make sure you know the key arguments of the social model and biomedical model views of disability, and can explain what CAM is and why it's increasingly popular. Then maybe relax, have a cup of coffee, and do whatever you'd normally do.

Religious Movements

Religious groups organise themselves into different forms. They differ in leadership, relationship to the state and politics, how they worship and who they appeal to. Sociologists have put forward different classifications of religious organisations. **This section is for OCR only.**

There are Four Key Concepts in the Study of Religion

Religious Belief	Thinking that the world is controlled by supernatural forces — normally a god or group of gods.
Religious Commitment	Carrying out religious actions, such as praying or singing religious songs.
Religious Membership	Being part of a formal religious institution — a church, sect or cult.
Religiosity	The level of an individual's connection with all aspects of religion — belief, commitment and membership.

1) A person's religiosity is the **balance** between their **religious experience** and their **religious beliefs**.

2) Some people attend church for social reasons, even though they don't believe in a god — their religiosity emphasises **membership** and **commitment**.

3) Others believe in a god but never go to church — their religiosity emphasises **belief**.

A Church is a Well Established Religious Organisation

Social historian **Ernst Troeltsch (1912)** distinguished between different kinds of religious organisation, and used the word **church** to mean a **large religious organisation**. He said churches usually have four main features:

1) A church claims **monopoly over the truth** — it says its claims are **absolutely true** and others are **false**.

2) Churches have a **complex rigid hierarchy** and a **bureaucratic structure** with lots of **rules and regulations**.

3) Churches often have a **close relationship** to the **state**. Some nations have an official national religion — Weber used the term "**ecclesia**" for this.

4) They are closely integrated into **mainstream society**. Churches act as a **conservative** force, resisting change. This is why the **upper classes** are more likely to join — even though churches are **universal** and **inclusive in principle**.

Examples of churches include the **Roman Catholic Church**, the **Church of England** and the **Episcopal Church**.

Troeltsch studied churches in **16th century** Europe. **Steve Bruce (1995)** says that Troeltsch's points don't always apply to today's churches because there's **religious pluralism** these days. The Church of England doesn't claim a monopoly over the truth and it isn't always conservative.

Religious pluralism = lots of different types of religious groups.

Sects are Small, Radical Religious Movements

Troeltsch defined sects as being almost the **opposite of churches**. Few religious groups fall into the category of sect.

People who are **dissatisfied** with mainstream religion can be attracted to a sect. Sects are often formed by people **splitting off from a church** because they **disagree** with the church's **practices** or **theology**.

1) Sects claim a **monopoly over the truth** and are intolerant towards other religious organisations.

2) Sects have **no complex hierarchy**. They often have a **charismatic leader** who **persuades** members to **follow his or her teaching**.

3) Sects are **small**. Their members follow with **total commitment**, and they can be **manipulated** by the sect's leader.

4) Sects are separate from the state — they're in **opposition** to mainstream society. Sects can sometimes offer an alternative way of life for **deprived** and **marginal** groups.

Examples of sects include the **early Methodists** and **Calvinists** (although over time these have become more mainstream). This category also includes **extremist** groups like the **People's Temple** in America who were led to mass suicide by Jim Jones, or the **Branch Davidians** led by David Koresh.

These extremist groups are generally called cults in everyday language. Watch out though — in sociology, cult means something else...

All hail the glorious leader of the oddly-patterned dungaree-ologists.

Religious Movements

Denominations are Subsets of Churches

Troeltsch **originally classified** religious organisations into **churches** and **sects**.
The term "**denomination**" was added later.

1) Denominations don't usually claim **a monopoly over the truth**. They see themselves as a **possible route to the truth**. They are **tolerant** towards other religious organisations.

2) Like a church, they have a **hierarchy** and **bureaucratic structure** but it isn't as complex.

3) They have a reasonably **large membership**, but not as large as an established church.

4) Members of denominations are usually **not as loyal** as members of churches.

5) Denominations **aren't closely connected to the state**. They get involved in society and **comment** on **current events**.

Examples of denominations are **modern Methodists** and **Baptists**.

Cults are Mystic Movements — Often Wrongly Defined

Bruce (1995) defined cults as movements without a fixed set of beliefs. They emphasise the **inner power** of the **individual** and **mysticism**. Cults are usually loosely knit and don't have a hierarchy.

Fundamentalism Provides Meaning and Certainty in Periods of Uncertainty

Fundamentalism involves the **fundamental, literal interpretation** of religious texts. Fundamentalist groups **strictly** and **fervently** follow their beliefs. These groups often have **charismatic leaders**.

In both of the following examples, **fundamentalism** provides **certainty** and **meaning** in periods of **uncertainty**.

1) Islamic Fundamentalism in Iran

Iran was a **traditional** society that **quickly modernised** under the **Shah**. **Women** wore **Western clothes**, alcohol was freely available and there was **secular education**. There was also **inequality** in society — the upper class were **very rich**, and working class areas were **neglected**. **Traditional Muslims** were **unhappy** about the direction that Iranian society had taken, and saw the Shah as **corrupt**. They started to oppose the Shah, led by a **fundamentalist** religious leader called **Ayatollah Khomeini**. There was a revolution in 1979 and the Ayatollah came to power. He established a society based on **Islamic Sharia law** — alcohol was banned, there were harsh punishments for crime, and women were required to cover their bodies in public.

2) Christian Fundamentalism

The **New Christian Right** in **America** argues that American society is in **decline** and in a state of **moral crisis**. They think this is caused by **liberal reforms** — e.g. easy **divorce**, legalised **abortion**, **gay rights** and **secular education**. The New Christian Right **oppose** the teaching of **evolution** in schools, because it disagrees with their fundamentalist interpretation of the Bible. They started some **universities** that offer not only degrees, but also a strict **Christian education**. They promote their views through **mass communication** e.g. TV and Christian publishing.

Practice Questions

Q1   Give the key characteristics of a cult.

Q2   Give two examples of fundamentalist religious movements.

Q3   What do sociologists mean by 'religious commitment'?

Exam Questions

Q1 Identify and explain two features of a church.	(17 marks)
Q2 Identify and explain two features of a denomination.	(17 marks)

Lots of religions don't condone sects before marriage...

*Don't assume you already know what a church is, what a sect is, etc. Sociological definitions can be a bit different from the everyday definitions. So **learn them**. Obviously, not all religious groups will fit neatly into one of these categories — but most will.*

New Religious Movements

The term "new religious movement" (or NRM for short) includes a huge range of movements from diverse sources. They've increased significantly in number since the 1960s. They don't always fit the old church-sect-denomination-cult divisions.

New Religious Movements can be Affirming, Rejecting or Accommodating

Sociologist **Roy Wallis (1984)** identified three types of new religious movement:

World-rejecting movements cut themselves off from society — similar to sects

1) World-rejecting movements are very **critical** of wider society and are often in conflict with the state.

2) **The Unification Church**, better known as the **'Moonies'**, is one example of a world-rejecting movement.

3) World-rejecting movements require **total commitment**. They demand **significant lifestyle changes**. Members often turn away from family and friends — world-rejecting movements have developed a reputation for "**brainwashing**" members. It's often hard to leave a world-rejecting movement.

World-affirming movements are tolerant of other beliefs — similar to cults

1) They're similar to **self-help** and therapy groups — they try to "**unlock spiritual power**". **Transcendental Meditation** is an example of a world-affirming movement.

2) World-affirming movements seek **wide membership**.

3) World-affirming movements **don't require** especially high levels of **commitment**.

World-accommodating movements are traditionally religious — similar to denominations

1) World-accommodating movements often come from **traditional** religions.

2) They try to rediscover **spiritual purity** lost in traditional religions. **Pentecostalism** is a movement within Christianity that aims to bring the Holy Spirit back into worship.

3) World-accommodating movements allow people to carry on with their **existing lifestyle**.

The Growth of New Religious Movements isn't Easy to Explain

The **interpretivist** idea is that **new religious movements (NRMs)** provide **certainty** in times of **uncertainty**. When there's uncertainty, new religious movements have **greater appeal** and **grow** in numbers. Here are some of the **uncertainties** that people face:

1) **Marginality** — inequality, immigration and racism may **marginalise** some groups. So, some new religious movements may help marginalised people **make sense** of their situation, and may promise a better life after death as **compensation**. **Weber** called this the "**theodicy of disprivilege**".

2) **Relative deprivation** — the concept of marginality doesn't explain why **white, middle class groups** join new religious movements. Although they aren't absolutely poor or deprived, some middle class people may see themselves as **deprived in comparison to their peers**.

3) **Social change** — transformation of society can result in **anomie** and **uncertainty**. The breakdown of **community**, the process of **secularisation** (see p.88), **cultural diversity** and bad news such as **terrorist attacks** may generate uncertainty.

anomie = a state of confusion where there is a lack of agreed norms and values.

4) **Modernity and post-modernity** — the **alienation** of capitalism, the increasing amount of **red tape**, bureaucracy and disillusionment with work may create **uncertainty**. The choice people have in constructing their identity may create **uncertainty** and a **crisis of identity**.

Melton (1993) didn't agree that NRMs emerged in periods of uncertainty. He looked at the founding dates of non-conventional religious organisations in the US. **Rapid growth** took place in the **1950s** — in a period of **stability** and **certainty**. Why do these sociologists never agree...

Wallis (1984) explains the appeal of the three different kinds of new religious movement

1) **World-rejecting movements** grew in numbers in the 1960s. There was a lot of **freedom** for people, but also **uncertainty**. It was a period of **radicalism** with lots of alternative world views — often called the "sixties counterculture". Some people got **disillusioned** with this counterculture and wanted more **concrete** beliefs.

2) **World-affirming movements** develop as a means of coping with a **crisis of identity** in more successful groups (e.g. the middle class). They try to unlock **human potential** and help people solve their problems. **Bruce (1995)** claims that they're a response to the **rationalisation** of the modern world where it's hard to find satisfaction from work.

3) **World-accommodating movements** appeal to those who are dissatisfied with existing religion.

New Religious Movements

Millenarian Movements Look Forward to the Apocalypse

1) **Millenarian** movements are a type of NRM that claim that members will achieve **salvation** through a **cataclysmic** event — a major disaster. Millenarianism is connected to **apocalypticism**, which is the belief that **divine forces** will **overthrow** the existing social order.

2) The **Ghost Dance** of the indigenous **Plains Tribes** in **North America** is a traditional example of a **Millenarian** movement. The tribes believed storms and earthquakes would return the buffalo to the prairies and end ethnic divisions.

3) Millenarian movements are associated with **deprived groups** or areas where there has been **radical social change**.

The return of Changing Rooms.
Enough to make anyone believe the end is nigh.

New Age Movements are Cultural

1) **New Age movements** are close to cults and world-affirming movements. New Age ideas often aren't linked to an organisation, but spread through a **culture** e.g. **dowsing**, **feng shui**, **crystal healing**, **neopaganism** and **reiki**.

2) **Heelas (1996)** claims that New Age beliefs are dedicated to "**self-spirituality**" and the development of the self.

3) **Bruce (1995)** highlights **three themes** to New Age movements: **New Science** rejects many claims of traditional science, **New Ecology** is concerned for the environment, and **New Psychology** sees the self as sacred.

New Age Movements Appeal to People Already Examining their Identity

1) New Age beliefs appeal to people who have **turned away from traditional religion**. New Age beliefs say that people can find salvation, peace or perfection **inside themselves**. Modern society is more **individualistic** than before — **individual beliefs** are **trusted more**, and **authority** is **trusted less**.

2) New Age movements help some people cope with the **uncertainties** of modernity. In the modern world, people have a lot of **different roles**. New Age beliefs can help people find a sense of **identity**.

3) New Age beliefs often appeal to middle class people working in "**expressive professions**" — actors, writers, social workers, counsellors, therapists etc. New Age beliefs appeal to **women** more than men, and **middle class** more than working class.

4) New Age movements may also reflect a **cultural change** in mainstream society. People are surrounded by non-conventional ideas like horoscopes, feng shui and homeopathy. **Mass communication** gives us an awareness of different movements.

5) New Age is quite a **postmodern** thing. In a **postmodern** society of **choice** and **diversity** people can **pick and mix** from all kinds of New Age philosophies to help them construct their own identity.

> There are more and more belief systems in society. "**Spiritual shoppers**" are people who **sample** different systems of belief to find the **best fit**. This is an **individualistic** and **consumerist** attitude.

Practice Questions

Q1 What are the three types of New Religious Movement that Wallis identified?

Q2 Give two examples of New Religious Movements.

Q3 Give two of the 'uncertainties' that help make New Religious Movements popular.

Q4 What three themes did Bruce identify in New Age movements?

Exam Questions

Q1	Identify and explain two characteristics of New Religious Movements.	(17 marks)
Q2	Outline and evaluate the view that New Religious Movements are created in periods of uncertainty.	(33 marks)

Yup, moving your furniture around counts as religion...

It's not just going to a traditional place of worship that counts as religion. Deranged groups who think the world's going to end tomorrow, and all sorts of wishy-washy lifestyle stuff is also seen by sociologists as evidence of religious belief.

Religion and Sociological Theory

The old "founding fathers" of sociology were all interested in the role of religion in society. Marx and Durkheim thought that religion stopped social change. Weber thought that religion could start social change.

Marx Said Religion Inhibits Social Change and Helps to Oppress Workers

1) Karl Marx said that in **capitalist** society there was **conflict** between the **ruling class** and the **working class** because the ruling class **exploit** the working class to get the most profit out of them.

2) But — there's **something stopping** the working class from **uniting** and **overthrowing** the ruling class. Marx says the working class are in a state of **false consciousness**. This means they're **not aware** of **how unfair** society is.

3) This is where **religion** comes in. Marx is **very critical** of religion. He says it **keeps** the working class in a state of **false consciousness**. He said, "**Religion is the opium of the people**". This means that it **dulls the pain** of oppression like **opium** — a **drug** which kills pain. It doesn't take the oppression away, though.

> **Marx says that religion justifies social inequality**
>
> 1) People have **heaven** to **look forward** to if they're **good**, so they **don't break the rules** and don't challenge the capitalist system.
>
> 2) Religion **consoles** people with the **promise of life after death** and so they **put up** with their **suffering** here **on Earth** more easily.
>
> 3) Religion often tells people that their **position is decided by God**. This encourages false consciousness by blaming God instead of **blaming capitalism**.
>
> 4) If **God is all-powerful** he could **do something** about the suffering **if he wanted to**. He **doesn't** do anything — so this must be **how society is meant to be**.

So, Marxism says that religion **passes on beliefs** that **oppress the working class**. Religion is a **conservative** force which prevents revolution. The **rich stay rich** and the **poor** keep on working. It's a **mechanism of social control**.

> **But... there are problems with applying this Marxist view to today's society**
>
> **Fewer people go to church** than in the past. The idea that religion is an **ideological device** just doesn't seem **relevant** in Britain today. If people **don't go to church**, it's **hard** for them to be duped by religious ideology.

There's Evidence that Religion is a Conservative and Oppressive Force

1) **Hymns** like *All Things Bright and Beautiful* contain **really clear ideologies** like "the rich man in his castle, the poor man at his gate, **God made them high and lowly** and **ordered their estate**". Blimey.

2) Monarchs in medieval Europe ruled by **divine right**. People believed they had the **God-given right** to rule — so they had total power. No one could challenge them.

3) **Halevy (1927)** claimed that **Methodism** prevented revolution in the 19th century. Dissatisfied workers turned away from the established state church to find enlightenment with the Methodists. Although they **changed denomination**, they **kept on working**.

4) **Hook (1990)** points out that the **Catholic Church** has a **conservative** view on contraception, abortion and homosexuality.

"This church has always been made of mud! You can keep your newfangled bricks and mortar".

But in Some Cases Religion can Encourage Social Change

1) Marx's good pal **Engels** reckoned that in **some circumstances** religion could actually be a **revolutionary** force. Sometimes **religion** is the **only means of change** because all other routes have been blocked.

2) **Early Christian sects** opposed Roman rule and brought about change. **Jesus** encouraged social change.

3) Neo-Marxist **Otto Maduro (1982)** also claimed that religion isn't always a conservative force. In the 1960s and 1970s, **Catholic priests** in **Latin America** criticised the bourgeoisie and preached **Liberation Theology** — using religion to free people from their oppression. This led to **resistance** and **social change** — in 1979, Catholic revolutionaries threw out the oppressive government in **Nicaragua**. Maduro said religion is "often one of the main available channels to bring about a social revolution".

4) Reverend **Martin Luther King** and the **Southern Baptist Church** resisted oppression and segregation, bringing about **political** and **social rights** for black people in **1960s America**.

Religion and Sociological Theory

Functionalists see Religion as Maintaining Harmony and Social Cohesion

Functionalists see religion as something that **inhibits change** and helps **keep society as it is**. They think this is a positive role, which creates **social order** based on **value consensus**. Here are those key functionalist's views:

1) **Durkheim** studied Australian **Aboriginal** society and thought that the **sacred worship of totems** was equivalent to **worshipping society itself**. Durkheim said that sacred religious worship encourages shared values.

2) **Malinowski (1954)** looked at how religion deals with situations of **emotional stress** that **threaten social order**. Unpredictable or stressful events like births and deaths create **disruption**. Religion **manages these tensions** and recreates stability.

3) **Parsons** wrote in the 1950s and 1960s that religion provides **guidelines** for human action in terms of "**core values**". Religion helps to **integrate** people into a value consensus and allows them to **make sense of their lives**.

There's also a functionalist idea of **Civil Religion**, which is when secular (non-religious) symbols and rituals create **social cohesion** in a similar way to religion. **Flags**, famous **political figures** and even **royal deaths** bring about some kind of **collective feeling** that generates **order** and **stability**.

> Functionalism ignores **dysfunctional** aspects of religion. There are **religious conflicts** all over the world. Religion can be a source of **oppression**.
> Religion can also bring about **change**, and functionalism ignores that as well.

Weber said that Religion can Indirectly Cause Social Change

Weber's book *The Protestant Ethic and Spirit of Capitalism* looked at how the **religious** ideas of **Calvinism** brought about social change. Weber spotted **two important things** in Calvinism:

1) **Predestination:** Early Calvinists believed in **predestination**, which says your **life** and whether you have a place in heaven is **predetermined** by God. Only a **specific few** were **chosen** for heaven. This created **anxiety** — you didn't know if you'd been chosen.

2) **Ascetic Ideal: Working hard** in your job was a **solution** to this anxiety. Success might be a sign that you were chosen for heaven. Early Calvinists lived a **strict** and **disciplined** life of hard work and simple pleasures.

Weber claimed that the ascetic ideal created an ethic of **disciplined hard work**. This is the **spirit of capitalism**. Not only was there a build-up of **capital** and **business**, but there was the right **work ethic** for capitalism. Religion **indirectly** brought about change.

However — **Eisenstadt (1967)** contradicts Weber's theory by claiming that capitalism occurred in **Catholic** countries like Italy **before** the **Protestant Reformation happened** and **before** the ideas of **Calvin ever came out**.

Postmodernism says There's No Such Thing as Truth

According to postmodernist thinkers, such as **Lyotard (1984)**, there's no such thing as **truth**. All that exists is **discourse** — attempts to explain the world through language. Religious belief is one type of discourse and science is another. These beliefs **compete** with each other in society, but none of them are actually "true".

Practice Questions

Q1   What role did Marx think religion played in the capitalist system?

Q2   What did Malinowski and Parsons say were the social functions of religion?

Q3   What did Weber claim was indirectly brought about by Calvinism?

Exam Questions

Q1   Identify and explain two ways in which religion creates social harmony.   (17 marks)

Q2   Outline and evaluate the view that religion works against social change.   (33 marks)

Learn the different theories — don't lose Marx...

Traditional Marxism sees religion as a conservative force that inhibits change and keeps the working man down. Engels and Maduro see religion as sometimes being the only way you can have social change. Weber suggests that religion indirectly brought about change and functionalists see religion as something that keeps order and stability. Confusing or what...

Religion and Social Position

Religiosity is related to age, gender, ethnicity and social class.

Religiosity varies by Age

Age affects how religious people are.

Lisa follows the cult of the Flying Spaghetti Monster. Well, it's hard not to believe in the thing when it's sitting on your head.

1) People **under 15** and **over 65** are more likely to be involved in religious activity. However, participation by those under 15 usually takes the form of **Sunday school** and **religious playgroups**.

2) The **over 65** group is the **most religious** in terms of **belief**. They aren't necessarily the most likely to practise their religion by going to church, because of difficulty with mobility.

3) However, some recent studies claim that the **elderly** are **increasingly losing faith** in God.

4) **Middle aged** groups are more likely to get involved in **world-affirming movements**.

5) **Sects** and **cults** are more likely to be populated with **young adults**.

- **Sects** often appeal to young adults by messages of **friendship** and **companionship** — this can be attractive to those who are experiencing forms of **anomie** (lack of social/moral standards) and **detachment** from the world, and those who have few responsibilities (e.g. marriage).

- **Cults** appeal to the **inner thoughts** and **feelings** of young adults who are often alienated from the primary cultures of society. **Cults** are attractive to individuals who are often already engaging in **counterculture** activity.

6) Young adults may be less religious than older people because of the way that society is changing. An increase in **rationalisation** means they feel less **need** for religion to explain things.

Religiosity varies by Gender

1) **Women** are **more likely to attend church**, and more likely to say they belong to a religion (British Social Attitudes Survey, 1991). This has often been explained by women's traditional role as **primary caregiver**. Going to **church** and **raising children** to be **religious** is traditionally seen as an **extension** of that role.

2) **Differential socialisation** is also a factor. The argument goes that girls are socialised to be **passive** and to **conform** — which fits in with the behaviour of more **traditional** and **conservative** religious groups.

3) Another argument is that **women** simply **live longer**. More women are on their **own** as they get older, and they may **turn to religion** for a sense of community. **Older** people are **more religious anyway**.

4) More **men** than **women** have **turned away** from organised religion in the 20th century.

Simone de Beauvoir wrote that religion creates a **theodicy of disprivilege**. She said that society keeps women in low status by promising them a reward in Heaven. Women show more religiosity than men because otherwise they'd have nothing on Earth and nothing in Heaven.

Women often have Significant roles in New Religious Movements (NRMs)

1) Women generally **participate** in **sects** more than men.

2) Also, many sects and NRMs were **established** by **women**, e.g. one of the founders of the Seventh Day Adventists was Ellen White, and the Christian Science movement was founded by Mary Baker Eddy.

3) **Glock and Stark (1965)** have argued that the gender difference in membership of NRMs is because **deprivation** (social, physical and mental) is **disproportionately** experienced by **women**.

4) **Bruce (1995)** suggests that men are more interested in NRMs that advocate **esoteric knowledge**, whereas women are more interested in subjects that can be classified as **New Science**, **New Ecology** and **New Spirituality**.

esoteric = elitist and specialist

5) Some sociologists claim that **New Age** movements appeal more to women, because they emphasise "**feminine**" characteristics such as healing, caring and cooperation.

Remember, some NRMs have **narrow beliefs** about **women's role** in society, and therefore may **not appeal** to women. For example some new evangelical right wing Christian movements believe that women should not work outside the home.

Religion and Social Position

Religiosity Varies by Ethnicity

The 1994 PSI Fourth Survey of Ethnic Minorities (**Tariq Modood et al**, published **1997**) found that, in England and Wales, nearly all **ethnic minority groups** are **more religious** and participate more in religion than white groups.

1) Religion maintains a sense of **community** and **cultural identity** within ethnic minority groups.

2) **Johal (1998)** claims that in a multi-faith society such as the UK, **religious identity** has become of key importance to members of ethnic minorities.

3) **Davie (1994)** argued that identification with a **religious organisation** was important to Indians, Pakistanis and Bangladeshis in the UK because it gave a sense of cultural identity and a feeling of **belonging**.

- **Modood** found that Pakistani and Bangladeshi Muslims in the UK identified themselves primarily as **Muslim**.
- Many young Muslims have a deeper **knowledge of Islam** than their **parents** do.
- Many Muslim girls feel more **liberated** by wearing headscarfs and dressing modestly because they are not subjected to the same **stereotypes** and values as non-Muslim girls.

i.e. rather than British, Pakistani, or Bangladeshi

4) **Afro-Caribbeans**, who are mainly Christian, attempted to incorporate themselves into the established churches of the UK but found **racism** within many congregations. One way to tackle this was to develop their own churches and ways of worshipping — e.g. Pentecostal churches.

5) **South Asians**, however, had to establish their faith in a country with **radically different** systems of belief. Religion acted as a **support mechanism** for new immigrants, allowing them to share their culture. South Asians **quickly established** religious organisations — mosques, Sikh gurdwaras, etc. **Bruce (2002)** calls this **cultural transition**.

6) **Modood (1994)** and **Saeed (1999)** found some evidence for a decline in religious practice among Asians in the UK.

Religiosity Varies by Class

1) The **middle class** is disproportionately **Anglican** and **Quaker** compared with a more **Roman Catholic** or **Methodist** working class (this can be partly explained by their popularity in Victorian industrial areas). This pattern can be seen across many countries such as the U.S. and this would seem to back up Marx and Weber's opinions on Protestantism and capitalism.

2) Religious participation is greater in the **middle classes**, partly because religious affiliation is seen as a **desirable** social characteristic. Church is an opportunity for **social networking**.

3) Some argue that participation in **denominations** and **sects** is based on **class position**, claiming that there are middle class denominations and working class denominations.

4) **Bruce (1995)** found that cults are primarily middle class — in his opinion because they fulfil spiritual needs for people who have little financial pressure.

Practice Questions

Q1 Suggest why young adults participate more in sects and cults.
Q2 What role does religion play in upholding patriarchy according to feminists?
Q3 Suggest why middle class people participate more in cults.

Exam Questions

Q1	Identify and explain two gender differences in religiosity.	(17 marks)
Q2	Outline and evaluate the view that religious identity is of key importance to ethnic minorities.	(33 marks)

"Ah no, this is the women's church. Men's church is next door"...

Well, obviously it's not quite like that. The examiners will expect you to know how religion relates to age, gender, ethnicity and class, and also how religious participation relates to those things. You should mention a few studies too — no, don't kid yourself that you can remember them all — what did Glock and Stark argue? What about Johal? Davie? Saeed? Ha!

Secularisation

That's me in the corner...

Secularisation is When Religion Loses Its Influence Over Society

Bryan Wilson (1966, *Religion in Secular Society*, London: CA Watts) defined secularisation as a "**process whereby religious thinking, practice and institutions lose social significance**". Secularisation is said to be a result of the social changes brought about by **modern**, **urban**, **industrial society**.

The "founding fathers" of sociology **predicted secularisation**.

1) **Auguste Comte** claimed that **science** was the **final stage** in the **development of human thought**.
He said modern society would be dominated by **science** and not religion.

2) **Max Weber** believed that **modern society** would be the age of **technology**, **rationality** and **bureaucracy**.
He said rationality and efficiency **sweeps away magic**, **myth** and **tradition**.

Church Attendance and Membership is in Decline

Counting bums on pews gives **supporting evidence for secularisation**:

1) **UK church membership** and **attendance** has gone down — the number of people who **go to church** has fallen by almost 1 million in the last 20 years.

2) Attendance at ceremonies such as **baptisms** and **marriages** has also dropped. Just **27%** of babies were baptised in 1993, compared to **65%** in 1900.

Measuring secularisation by counting **bums on pews** has **limitations**:

1) People may **attend church** but **not believe in God**. They might attend a service, baptism or wedding out of friendship for the people involved, for respectability or because of family duty. Or even to get their kids into a certain school.

2) People may **not attend church** because of their **lifestyle** even though they believe in God. **Not being in church** doesn't tell you about **belief**. The last census found that 72% of the population identified themselves as Christians.

3) To make comparisons with the past you have to use **old statistics**, which may not be reliable.

Pluralism Gives People Choice

Religious pluralism means **diversity** in types of religious organisations and beliefs in society.
As a result of this diversity the **established, national church loses its influence** in integrating people into **shared values**. **Multicultural** societies are more likely to have religious pluralism.

Some sociologists see pluralism as evidence against secularisation

1) The increase in **New Age movements** since the 1980s can be seen as proof that the **sacred** is becoming **important** again — this is called **resacrilisation**, by the way.

2) It can be argued that pluralism is evidence of religion being **transformed**. It shows a trend towards **individuation** — people being free to search for their **own religious meanings** (to become "**spiritual shoppers**").

Other sociologists see pluralism as supporting evidence for secularisation

1) Pluralism gives people **choice**. People might feel freer to choose to **reject religion altogether**.

2) Although some people in modern society have joined **new religious movements**, they are still a **small proportion** of the population. Some sociologists claim the **growth** in NRMs has been **overestimated**.

Desacrilisation is Where Supernatural Belief is Less of a Force in Society

1) Weber **predicted desacrilisation** (see glossary) in his idea of **disenchantment**. He thought that magic and myth were less important in modern society. Similarly, **Bruce (1995)** sees **science** and rational explanations as **undermining religion**.

2) Instead of turning to the supernatural or religion to **explain our problems** we might turn to **science**.
We demand pills when we are ill and we use science to explain natural disasters.

3) However, the **death** of a loved one, **injustice**, **natural disasters** and **terrorist atrocities** still sometimes lead people to prayer and faith in the supernatural. Modern science **can't explain everything** to everyone's satisfaction.

4) **Postmodernists** claim that we've moved **beyond scientific** rationality and we now **mistrust science**.

5) Belief in **astrology** and **lucky charms** and **fanatical interest** in magical fantasy like **Harry Potter** and **Lord of the Rings** demonstrates that people still have an interest in **magic**, **myth** and the **irrational**.

Secularisation

Some Religious Institutions have Become Secularised

1) **Secularisation** of **religious institutions** is when the church becomes **less religious** in its beliefs to **fit in** with the rest of **society**. For example, many churches will now allow divorced people to marry.

2) American sociologist **Herberg (1956)** thinks church attendance shows **commitment to community** and not religion — people go to church to **meet up with friends** and feel like **part of something**.

3) Remember that **not all religious institutions** have become more **secular**. The **New Christian Right** don't compromise their beliefs to fit in with society — they're against divorce, homosexuality and premarital sex. The more extreme end of the religious right are also against women working outside the home.

The Church May have Lost Some Functions and Become Disengaged

Differentiation is where society becomes more specialised so each institution in society has fewer functions than in the past. For example, the church used to have an important educational function. But since the 19th century more separate institutions have developed for this role and state involvement has increased. Religion becomes less important in society as some of its previous functions are taken over.

Disengagement is when the church becomes separated from the state. As a result, it has less influence.

1) Although the church may have lost its functions and become disengaged from the state and politics, religion can still be **significant in everyday life** and encourage **shared values** in society.

2) Religion is still closely linked to **politics** in the **Middle East** and **Northern Ireland**.

Secularisation is Very Difficult to Measure

1) There are lots of different **measures of secularisation**. Some are more valid and reliable than others. **Surveys** show **high levels of religiosity**, but **quantitative measurements** of **church attendance** are **low**. **Different religious groups** measure membership in **different ways**, anyhow.

There's more about sociological research methods in Section 8.

2) The term **secularisation** is a general term that's sometimes applied just to Christianity. It's important to know **what's being measured** — the decline of **religion in general** or the decline in **Christianity** in particular.

3) It's difficult to measure the significance of religion and make comparisons because sociologists use **different definitions of religion**. Some sociologists use **substantive definitions** which say **what religion is** — e.g. "religion is belief in the sacred". Some sociologists use **functional definitions** saying **what religion is for** — e.g. "religion is for creating value consensus".

4) To measure whether society has become **more secular** you have to compare it to **the past**. Some sociologists argue that we see the past as a **golden age** of religion where **everyone** believed and **no one** was sceptical. This is **far too simplified**.

5) Research into secularisation can also be rather **ethnocentric** — e.g. focusing on **Christianity** and what the **predominantly white British mainstream** does. Islam, Hinduism and Sikhism are also changing and developing in different ways.

Practice Questions

Q1 How did Bryan Wilson define secularisation?
Q2 How does religious pluralism provide supporting evidence for secularisation?
Q3 What is meant by desacrilisation?
Q4 Using the measure of church attendance, give one piece of evidence to support secularisation.
Q5 Define the term disengagement, with reference to religion.
Q6 Give one reason why it can be difficult to measure the importance of religion.

Exam Questions

| Q1 | Identify and explain two problems with measuring secularisation. | (17 marks) |
| Q2 | Outline and evaluate the view that the influence of religion is in decline. | (33 marks) |

...that's me in the spotlight, losing my religion...

There are lots of different sides to secularisation, and lots of ways to measure it. There's some clear evidence both for and against the secularisation thesis — which you need to learn. Oh, and by the way, the Bryan Wilson with the theory on secularisation isn't the Brian Wilson who was in the Beach Boys. Not that you thought he was. I'm just saying, like.

Social Construction of Youth

*Youth is the period in a person's life between childhood and adulthood. Roughly speaking, it's your teenage years —
but some people start early and some finish late. Sociologists see it as a crucial period in the socialisation process.*
This section is only for OCR, so skip it if you're doing AQA.

Youth Culture *is a* Different Thing *from* Culture...

Culture means **language**, **beliefs**, **values and norms**, **customs**, **roles**,
knowledge and **skills** — the "**way of life**" of a **whole social group**
or **society**.   Culture is **socially transmitted**. That means it's passed
on through socialisation from one generation to the next.

See pages 10 and 11 for a more detailed
look at the idea of socialisation.

> **Youth culture** is different because it often **opposes mainstream society**.
> It **rejects** the norms and values passed on by previous generations. Rejecting
> society's values can range from **minor differences** to **total rebellion**.

Sociologists say youth
culture is "<u>oppositional</u>".

> One of the defining features of youth culture is that most youth
> **individuals** are part of a **group**. These are known as **peer groups**.

...But There Isn't Just One Youth Culture

Sociologists say that young people form **lots of different subcultures**.

> A **subculture** is an **identifiable group** whose members **share values**
> and **behaviour patterns** which are **different** from **mainstream norms**.

Dressing like your mates
and listening to music your dad
hates. All part of growing up.

Sociologists Have Tended to Focus on "Spectacular Subcultures"

These are **dramatic subcultures** that attract the **attention** of the public and the **mass media**. They dress
flamboyantly and **distinctively**, and often appear to **behave** in ways that **break the norms** of society.
Examples include **Teddy boys** (1950s), **mods** and **rockers** (1960s) and **punks** (1970s).

> **Stan Cohen (1972)** examined the way the media encouraged
> spectacular subcultures in the mid 1960s.
>
> 1)   His research looked at a number of disturbances in English
>   seaside towns involving **mods** and **rockers**.
>
> 2)   **Exaggerated media reporting** of fairly **minor** incidents
>   encouraged an **exaggerated reaction**. The **police** and **court**
>   responses to the fights grew stronger.
>
> 3)   More young people were **encouraged to join in** the fights. This
>   **seemed** to **justify the fear** that the media had expressed.
>
> 4)   Cohen called this a **moral panic**.

A <u>moral panic</u> is a strong public reaction to a particular group of people or a social phenomenon.
Cohen reckons that these moral panics come from deliberate <u>media exaggeration</u>.

Some Say this Distorts the Truth about Most Young People

1)   Spectacular subcultures are **interesting** to sociologists because they're **dramatic** and **kind
       of fun to study**. Some sociologists have said that it's a **mistake** to focus on these groups.

2)   The term "**ordinary youth**" is used to describe young people who **generally accept
       mainstream norms** and **values** and don't belong to any identifiable subcultures.

3)   According to a **1990** study by **Paul Willis**, only **13%** of young people claim to belong to
       a **spectacular youth subculture**. This means most young people are "ordinary youth".

Social Construction of Youth

Sociologists **Disagree** on the Reasons for the **"Invention of the Teenager"**

1) The idea of a **youth culture** first appeared in the **early 1950s**. At the time teenagers seemed to have a **rebellious spirit**.

2) The **school leaving age went up** to 15 in the 1940s, so people stayed as "youth" for longer.

3) The post-war period was **relatively affluent**. Young people had **disposable income** to spend on **leisure activities**. A **youth culture** based around **popular music** and **fashion** started to develop.

Pilcher (1995) says that youth became more important in the 1950s because of **demographic changes** — the return of millions of men at the end of the Second World War caused a **massive jump** in the pregnancy rate, known as the **baby boom**. That meant that by the late 1950s there were **a lot more youths** about than before.

Abrams (1959) says that the teenager was created by **economic factors**. In the 1950s, people left school at 15 and it was easy to **find a job**. This led to a large number of young people with **money to spend** and **limited responsibilities**.

Frith (1984) and others link the creation of the teenager with **consumption**. There was a need for people to buy certain products, such as those produced by the fashion and media industries, so youth culture created a market for these industries.

In the 1950s young men had to do 18 months of National Service in the armed forces between the ages of 17 and 21. Boys leaving school had a couple of years of freedom before being forced to join up...

Youth Culture is Strongly **Linked** to the **Mass Media**

Hollywood films like *Rock Around the Clock* in the 1950s, *Bonnie and Clyde* in the 1960s, *Saturday Night Fever* in the 1970s and *Boyz n the Hood* in the 1990s were all influential on youth audiences, affecting **clothing fashions** and **trends in music**.

TV shows, particularly comedy and music television (e.g. The Mighty Boosh, MTV), affect the **way** that teenagers talk to each other and **what** they talk about.

The internet, especially **social networking** sites like MySpace and Facebook, has become a big influence on youth culture, particularly on how young people **communicate** with each other.

Youth Culture is affected by **Globalisation**

1) **Guibernau and Goldblatt (2000)** identified an increase in **American** control over world culture, including youth culture.

2) The biggest **media influences** on young people tend to come from the USA, e.g. Hollywood, Facebook and MTV. The **big brands** associated with most teenage interests are American-owned — clothing and footwear, soft drinks, fast food, music, TV and films are all dominated by American companies.

Practice Questions

Q1 How is youth culture different from culture?

Q2 What is a subculture?

Q3 What do sociologists mean by 'spectacular youth subcultures'?

Q4 How did Abrams (1959) explain the rise of youth culture?

Exam Questions

Q1 Identify and explain two reasons for the development of youth culture in Britain since the 1950s. (17 marks)

Q2 Outline and evaluate the view that economic change is the main influence on youth culture. (33 marks)

Das Boot — a great German sub culture film...

...cos it's set on a submarine. Ha ha ha. Ha ha. Ha... Er, anyway, you've got your mainstream culture, your youth culture and your subculture. These pages really aren't that hard to get your head around. It's fairly likely that you've already got a working idea of what a subculture is. We've all seen a punk, a hippie, a goth etc.

Theories of Subculture

So now you know what a subculture is, the next thing to look at is why young people join them. Sociologists have worked out various reasons. A big point of difference is between the functionalists, who think everything in society exists for a good reason, and the Marxists, who think that everything is a reaction to the oppression of capitalism.

Functionalists *say the* Generation Gap *creates a* Need *for* Subcultures

1) There are many social and cultural **differences** between **childhood** and **adulthood**. Getting across the **generation gap** from child to adult can be an awkward and stressful experience. According to functionalist thinkers like **Talcott Parsons (1956)**, subcultures can provide a bridge over that gap. They give young people something to belong to while they're in a **transitional state**.

2) **Eisenstadt (1956)** said subcultures are to do with **ascribed** and **achieved status**. In pre-industrial society every individual's status was **ascribed** from birth. In today's society, people have to **achieve** their status for themselves. **Adolescence** is the time when young people are often **uncertain** about what their status is going to be in the **future**. Eisenstadt believed that **subcultures help young people to cope** with this uncertainty by giving them a **nice, clear status**. You know where you are in a subculture.

3) **Albert Cohen (1955)** was influenced by **functionalist** ideas, but he added a **new twist**. He says working class boys join subcultures to overcome **status frustration**. In **school** they might feel like **failures**, but in a subculture they can have **high status**. They can **feel superior** to less important members of their own group and to people who aren't members of the subculture.

Fuzzy about the difference between functionalist and Marxist perspectives? Check out pages 2 and 3. Need to know about ascribed and achieved status — it's on page 11.

Marxists *see subcultures as a form of* Resistance *against the* Class System

1) **Young, working class males** are at the **lowest level** of society and often have **little to look forward to** in life. It's quite likely that they'll end up in **dead-end jobs** and be tied down by families.

2) According to Marxist sociologists, this **explains** why **spectacular subcultures** attract working class male youth. The subculture gives them **status** and **independence** which they wouldn't get anywhere else.

3) Sociologists at the **Centre for Contemporary Cultural Studies (CCCS)** at Birmingham University took a **Marxist** approach to the study of youth subcultures. Here are three examples:

Tony Jefferson (1976) researched **1950s Teddy boys**. Teddy boys wore **Edwardian style jackets**, **suede shoes** and **bootlace ties**. Jefferson reckoned that the **bootlace ties** were from characters in **Western** films who had to **live off their wits** — the sort of character who **working class lads** would **admire**. He thought that the Teddy boys wore clothes that they felt would give them **higher status**.

Phil Cohen (1972) studied **skinheads**. Cohen thought skinhead style was a **reaction** to the **decline of working class communities**. He said **skinheads** tried to **recreate working class culture** by dressing in grandad shirts, work boots and braces, and by acting in a way that valued **masculinity** and **aggression**.

Dick Hebdige (1979) studied **punks**. He looked for the meanings behind the **clothes** they wore. He said that punk was a form of resistance to the dominant cultural values of British society in the late 1970s. The symbolism and style of punk, such as safety pins stuck in the nose, and bin liners for clothes, stood for a **rejection** of **common norms** and **values**. Rather than trying to look attractive, punks went out of their way to shock.

Hebdige believed that punk was a rejection of available **identities**. Instead of accepting the patterns of behaviour, dress and future career that were expected by society, punks chose a different path. They dressed and acted in a way that told the world they wouldn't conform.

Some feminist sociologists describe the theories above as **'malestream sociology'** — focusing on a **masculine point of view** and ignoring the role of gender in subcultures. They argue that this is because **sociology as a whole** is **male-dominated**, and subcultures have been of particular interest to **male** researchers. There's more about the relationship between gender and subcultures on page 94.

Theories of Subculture

Postmodernists Say There's No Such Thing as Subcultures Any More

Spectacular subcultures seem to be a **thing of the past**. In the 1980s and onwards, youth subcultures **fragmented** into lots of small movements and trends, like rave and hip hop. They didn't seem to involve huge numbers of young people in the same **spectacular** way as the old subcultures. Maybe there are **no real subcultures** any more. Or perhaps there are **so many subcultures** that it's **hard to tell them all apart**.

> **Hetherington (1998)** believes that the fashions and musical styles of the 1980s were **too bitty and too varied** to be described as subcultures.

Youth culture is an expression of individuality. And iffy taste...

1) **Paul Willis (1990)** says there are now a wide range of "style and taste cultures" so young people have lots of different ways to define their identity. There's **too much diversity** these days for any **single youth subculture** to **dominate** society.

2) He says that most young people don't want to join uniformed subcultures like the teddy boys or punks any more. Instead, they have a much **more individualistic** approach.

3) Willis believes that the **old spectacular subcultures** were quite **passive** — members accepted norms and styles of the group as a whole. Young people today are **active** and **create** their own **individual styles** by **mixing up** whatever's available. Willis calls this "**symbolic creativity**".

> **Examples of symbolic creativity include:**
>
> 1) **Mixing up clothing** from **high street stores** and **charity shops**.
> 2) **Sampling** and **scratching** existing music to create **new music**.
> 3) Using **religious iconography** such as **crosses** or rosary beads as **fashion items**.

Bennett Said "Young People Don't Form Subcultures"

Bennett said we **shouldn't talk about subcultures** any more. He invented the term **neo-tribe**. This means a loose group based around **fashion** and **lifestyle**, but **without** the **shared values** that members of a **traditional subculture** would share. He implied that youth culture no longer has much meaning and that young people value **style over substance**.

Bennett (1999) researched clubs in Newcastle

Bennett found that young people formed brief, **temporary associations**, instead of subcultures. Friendship groups included people with a **wide range of class backgrounds** and musical tastes. This was unlike the mostly working class subcultures of earlier generations.

Individuals **mixed and matched fashion influences** and didn't feel they belonged to any definable group. They didn't identify with just one lifestyle and set of ideas. Bennett concluded that **youth identity** is now very **fluid** and doesn't involve fixed commitments or norms and values.

Practice Questions

Q1 According to Albert Cohen, why did working class boys join subcultures?

Q2 Give two examples of the symbolism and style of Punk.

Q3 What group of sociologists think that subcultures have died out?

Q4 Who introduced the idea of 'neo-tribes'?

Exam Questions

Q1 Outline and evaluate the view that subcultures are a form of resistance to capitalism. (33 marks)

Q2 Outline and evaluate the view that subcultures no longer exist. (33 marks)

Grungers, punks, chavs, ... whatever happened to the good old hippie?

When you write about these theories, you may need to evaluate them — explain their weak spots as well as their strengths. One of the easiest ways to identify weak points in a theory is to discuss the alternative theories/viewpoints. For example, you could criticise a Marxist theory by looking at the alternative feminist and postmodern viewpoints.

Gender and Youth Culture

Early sociological studies on youth culture focused on working class white males in spectacular subcultures. Later sociologists have questioned this narrow focus.

McRobbie Says Girls Have Been Involved in Youth Subcultures

1) There aren't as many girls in subcultures, and their role is often as **girlfriend** to a male in the group. This is linked to the **social control** of girls, who have generally been given **less freedom** than boys.

2) **Angela McRobbie and Jenny Garber (1976)** write about the **bedroom subculture**. This is where girls spend a lot of time in their bedrooms with friends, listening to music, experimenting with make-up and discussing pop music. This means that girls **accept social control** but still have a **private space**. This is **not spectacular**, but **it is a subculture**.

3) On the other hand, there were **plenty of girls** in the 1980s and 1990s **Goth** subculture. Some elements within the Goth subculture are **particularly feminised** — e.g. both male and female **Romantic Goths** wear lace clothing and lots of eye make-up.

I guess you could say there's a "hanging around outside McDonald's" subculture too.

Mainstream Youth Cultures are part of Gender Socialisation

According to **Angela McRobbie (2000)**, youth culture often pushes young people towards **traditional gender roles**. McRobbie discusses the difference between 'teenybop' music directed at girls and 'cock rock' directed at boys.

> **'Teenybop' music — aimed at girls**
>
> Teenybop music uses **romantic lyrics** and a **gentle presentation** to present **vulnerability** and **emotional depth**. Teenybop songs often emphasise **lyrics** over music, e.g. James Blunt, Take That.

> **'Cock rock' — aimed at boys**
>
> Cock rock music uses **sexual lyrics** and a **hard, aggressive presentation** to present **toughness** and **physical strength**. Cock rock songs often emphasise **musical ability** rather than lyrics, e.g. Klaxons, Bloc Party, Cold War Kids, The Gossip.

What you looking at, punk?

Girl Youth Culture has Changed Over Time

1) In **1977, McRobbie** produced a study of *Jackie*, a teenage girls' magazine. She found that it encouraged its readers to see female friends as '**catty**' and '**bitchy**', and to look instead for the **safety of a boyfriend**.

2) By the 1990s, female music stars like the Spice Girls and Destiny's Child were promoting the idea of '**girl power**' — a simplified type of **feminism**, encouraging girls to **make their own choices** and **enjoy their lives**.

3) In the late 1990s, '**ladettes**' developed — girls who take on behaviour traditionally **reserved for males**, such as noisy public drinking, swearing and boasting about sex.

Some Postmodernists say Gender is Determined Creatively

1) Research on secondary school girls by **Valerie Hey (1997)** showed that gender identities are not imposed on individuals from outside.

2) She studied the way teenage girls **communicated** by passing each other **notes** in class. She found that most of the notes were about their **friendships** and **fallings out** with each other. **Very few** of them were about **boys**.

This research could be carried out today with text messaging.

3) She thought that through this process the girls were **inventing** their **own version** of femininity by comparing themselves with each other.

Ethnicity and Youth Culture

Sociologists have sometimes been Ethnocentric

Ethnocentric means seeing things from a **certain ethnic point of view**.

In the past, **white sociologists** have sometimes **misunderstood** and **misrepresented** non-white ethnic groups.

1) Sociologists have often seen the **whole ethnic group** as a **subculture** — that means if you're a young Asian, sociologists have tended to focus on the "Asian" part and ignore the fact that you're young.

2) There are Asian youth subcultures, but they **haven't had as much attention** from sociologists as, say, Punk.

3) Some sociologists like **Maria Gillespie (1995)** have started looking at "**hybrid identities**" which bring together influences from **various cultures** and media.

Rastafarianism is an Important Black Subculture

Although Rastafarianism is a **religion**, it does have several of the **characteristics** of a **spectacular youth subculture**.

1) It's **oppositional**. Rastafarians rejoice in being black and believe **mainstream white society** is **corrupt**.

2) It requires **illegal activity**. Smoking **marijuana** is a part of Rastafarian **religious meditation ritual**.

3) It has a **spectacular style**. Some Rastafarians wear **dreadlocks**, often with a cap in red, green, gold and black.

4) It's associated closely with a **distinctive music**. Reggae and Dub are strongly linked to Rastafarianism.

Because the **stylistic elements** of Rastafarianism are so **strong**, they've sometimes been taken up by **non-Rastafarian black youth** in a more **subcultural** way. They've also **attracted** young people from **other ethnic groups**.

Racism in Society Creates Subcultures

1) Youth subcultures in ethnic minority groups are often linked to the **racism** of mainstream society — young black or Asian people often stick together as **protection** against possible racist abuse or violence.

2) **Mercer (1995)** and **Gilroy (1987)** both found that black youth subcultures often involve direct **resistance** to racism. For example, the lyrics of **rap music** frequently attack racism, especially racist police.

3) Sociologists such as **Bullock and Tilley (2002)** have connected the idea of **resisting racism** with **youth deviance**, such as joining criminal gangs.

Hybrid Youth Cultures Combine Ethnicities

1) **Paul Gilroy (1993)** writes about **hybridisation** of youth cultures — where youths borrow styles, music and language from other cultures instead of focusing on one set of influences.

2) **Bhangra music** combines influences from traditional Indian folk with pop and reggae.

3) **White rap music** from artists like Eminem and The Streets borrows black music styles to express white working class concerns.

Practice Questions

1) What is the 'bedroom subculture'?
2) What was 'girl power'?
3) What is ethnocentrism?
4) Give two examples of hybrid youth cultures.

Exam Questions

Q1	Identify and explain two types of female youth culture.	(17 marks)
Q2	Outline and evaluate the view that sociologists have focused too much on white male youth subcultures.	(33 marks)

A goth, a ladette and a Rastafarian walk into a bar...

Several hybrid youth cultures result — and none of them read Jackie. One of the problems with existing research on youth culture is that studies on girls tend to be rare and studies by white sociologists can be quite ethnocentric. So as well as learning the key sociological theories, you also need to remember the flaws in this area of research.

Youth and Deviance

Young people's behaviour sometimes breaks the rules. Sociological theory and research has tried to explain why this is and what sorts of deviant behaviour are typical of the young.

Deviance is Behaviour which Goes Against the Norm

OK, remember the idea of **social norms** from page 2. Norms are **ways of thinking and behaving** that are **shared** by most people in **society**. **Normative** behaviour **follows** these "rules", **deviant** behaviour **breaks** them.

Juvenile crime is where young people break the law

Some types of crime such as **vandalism** and **joyriding** are more likely to be committed by the **young**.

Juvenile delinquency is all disruption caused by young people

This includes **serious crimes**, such as rioting or burglary, **less serious crimes** like graffiti and public drunkenness, and **non-criminal misbehaviour** like being cheeky or truanting from school.

Official statistics show a **pattern** of **crime** and **delinquency**.
It seems that **most criminals** are:

1) **male**   2) **adolescent (young)**   3) **working class**   4) **urban**

Some Functionalists link Youth Crime to Subcultures

Quite a few **functionalist sociologists** tried to explain why crime tended to be committed by young working class men. Many based their ideas on **Robert Merton's work** from the 1950s and 1960s. They thought that crime and delinquency occur because **society seems to expect more** from **young men** than they can ever **achieve**. They called this "an **imbalance** between **culturally prescribed goals** and **opportunity structures**". Here's what it means:

1) **Young working class males** are **taught** through primary and secondary socialisation that **hard work** brings **material rewards**.

2) They're bombarded with **images of success** — through advertising, for example.

3) They **realise** they **don't have** any **real opportunity** to **achieve** this success.

4) They **rebel** against social norms and look for status from delinquent peers.

1) **Albert Cohen (1955)** saw that young people often committed delinquent acts in **groups** or **gangs**. He called these groups "**delinquent subcultures**".

2) Cohen believed that **working class youth** were **judged** according to **middle class goals** and **values**, which made them **frustrated** with their **status** and gave them a sense of failure.

3) Delinquent subcultures gave these young people a **different source** of **status**. In **delinquent subcultures**, individuals **get status** from their **peers** for doing **deviant** acts like vandalism and shoplifting.

4) **Miller (1962) disagreed.** He said delinquents **weren't rejecting middle class values** — they were **accepting working class ones**. According to Miller, working class communities value masculinity, toughness and thrill-seeking.

Status frustration is the feeling that you can never achieve a position of respect in society. Functionalist sociology says that status frustration happens when a person is given a set of goals that they know they can't reach.

Marxists link Deliquency to Economic Inequality

1) **Mike Brake (1980)** suggests that youth crime comes about because working class youths know that they have **little chance** of becoming **affluent** by legal means. Instead they seek an alternative path.

2) Many of the CCCS sociologists saw youth deviance such as drug-taking, street violence and vandalism as part of an overall pattern of symbolic **resistance to capitalism**.

There's more about the CCCS on page 92.

Youth and Deviance

Left Realism *Tries to Explain* Causes *and* Consequences *of* Delinquency

Left Realism is a viewpoint in sociology which tries to focus on the real world and **not be too theoretical**. Left realist sociologists **Lea and Young (1984)** say inner city **youth crime** is a big problem which damages working class communities. They say crime happens because **working class** and **black** youth **interpret** their situation **negatively**.

1) These groups feel **relatively deprived** because their job potential, income, standard of living and status are all **lower** than **middle class** and **white** youth.

2) They feel **marginalised** (pushed to the outside of society), believing that **nobody listens** to them, the police **harass** them, there are **no places** designed for them, teachers **label** them and so on.

This leads some youths to **look for status** in subcultures. **Positive subcultures** such as **sports clubs** offer **status** for **normative** (socially acceptable) behaviour. **Negative** ones give **status** for **delinquent** behaviour, including crime.

Labelling Theory *Says it's All About* ... Labelling

Some studies suggest that certain young people are **labelled as delinquent** by the **media** and the **police** — for example, young black men. This means they're **more likely** to be **stopped**, **searched** or **arrested**.

Some sociologists argue that **deviant values** and behaviour appear **throughout society**, but **working class** youth is more likely to be **negatively labelled**. They get **more media attention** and are arrested more, though maybe they don't actually commit any more crime than other social groups.

Labelling theory says "**deviance**" is a **master status**. Once you're labelled as delinquent, that becomes the most **important aspect** of your identity. **Everyone** sees you as a **delinquent**, and that's how you **see yourself** too. So, you **behave like a delinquent**. It ends up as a **self-fulfilling prophecy**.

Feminists *Point Out That These Theories* Don't Refer *to* Women

Feminists also say that the studies, which are mostly **just of male youth**, are presented as studies of **all youth**. **Merton's theories** about **expectation** and **failure** would suggest that **young, working class women** would commit a lot of crime — but they **don't**.

1) **Some sociologists** think that **women** have a **civilising influence** on men. When they want to develop **stable relationships** with **women**, young men often have to **give up delinquent activity**.

2) This is because **young women** are more likely to have **normative goals** — in other words their goals and aims are more likely to be in line with the norms of mainstream society.

3) This argument says that although **delinquency** is mostly a **male** activity, you can't understand it properly without looking at **gender relations**.

Practice Questions

1) What is the difference between normative behaviour and deviant behaviour?
2) What is juvenile delinquency?
3) What four characteristics do most criminals have, according to official statistics?

Exam Questions

Q1   Identify and describe two functionalist explanations of delinquency.   (17 marks)

Q2   Outline and evaluate the view that youth crime is a product of labelling.   (33 marks)

All this talk of deviance is making me feel positively... dirty...

As usual, there are several different explanations of why people do naughty things which society doesn't like. Some sociologists say that people feel they can't measure up to society's standards, so they kick against society — maybe out of some kind of spite. Others say it's about self-fulfilling prophecies — give a dog a bad name. Others say it's personal choice. Hmm...

Youth and Deviance

Lots of the sociology on youth crime has (no big surprise here) looked at social class, gender and ethnicity. Page 96 was all about social class. So that leaves... dun dun daaaaahhh...

Statistics Show That Females are Less Involved in Crime

1) **Frances Heidensohn (2002)** found that females **commit fewer crimes**, commit less serious crimes and are less likely to become repeat offenders.

2) **Heidensohn (1986)** says that **gender socialisation** explains why females do less crime.

3) **Male gender roles** emphasise things like **toughness**, **aggressiveness** and **physical strength**. These qualities are associated with **delinquency**.

4) **Female gender roles** include elements like **prettiness**, **softness**, **emotion** and **domesticity**. These aren't the sort of qualities that go with delinquent behaviour.

5) To make sure that girls are **successfully socialised** into female gender roles, they're given **far less freedom** than **boys** are. During adolescence, for example, they're more likely to be **confined** to the **home** by their parents — not allowed to go out.

6) This **social control** often leads to girls developing a "bedroom subculture" where **girls visit each other** to **listen to music**, **practise dance moves**, share **teen magazines** and chat. Unlike male adolescent subcultures, this all happens **indoors**, not out on the streets where there are opportunities for delinquent behaviour.

> One result of **socialisation** is that girls are **less interested** in committing crime.
> One result of **social control** is that girls have **fewer chances** to get involved in crime.

Some Sociologists Say Females Commit More Crime than People Realise

Anne Campbell (1981) asked males and females to fill in a **self-report survey** by ticking which deviant activities they'd done. She found that **official statistics** show **less female crime** than **actually happens**.

In recent years, statistics have shown that the **female crime rate** has **increased**. **Ann Hagell (1998)** says one explanation is a **reduction in social control**. Girls are **supervised less** than they were in the past.

Statistics Suggesting Links Between Ethnicity and Crime are Criticised

1) According to official statistics from 2000, **Afro-Caribbean** people are **four times more likely to be arrested** than other ethnic groups. Based on the UK population, you'd expect 8% of prisoners to be from ethnic minorities. In fact it's 18%.

2) Sociologists such as **Stuart Hall**, **Paul Gilroy (both 1982)** and **John Solomos (1993)** have all said that **racism** in the **police**, the **media** and the **white population** means that black criminality is exaggerated.

3) **Afro-Caribbean** and **Asian** youths are much **more likely** than white youths to get **stopped** or **arrested**. Some say this shows that the police deliberately **target ethnic minorities**. The **MacPherson report (1999)** stated that the (London) Metropolitan Police were "**institutionally racist**".

4) In 1981, Lord Scarman's **report on the Brixton Riots** discussed the police tactic of **stop and search.** Because they had a **strong street culture**, and were out on the streets more than other ethnic groups, **Afro-Caribbeans** were **more likely** to be **stopped and searched**. Stop and search was **racially discriminatory**.

Some Sociologists Say There are Social Reasons for Black Crime

Paul Gilroy (1982) thinks that black street crime reflects young black people's **anger at white society**. He says it's a **rational political response** to **prejudice** and **discrimination**, especially **police harassment**. He also links it to black people's anger at the **history of slavery** and colonialism.

Left Realists (look at page 97 for more on them) say black youth commit more crime because they're suffering from **relative deprivation** and a feeling of being **marginalised**.

1) Sociologists like Lea and Young also say that youth crime often **damages its own community** or **other underprivileged communities**.

2) Data shows that people from Afro-Caribbean backgrounds are **twice as likely** to be **victims** of **burglary**. They're also **more likely to be assaulted** than the white population.

3) *But* the **mass media** tends to portray black people as more likely to commit crime, not more likely to have a crime committed against them.

Youth and Deviance

Sociologists have been Very Interested in Gang Culture

Youth gangs are subcultural groups who aim to control a geographical area called a "territory".
They're usually involved in delinquent behaviour, such as crime and violence.
Everything you've learnt so far about deviant youth subcultures can be applied to gangs.

1) Most gangs are male.

2) Mostly, gangs are formed in poorer urban communities where there aren't many opportunities for young men to get status through education or a career.

3) Gangs are often linked to boredom. Gangs form because kids feel there's "nothing to do".

4) Gangs often start off with low-level delinquency such as vandalism and fighting. As they get more organised and older, gangs can move into more serious criminal activities like rape and gun crime.

5) Gangs often have very strict rules and status systems. Sociologists of subculture and deviance see this as a way young people can replace the norms and values of mainstream society with their own.

Most Sociological Work on Gangs Comes from the USA

1) In big American cities, there's often been a strong gang culture.

2) In the 1920s, Frederick Thrasher said that gangs were an important part of socialisation in all poor communities, helping young people to learn about "group awareness", and giving them a sense of belonging.

3) By the 1970s, US sociologists like Malcolm Klein were looking at it in a different way. They saw gangs as basically criminal groups which are often tied in with specific ethnic groups — Italian, black, Mexican, Puerto Rican etc.

4) In Britain, Bullock and Tilley (2002) did research which backed up this idea of ethnic selection in gangs. They found that known members of four main South Manchester gangs were mostly male and black.

Because gang members are mostly from specific ethnic groups, a lot of the sociology of ethnicity and youth crime applies, and you can use it in your answers. Also, since gangs appear in poorer communities, all the stuff on social class is relevant too.

Gangs Aren't Just Male

1) Mary Celeste Kearney (1998) looked at the recent growth in the numbers of girl gangs. She says this reflects wider changes in gender roles.

2) Anne Campbell (1986) studied New York gangs. She found that females were full members of gangs and that they were involved in a wide range of delinquent activities — violence, drug dealing etc.

3) However, Rutter, Giller and Hagel (1998) suggested that girl gangs in the UK had been exaggerated by the media, though girls were now more likely to have the opportunity for crime or be in the company of other people committing crime, as the bedroom subculture had moved out onto the streets.

Don't mess with the Rollerblade Crew. They'll, uh, nick your water bottle.

Practice Questions

Q1 How did Frances Heidensohn explain the fact that statistics show fewer female criminals than male criminals?

Q2 What did Anne Campbell's self-report survey show?

Q3 According to Lord Scarman's Report (1981), why were Afro-Caribbean youths more likely to be stopped and searched by the police?

Q4 What did Bullock and Tilley (2002) find about the sex and ethnicity of some South Manchester gang members?

Exam Questions

Q1	Identify and explain two reasons why girls tend to be less involved in crime than boys.	(17 marks)
Q2	Outline and evaluate the view that there is a link between youth crime and ethnicity.	(33 marks)

So what's Cell Block H full of then — blokes?...

This link between gender and delinquency isn't as clear-cut as you might think. Seems that girls don't tend to go off the rails, but when they do, they can go as far as the guys and get involved in gang violence. Ethnicity and crime is a biiiig hot-button topic in society. It's all tied up with the relationship between the police, black communities and the media.

Youth and Education

Young people respond differently to schooling — some accept the authority of teachers, but some don't. Many sociologists think it's all to do with which subculture you belong to.

There are **Pro-school Subcultures** and **Anti-school Subcultures**

And, guess what... **Anti-school subcultures** are **negative** about school. They **reject school rules** and don't conform in school. They get **status** from their **friends** by **not conforming**. These pupils tend to be **working class**.

Pro-school subcultures are **positive** about school. They **accept school rules** and **conform**. They gain **status** from the **school**, from **adults** and from their **friends** by working hard and **achieving highly**. They tend to be **middle class**.

These are all common forms of nonconformity in schools:

1) **Truancy** — skipping school   2) **Resistance** — not doing school work
3) **Challenging teachers' authority**   4) **Damaging school buildings** or **property**   5) **Fighting**

Research Suggests **Anti-school Subcultures** are **Working Class** and **Male**

David Hargreaves (1967) studied working class pupils

He found that **working class** pupils were **more likely** to be placed in **lower sets** and feel **labelled** as **failures**. Because of this they were likely to **reject the school's values** and follow their own set of **delinquent values** instead. This gave them a chance to **feel successful** in the eyes of **their peers**.

Paul Willis researched lad subcultures in the 1970s

He found that **working class boys rejected** the **values of school** because they associated being a "good pupil" with being "**girly**". The working class lads thought that education offered them nothing. Middle class pupils expected to stay on at school and get higher qualifications. Willis reckoned that because the working class boys didn't achieve in school they got **trapped** into **working class jobs** when they left.

Máirtín Mac an Ghaill (1994) studied low-achieving boys

He looked at a group of low-achieving white working class boys, who he called the "**macho lads**" because they were very keen to seem masculine. They were in bottom sets for all subjects, and their behaviour was difficult and aggressive. Mac an Ghaill said they were suffering from a **crisis of masculinity**. They knew that their failure at school meant their future wasn't looking great. They decided all the values of school were effeminate. They linked successful, pro-school boys with homosexuality and insulted them a lot. Which was nice.

Mac an Ghaill took Willis's ideas a bit further.

Ethnicity can Affect Your Experience of Schooling

Labelling theory says that teachers have **different expectations** of **different ethnic minority groups**. **Gillborn (1990)** found that teachers sometimes **negatively label black students**. Afro-Caribbean students were seen as a **challenge** to **authority** — and were more likely to be excluded from school. Negative labelling could result in a **self-fulfilling prophecy** of **failure**. In contrast, teachers had high expectations of Asian students.

There's also an issue about whether the school curriculum is **ethnocentric** — i.e. that it might fit the mainstream, white, middle class culture better than other ethnicities. It could be **Europe-centred** too. Languages in the National Curriculum are mainly **European** — kids usually learn French and German, not Gujarati or Chinese. **Assemblies**, **school holidays** and even **history lessons** may not fit with the culture and history of particular groups.

Some sociologists see British education as "**institutionally racist**". This is where **policies** and **attitudes** unintentionally discriminate against ethnic minority groups. **Wright (1992)** found that even though members of staff said they were **committed to equal opportunities, Asian girls** got **less attention** from teachers and felt their cultural traditions were disapproved of (e.g. they might get told off for wearing a headscarf if it isn't part of the school uniform). **Afro-Caribbean boys** were thought to be "likely to misbehave" so were more likely to be punished and **sent out of class**. These boys often **felt they'd been unfairly treated** and quickly started to **resent school**.

Youth and Education

Boys and Girls Choose Different Subjects at School

Girls are **more likely** to take **arts subjects**, like English literature, foreign languages and sociology.
More boys choose **scientific** and **technological** subjects. This starts at **GCSE** and gets **more obvious** at **A-Level**.

Some Scientists Say It's Because of Biology...

Some **scientists** believe that boys and girls choose different subjects because their **brains work in different ways**.

The idea of "**biologically programmed**" gender differences has been connected with the fact that **girls** now tend to do **better** than boys at school.

Boys are "biologically programmed" for:	Girls are "biologically programmed" for:
Competition	Cooperation
Physical Construction	Language
Factual knowledge	Conceptual knowledge

...But Sociologists Say It's Because of Socialisation

Sociologists reckon that **gender socialisation** is a **much better explanation** for these differences.

It starts with primary socialisation

For example, boys and girls are **encouraged** to play with **gendered toys** — Lego and Meccano sets for boys, dressing-up and dolls for girls. This encourages boys to become interested in technical and science subjects.

Secondary socialisation in school carries on gender stereotypes

1) The **advice** teachers give about **choosing GCSE options** may **reflect gender stereotypes**.
2) **Science** and the science classroom have a **masculine** image. According to **Alison Kelly (1987)** boys dominate science classrooms, **grabbing equipment** and answering questions first.
3) **Anne Colley (1998)** found that **girls did better at science** and technology in **single-sex classes**. Her research showed that many subjects **still** have **gendered images**. For example, ICT is seen as more **masculine** because there's **not much discussion**, students **work in isolation** on machines and the teaching is very **formal**. **Sociology** is seen as **more feminine** — lots of talking.

Gender might be Less Important than People Think

You can **criticise** this **whole debate**. Gender is an **important issue**, but it **can be overemphasised** — it's **only one** of the factors which affect children's education, after all. In lots of ways, boys and girls have **very similar experiences** at school — same teachers, same classrooms, same National Curriculum, same tests.

Practice Questions

Q1 How do members of anti-school subcultures gain status?
Q2 What is the usual social class and gender of members of anti-school subcultures?
Q3 Why did the boys Willis (1977) studied feel that education offered them nothing?
Q4 Why did Mac an Ghaill (1994) call the boys he studied "the macho lads"?

Exam Questions

Q1 Identify and explain two reasons why working class boys underachieve at school. (17 marks)

Q2 Outline and evaluate the view that gender differences in education have a biological basis. (33 marks)

Hide this book behind a magazine — they'll never know you're studying...

Kids have different reasons for thinking it's good to fail at school. The thing is that they don't decide based on what parents or teachers say, but based on what their own peer group will think. Sociologists haven't decided which comes first — boys' anti-school subcultures or boys feeling useless at school. Check out the AQA Education section if you like.

Key Issues in Research and Methods

These pages are for OCR and AQA. *Sociologists do research to get evidence which helps them understand society. Unfortunately, it's not all that straightforward to study human behaviour. If only we were ants in an ant farm.*

Sociologists Have Three Aims When Collecting and Using Data

1) Sociologists try to make their research **valid** and **reliable**. Research is **valid** when it gives a **true picture** of what's being measured. Research is **reliable** if other sociologists using the **same methods** get the **same data**.

2) You can't research the whole population. You have to take a **sample** (see page 106). Sociologists try to make sure that their **sample represents the population** — it needs similar proportions of different ages, gender, class and ethnic groups. If a sample is **representative** then sociologists can **generalise** — i.e. conclude that the results are likely to apply to the entire population.

3) Sociologists aim to be **objective** and **avoid bias**.

If a study focuses on a particular group, e.g. teenagers or working class people, researchers must still ensure that their sample is representative of that particular group.

Sociologists get data from different sources

1) **Primary sources of data** involve **first-hand research** — things like interviews, focus groups, questionnaires or observations (see pages 107-111).

2) **Secondary** data includes things like **official statistics**.

Data can be either quantitative or qualitative

1) **Quantitative data** is **numbers** and **statistics**. You can easily put quantitative data into a graph or a chart.

2) **Qualitative data** gives a detailed picture of what people do, think and feel. It's **subjective** — it involves **opinions**, **meanings** and **interpretations**. You can't turn qualitative data into a list of numbers or a graph.

Positivists Use Reliable Methods That Give Quantitative Data

1) **Positivists** say behaviour is influenced by **external social factors**.

2) They think sociology should be **scientific** and **analyse social facts**. Social facts are things that **affect behaviour** and can be **easily measured**. They're **external** things like laws, **not internal** things like people's opinions.

3) So positivists measure human behaviour using **quantitative data** — data that turns everything into **numbers**.

4) They use **statistics** to measure the **relationships** between different factors. They're interested in **cause and effect** relationships, e.g. the factors that cause underachievement in schools.

5) They use sources like **questionnaires** and **official statistics**. These are **objective** and **reliable**.

Interpretivists Use Valid Methods That Give Qualitative Data

1) **Interpretivists** (also called **interactionists**) believe that you can only really **understand** human behaviour using **empathy** — by putting yourself in **other people's shoes**. They think that it is important to uncover and understand the **meaning** individuals give to **their actions** and to **the actions of others**.

2) **Interpretivist sociologists** use methods that let them discover the **meanings**, **motives** and **reasons** behind **human behaviour** and **social interaction**.

Participant observation means being actively involved in the research as both participant and observer.

3) Interpretivists reckon that the **scientific** methods used in **positivist** research **don't tell you much** about how **individual people** act in society.

4) Interpretivists say you can't count meanings and opinions and turn them into statistical charts. They reckon **sociology isn't scientific** because **humans can't be measured** like ants in an ant farm. People don't always understand questions in questionnaires and they don't always tell the truth to researchers.

5) Interpretivists like to use methods that produce **qualitative** data — they try to understand human behaviour from the point of view of the **individual person**. They use methods like **participant observation** and **unstructured interviews** to build up a **rapport** (a feeling of mutual trust and understanding) with individuals, so they can produce a valid and detailed picture of what they think.

6) **Max Weber** said it's important to use **empathy** to **get inside a person's head** to figure out **why** they're doing what they're doing. He called this "**Verstehen**". Interpretivists take this idea very seriously — they're big on empathy.

> **Positivism** looks at the **institutions** in society. It's called **macrosociology**.
> **Interpretivist sociology** looks at the **individual**. It's called **microsociology**.

Key Issues in Research and Methods

Theoretical Background Affects Your Choice of Method

Theoretical background	Positivism	Interpretivism
Explanation of behaviour	It's determined by **social forces beyond people's control**.	Humans **make sense** of **social situations** during human interaction.
Aims of sociology	Sociology should discover **what causes what**.	It should **describe** and **explain** how people **make sense** of situations — using **empathy**.
Research methods	**Questionnaires** and **structured interviews** — they give **quantitative data** and they're **reliable** and **objective**.	**Observations** and **unstructured interviews** — they give **qualitative data** and a more **valid insight** into society.

Ethical Factors Affect Your Choice of Method

Ethical considerations can be grouped into **four main areas**:

1) **Consent** — all participants must have openly agreed to take part.
2) **Confidentiality** — the details of all participants and their actions must remain confidential and private.
3) **Avoidance** of **harm** — participants should not be physically or psychologically harmed by the research process.
4) **Avoidance** of **deception** — researchers should be open and honest about the study and its implications.

The **British Sociological Association** gives **ethical guidelines** for research. Researchers should use **informed consent** — people should know who's doing the research, why they're doing it and what it's about. **Covert participant observation**, where people don't know a sociologist is watching them, should only be used when there's **absolutely no other way** of getting data.

> Researchers studying **sensitive issues** like domestic violence often choose to use **informal interviews** to put the person answering the questions **at ease**.

Practical Factors Affect Your Choice of Method

1) **Time** — Some methods need more time. **Covert participant observation** takes a **long time**. The researcher has to get into the group they're studying and win their trust before starting the actual research. A **social survey** doesn't need the researcher to participate all the time and the **workload can be shared** in a team.
2) **Money** — This affects the **length** and **method** of the research. Money is needed to **pay the researcher**, for **transportation** to interviews, and to pay for **resources** like computers. **Large-scale social surveys** are **expensive**. The 1991 census cost £135 million. A small focus group will cost a lot less.
3) **Characteristics and skills of the researcher** — It'd be difficult for a **female** researcher to be involved in a participant observation of **monks** in a monastery. Some researchers may be OK with **dangerous situations** and others may prefer to **stay at their desk** and do **detailed analysis** of statistics.
4) **Access and opportunity** — If researchers **don't have access** to certain groups to carry out interviews or observations then they have to turn to **secondary sources**.

Practice Questions

Q1 What is the difference between quantitative and qualitative data?
Q2 Name two characteristics of positivism.
Q3 What type of data do interpretivists prefer?
Q4 Briefly explain how practical factors can affect your choice of research method.

Exam Question

Q1 Give two factors which may influence a sociologist's choice of research method. (4 marks)

Ready, aim, research...

Sociologists use different methods to produce different types of data. Positivists and interpretivists prefer different research methods. There are also ethical and practical factors which influence which method you choose. Remember that funding is a huge factor — sociologists don't work for nowt, y'know.

Key Issues in Research and Methods

The first step in sociological research is figuring out what you're going to research. The second step is condensing your topic down into a single question, or a single hypothesis. **These pages are for OCR and AQA.**

Sociologists pick a *Topic* based on their own *Preference* and *Knowledge*

Well, obviously. But there's slightly more to it than the obvious, so here you go.

1) Sociologists often **specialise** in different fields of the subject and therefore will often choose a topic that they have experience or knowledge of — for example, **Steve Bruce** specialises in **religion**.

2) Sociologists try to pick a topic that they think they'll find **enjoyable** and **interesting** to research.

3) Also, certain topics become popular in sociology at different times. For example, research in the **mid twentieth century** focused on **stratification** and the **class system**. **Nowadays**, the focus of sociologists has moved on to other topics such as **world sociology** and **medical sociology**. To gain **prestige**, **funding** and public or academic **interest**, sociologists are more likely to focus their research on topics that are currently **in vogue**.

4) Sociologists and other academics who want to make a **change** in society prefer research that could help develop **solutions** to **social problems**.

5) Sociologists may feel that a particular issue is **neglected** by other researchers, so they'll research the issue to try to **"plug the gap"** — and encourage others to embrace the issue as well.

Funding and Cooperation for Research have an impact on the choice of Topic

1) There are a wide range of potential **sources of funding**. Some research is funded by **charities**, e.g. the Joseph Rowntree Foundation. Some is funded by **industry**. Some is funded by the **government**. A lot of quantitative studies are done **directly** by **government agencies**.

2) The organisation which funds the research often likes to have some say in the **choice of topic**, or the **way** that the topic is **researched**. Government agencies often do research into areas covered by current or proposed **government policy**. **Industrial** grant providers tend to fund research that gives their industry some **practical benefit**.

3) Additionally, a researcher needs to decide whether they will be able to get the **cooperation** of the groups they'll be studying if they choose a particular topic. If potential subjects refuse to give their help for the research, then the topic may not be viable.

The researcher's *Career* in *Sociology* is another factor in selecting a topic

1) Sociologists have their eye on their **careers**, just like everyone else. Researchers would jump at the chance to conduct a study that improves their **employability**. Interesting, original or popular topics that are well researched, with good clear results, improve an academic's chance of having their work **published**. Getting work published, particularly in one of the **big sociological journals**, really **improves a researcher's standing** in academia.

2) A quick way for a sociologist to progress in their career is to respond to another sociologist's work. The aim can be either to **prove** the other sociologist **wrong**, or to **add something** to their research. Practically speaking, this could mean investigating the same topic, but using slightly different methods, or investigating a different group of people.

3) This can mean that particular social groups are researched a lot. For example, **routine office workers** are frequently researched in order to test out **theories of stratification** — some systems classify them as working class and some as middle class. Each sociologist who wants to **disprove** or **add to** earlier research on classification has to research **yet another** bunch of routine office workers. (Beekeepers **never** get this level of interest from sociologists.)

Reviewing the Field is crucial to a good research topic

1) **Reviewing** and **critiquing** existing **data** and **literature** is an important feature in any sociological report. It requires the researcher to spend time reading **articles**, **publications** and other sources of information already produced on the subject.

2) The researcher then **analyses** this material to help clarify the issues around the subject.

3) Reviewing the field gives the researcher useful information on the types of **methodology** used in **previous studies**. They can see whether specific methods, e.g. structured interviews, worked in the past. They can see if research samples were big enough, and form ideas about how big their own sample should be.

Not many research opportunities in this field.

Key Issues in Research and Methods

Research Questions give Focus to sociological research

1) Once the researcher has chosen a broad topic area, they need to **narrow down** the focus of their research so they don't spread their work out too thinly and end up with not enough detail.
They do this by coming up with a **single research question** that their research aims to **answer**.

2) A good research question should focus on **one part** of the topic, and it should be **clear** and **easy** to **research**.

3) Questions should be as **value-free** as possible. In other words they shouldn't be **biased**, or **suggest potential social changes**. So, "Should governments provide vocational education to 14-year-olds?" isn't a good research question because it asks for a **value judgement** on social policy. "What are the attitudes of employers, parents and teachers towards vocational education for 14-year-olds?" is **better**.

Hypotheses are Statements that make Predictions that can be Tested

1) A hypothesis is a **statement** that makes a **prediction**. A hypothesis acts as a **starting point** for research. The research will aim to either **show that the hypothesis is true**, or **show that it's false**.

2) A hypothesis states a **relationship** between **two factors** — e.g. "sociology teachers wear corduroy trousers" or "material deprivation causes educational underachievement".

Terms like "democracy" need to be Operationalised — i.e. Made Measurable

1) Sociology prides itself on giving names to **concepts** and **ideas** that aren't **easily explained** or measured. For example, it's **tricky** to measure things like "democracy", "development" and "culture".

2) You end up measuring these concepts by measuring **something else** that's **linked** to it — sociologists call this an **indicator**. This is called "**operationalising**" a concept. It means making it operational, or workable, by finding a way to measure it.

3) Researchers do this **every time** they conduct a piece of research, because you **can't research** something if you **can't measure** it. Each difficult concept needs an **indicator**, e.g. electoral participation or diversity of electoral results for democracy.

4) There's a **series of steps** that a researcher needs to go through in order to **operationalise** a concept properly:

Operationalising a concept	Example — "democracy"
1) Clearly **define** the concept.	Rule by the people
2) Define its **dimensions** — i.e. say what **other ideas** it's **made up of**.	Voting, freedom of speech
3) Define **potential indicators** to test the various **dimensions** of the concept.	Electoral **turnout, voting patterns**
4) Select the **most useful** indicators.	**Voting patterns**
5) Create **data collection techniques** for each indicator.	Compare successive **general election results**

5) Researchers need to be able to **justify** how they **operationalised** their concepts in their final report. This is often a **subjective** process and the way a researcher operationalises may be **criticised** by other sociologists.

Practice Questions

Q1 Give three factors to consider when choosing a topic for research.

Q2 Why is reviewing the field useful?

Q3 What is the "operationalisation of concepts"?

Exam Question

Q1	Explain and evaluate the various factors to be considered when choosing a research topic.	(24 marks)

The scarecrow award — for being outstanding in your field...

Now you know how sociologists plan research — they pick a topic, find funding, check out previous studies, formulate a research question, make some hypotheses and operationalise all the concepts. If I'd known it was that easy, I'd never have gone into publishing. Revise these pages and do well in your exam and maybe you can become the sociologist I can only dream of being.

Surveys

Sociologists can choose from many research methods when they carry out social research. Some methods produce quantitative data. Others produce qualitative data. There are lots of different methods and lots of different problems. **These pages are for OCR and AQA.**

Before *You Can* Start *— You* Need *a* Sample

1) It is **too expensive** and **time-consuming** for sociologists to involve the **whole population** in their research. They select a **sample**. Only the census includes everyone.

2) When they select the sample they usually try to make it **represent the population** — with similar proportions of people in terms of age, class, ethnicity and gender.

3) If the population is **homogenous** (all the same) the sample needs to be homogenous. If the population is **heterogeneous** (all different), the sample needs to be heterogeneous.

4) **Random sampling** is where names are selected at random from a list of names called a **sampling frame**. Random sampling is often more representative than non-random sampling.

How to do random sampling
1) **Simple random sample** — Pick names **randomly** from a list. Everyone has an **equal chance** of being selected.
2) **Stratified sample** — Divide the population into groups and make a **random selection** with the **right proportions** (if 60% of the population is male, 60% of the sample must be male).

How to do non-random sampling
1) **Snowball sample** — Find an **initial contact** and get them to **give you more names** for your research.
2) **Quota sample** — Pick people who fit into a certain **category** (say, 15 people between ages 30 and 40).

A *Pilot Study* Lets You Have a *Practice Run*

1) A pilot study is a **small-scale** piece of research used as a **practice run**. You might want to **test** the **accuracy** of your **questions**, or **check** to see if there are any **technical problems** in your research design. You do this to make the study **more valid** and **more reliable**.

2) You can also **test how long** the research will take, **train** your **interviewers** and get **research funding** — once you show your project is useful.

3) Pilot studies can be **time-consuming** and **expensive** and can create a **lot of work**.

Social Surveys *Give* Quantitative *Data*

1) **Social surveys** collect information about a large population, using **standardised questionnaires** or **structured interviews**.

2) Social surveys tend to be used by **positivists** as a **primary source** of **quantitative data**.

3) Standard questionnaires and structured interviews are **reliable**. They're used by **government agencies** and **research companies**.

4) Data collected using surveys can be analysed to discover overall **patterns** and **trends**.

Townsend used a 39 page questionnaire in his 1979 research on poverty.

Longitudinal Studies *are* Social Surveys *over a Period of* Time

Longitudinal studies are done at **regular intervals** over a **long period of time**. They're often **large-scale quantitative** surveys, and they tend to be used by **positivists**. Some TV programmes like *Seven Up* are more **qualitative**.

Seven Up was a TV documentary that asked 14 kids aged 7 what they thought about life, and what they wanted to be when they grew up. The programme makers came back to interview the children every seven years. The latest instalment was Forty-Nine Up.

Strengths of longitudinal studies
1) You can **analyse changes** and **make comparisons** over time.
2) You can study how the **attitudes** of the sample **change** with time.

Limitations of longitudinal studies
1) It's **hard** to recruit a **committed sample** who'll want to **stay** with the study.
2) It's **hard to keep contact** with the sample, which may make the study less valid.
3) You need **long-term funding** and you need to **keep the research team together**.
4) Longitudinal studies rely on **interviews** and **questionnaires** which might not be **valid** or **reliable**.

Surveys

Questionnaires *Mainly Give* Quantitative Data

Questionnaires mainly use **closed questions** and standardised **multiple-choice answers** —
e.g. "What's your favourite fish? Tick *cod, haddock, salmon, sea bass, tuna* or *other*".
Don't forget though that some questionnaires use **open-ended** questions.

Questionnaires mainly give you **quantitative** data which positivists like. **Standardised questions** make them **reliable**.
A questionnaire with **open-ended questions** can give you some insight into **meanings** and **motives**. They give you
qualitative data. The **reliability** and **validity** of a questionnaire depends on **how it's designed**.

Questionnaires should...

1) Use **clear, simple questions** which are **easy to understand**.
2) Give **clear instructions** and make it **easy** for the respondent.
3) Have a nice **clear layout** that doesn't **intimidate** people.
4) Give a **range of options** on **multiple-choice** questions.
5) **Measure** what **you want to measure**.

The person answering
the questionnaire is
called the <u>respondent</u>.

Questionnaires shouldn't...

1) Ask **embarrassing**, **threatening** or **complex** questions.
2) Ask **two questions instead of one**.
3) Be **too long**.
4) Use **sociological** terms that **no one understands**.
5) **Lead** the respondent to **answer a question** in a **particular way**.

Strengths of questionnaires

1) They're **quick** and **cheap**, and they can reach lots of respondents.
2) They're **reliable** because the questions are **standardised**.
3) They're **easy to analyse** with computer programs.
4) There's **no interviewer** to **affect** people's answers.
5) You can **spot patterns** in the answers and **make comparisons**.

Limitations of questionnaires

1) Respondents **may not tell the truth**.
2) Questions may be **misleading** or **mean different things** to **different people**. They may not measure what you actually **want to measure**.
3) Postal questionnaires have a **low response rate**. If it's **too low** it won't give a **representative** sample.
4) **Open-ended questions** make it **hard to quantify the data** into nice neat **numbers**.
5) No one can **explain** the questions if the respondent doesn't understand them.

1) Questionnaires can be used to investigate topics such as **TV viewing habits**, **purchasing habits**, **voting behaviour** and **experiences of crime**.

2) The **British Crime Survey** is a questionnaire that is carried out **continually** by the British government. They survey about **50,000** people a year and publish new results **annually**.

3) The **British Social Attitudes Survey** is carried out annually by the National **Centre for Social Research**. Each year they select **3,300** British adults at random and send them a questionnaire.

Practice Questions

Q1 Why do sociologists select a sample?
Q2 Briefly explain two types of sampling procedure.
Q3 What are the benefits of carrying out a pilot study?

Exam Question

Q1 Outline some of the reasons why sociologists use surveys. (12 marks)

I had to give a sample at the doctor's — don't say I need one here as well...

*Pick your sample first, then do a pilot study. Check that what you're doing is really as valid and reliable as you'd like it to
be. Questionnaires are harder to design than you might think — you've got to give sensible options for multiple-choice
questions, and you've got to make the questions really clear and easy to understand.*

Interviews

These pages are about getting primary data from interviews. **They're for AQA and OCR.**

An *Interview* is a *Conversation* Between a *Researcher* and a *Respondent*

1) An **interview** is a **conversation** between a **researcher** and an **interviewee** where the researcher asks a set of questions.

2) You have to pick the **sample**, organise the **interview**, select / train your **interviewers**, **ask the questions** and **record the answers**. **Bias** can get in the way at each stage. An interviewer should create a **friendly relaxed atmosphere**.

3) An **interview effect** is when the **response** given isn't what the interviewee **really thinks**. This can be caused by the **gender**, **age**, **class** or **personality** of the interviewer. The **opinions** of the **researcher** and **interviewer** can **influence** the interviewee.

4) There are two main types of interview — **structured** and **unstructured**.

Structured Interviews produce *Quantitative Data*

Structured interviews ask the **same standardised questions** each time. They're popular with **positivists**.

Structured interviews have similar advantages to questionnaires...

1) They produce **quantitative data** that can be **analysed mathematically** or **plotted on graphs**.

2) They're often the easiest way of collecting **simple, factual data**.

3) They have a high level of **reliability** — if you **repeat the survey** then it is very likely to produce **similar results**.

4) They're **relatively quick** to carry out and to analyse, especially compared with unstructured interviews. So they're also good for researching **large samples**.

5) The results are relatively easy to **generalise**.

... and similar disadvantages

1) The questions **limit** how the interviewee can respond — they're usually **closed** or **multiple-choice** questions. So the answers can be limited by the **expectations of the question writer**.

2) Structured interviews aren't very helpful for collecting **sophisticated detail**, such as anecdotes about a person's experiences.

3) The interviewer can't build up a rapport with the person being interviewed because the whole process is **mechanical** and **scientific**.

Structured Interviews can be **More Reliable** *than Questionnaires*

1) Questionnaires are a **cheap way** to collect the **same sort of information** as structured interviews.

2) But structured interviews have a **better response rate** than questionnaires. Postal questionnaires are often not returned and website questionnaires are often ignored, but people tend to respond **more politely** to a human interviewer.

3) Data obtained from structured interviews can also be **more reliable** than data obtained from questionnaires. Interviewers can check that the people being interviewed really do **fit into the sample criteria**. With questionnaires there's a risk of people **misrepresenting themselves** — e.g. people filling in internet surveys out of **curiosity** even though they're not part of the target group for the survey.

4) Respondents are more likely to answer a person **truthfully**, especially about basic information such as **their age**.

5) An interviewer can clarify any **ambiguous questions**, making **misinterpretations** less likely.

6) But structured interviews aren't perfect — they can suffer from the **interviewer effect**, when the person being interviewed tries to **please the interviewer** by giving them the answers **they seem to want** rather than **more honest ones**.

Structured interviews are often used in **large-scale social surveys**. **Norris et al (1999)** used this method as part of a survey of 3,615 people's responses to political campaigns in the 1997 general election.

Interviews

Unstructured Interviews produce Qualitative Data

An **unstructured interview** is like a **free-flowing conversation**. The interviewer needs to build up a **rapport** — a relationship of trust — with the interviewee.

Unstructured interviews have advantages...

1) They produce **qualitative data** that gives an insight into an interviewee's **emotional reactions**.

2) The person being interviewed is **more likely to be honest** if they feel a **rapport** with the interviewer. So responses tend to be **valid**.

3) The interviewer is able to **follow up** any **confusing or interesting responses**.

... and disadvantages

1) Unstructured interviews are **expensive**. They usually **take longer** than structured interviews, and it's hard to estimate how long each interview will take **in advance**.

2) Because they produce **qualitative data**, it's not easy to **make comparisons** between one respondent and another.

3) A **bad interviewer** can easily produce **poor results**, especially if the interview goes **off-subject**.

4) The results are not **reliable** — if you **repeat the study**, it will probably **produce different results**.

5) The research sample usually has to be **small** because unstructured interviews tend to produce long, unwieldly responses, e.g. hours of taped interviews.

6) It's usually difficult to **generalise** from unstructured interviews because answers tend to be **specific to individual subjects**.

Unstructured interviews are popular with **interpretivists**. For example, **Simon Charlesworth (2000)** wanted to create a valid description of working class experiences, so he performed several unstructured interviews with working class people.

Semi-structured Interviews Combine Some of the Strengths of Each Approach

1) A **semi-structured interview** is an interview in which a few **key questions** are used to **give shape** to the conversation. Unlike a structured interview, the interviewee **can answer in any way they like** and the interviewer can ask as many **follow-up questions** as they feel are necessary.

2) So semi-structured interviews are **less restricted** than structured interviews, but more likely to produce data that can be **compared** with other respondents than unstructured interviews.

3) For example, **David Muggleton (2000)** used semi-structured interviews to research the link between fashions and subcultures in postmodern society.

Practice Questions

Q1 What are the disadvantages of a structured interview?

Q2 Give four advantages of using a structured interview instead of a questionnaire.

Q3 Why do some sociologists choose to use unstructured interviews?

Q4 How are semi-structured interviews different from structured interviews?

Q5 What are the advantages of semi-structured interviews?

Q6 Give an example of a study that used structured interviews.

Exam Question

Q1 Outline and explain any two methods of conducting interviews for a sociological study. (16 marks)

When I want your opinion, I'll give it to you...

The goal of all interviews is to get information from the person being interviewed that will help you in your research. Sometimes that means asking them a series of multiple-choice or closed questions, sometimes it means just having a conversation. And then there's always a third option of doing something in between.

Observations

Some sociologists get data by watching and listening to people — by making observations. **These pages are for AQA and OCR.**

Observation is Watching Behaviour in Real-Life Settings

1) In **covert observation**, the researcher **doesn't tell the group** they're being observed. The British Sociological Association (BSA) advise that you should only use covert participant observation when there's **no other way** of obtaining the data. For example, **Nigel Fielding (1993)** used covert observation when researching the National Front (a far right-wing political party) because he believed he would encounter hostility if they knew he was a sociologist.

2) **Overt observation** (direct observation) is when the group is aware of the research and they know who the researcher is. For example, **Beverley Skeggs (1991)** used overt observation when studying female sexuality among students at a college.

3) **Participant observation** is when the researcher **actively involves themselves in the group**.

4) **Non-participant observation** is when the researcher **observes** the group but isn't actively part of the group.

<u>Interpretivists</u> prefer observation because the researcher can get to the action.
It tends to produce qualitative data that's more valid than questionnaires.

Participant and Non-Participant Observation Have Pros and Cons

Participant observation

1) Participant observation gets the researcher **right to where the action** is — so they can **check out the dynamics of a group** from **close up**. It's useful for studying **subcultures** and **lifestyles**.

2) **Participant observation** allows you to research the workings of deviant groups.

3) The researcher gets **first-hand insight** of people in **natural real-life settings**.

4) If it's **covert**, people **can't mislead** the researcher.

But...

1) The researcher may get too involved and find it **hard to stand back** and **objectively observe** the group.

2) **Overt research** may **influence** the behaviour of the group.

3) The researcher in a **covert observation** may join in with illegal acts if they're in a deviant group.

4) You **can't repeat the research**. It **lacks reliability**. A covert observer may find it difficult to remember all the events and accurately record them.

5) There are **ethical** and **practical** problems in **getting in**, **staying in** and **getting out** of the group.

6) The research usually includes a **small group** so it's not **representative** of the population.

7) It is **hard work**, **time-consuming** and **expensive**.

Non-participant observation

1) In **non-participant** observation, the researcher **isn't drawn into the group** so they can be more **objective** about the group's behaviour.

2) If you want to observe **deviant** groups, you have to be very **inconspicuous**.

But...

1) **Observing from the outside** stops you from getting to where the **action** is.

2) **Overt research** may **influence** the **behaviour** of the group.

Participant observation is useful for studying subcultures and lifestyles:

1) **Sarah Thornton (1995)** used participant observation to investigate the **clubbing subculture**. She dressed as a clubber and attended raves.

2) **Fran Abrams (2002)** took a series of **minimum-wage jobs** to explore life as experienced by the poorest workers in Britain.

Ethical Guidelines Apply to Participant Observation

1) The **British Sociological Association** has set out **ethical guidelines** for research that involves **participant observation**.

2) In most circumstances, subjects must give **full informed consent** — they should fully understand **what the research is about**, **how data is being collected** and **what the data will be used for**.

3) Sociologists must avoid doing any **physical**, **psychological** or **emotional harm** to their subjects during the research.

4) **Special care** must be taken when researching **vulnerable people** such as children or the elderly.

5) The **anonymity and privacy** of research subjects must be protected.

Observations

Ethnography Studies the Way of Life of a Group

1) **Ethnography** is the scientific description of a specific culture by someone with first-hand experience of observing that culture. It was first used by **anthropologists** to study **traditional societies**. They joined the community, learnt the language and noted their observations.

Anthropology is the study of humans.

2) It is based on small-scale fieldwork that tends to produce **qualitative** data. It's **valid** because you can study behaviour in **natural settings**.

3) You can use all sorts of methods to get **primary data**. You can use **unstructured interviews**. You can **observe** a community and see what they get up to.

4) **Case studies** are in-depth studies of **particular events** like **demonstrations**.

5) You can find out an **individual's life history** with **interviews** and **observations**.

6) **Time budgeting** is where you ask people to keep a **detailed diary** of their activities during a specified time. This can create **qualitative** and **quantitative** data.

7) Researchers may also analyse **diaries** and **letters**, which are **secondary data**.

- Ethnography is **in-depth research** which gives **inside knowledge** about a community.
- You get a **valid** picture from ethnography, but it relies on the **researcher's interpretations** of what people do and say.
- It's **difficult** to **make generalisations** from small-scale research.

Focus Groups are a Type of Semi-structured Observation

1) A **focus group** is a **small sample**, perhaps fewer than ten people.

2) The sample are **put in a room together**, and asked to talk about a particular issue or to try to answer a specific set of questions. The discussion is **observed by a researcher**.

3) Because this is more like a **natural conversation**, the subjects may feel **more able to express themselves** than if they were speaking **directly to an interviewer**.

4) Sometimes the focus group is **left alone** and a **video camera** or **audio recorder** is used to **record the discussion for later analysis**.

5) Sometimes researchers **stay with the group** and **take part in the discussion** — they use the focus group to conduct a **group interview**.

6) **Chahal and Julienne (1999)** researched the **effects of racism**. They set up focus group sessions in which respondents **discussed their experiences** of racism, explored their understanding of what a racist incident actually was, and **talked about the consequences** of such incidents.

The focus group's feelings were unanimous. Yes, they did look ridiculous.

Practice Questions

Q1 What is the difference between covert and overt observation?
Q2 Briefly explain two strengths of participant observation.
Q3 What is ethnography?
Q4 How did Chahal and Julienne use focus groups?

Exam Question

Q1 Examine the problems sociologists may face when using participant observation in their research. (20 marks)

Sociologists could be everywhere, watching us... shhhh...

Participant observation gives access to people in their normal social setting, but it's difficult to do and you won't necessarily get the same results twice. It can also be risky — I don't think I'd want to do a participant observation of serial killers. I'd be more tempted to put a bunch of them into a focus group and analyse their comments later from a video tape.

Experiments

You can use experiments to give you quantitative primary data.
You can get quantitative secondary data from statistics, and qualitative secondary data from documents.
Page 112 is only for AQA. Page 113 is for AQA and OCR.

Experiments Let You Find Cause and Effect

1) Experiments are used by **natural scientists** — biologists, chemists etc.

2) The researcher starts with a **hypothesis** and they use the experiment to **test** it out.

3) All the variables are kept constant, apart from the one you're interested in — the **independent variable**. Scientists **change the independent variable** and observe the effects on the **dependent variable**. If you were testing the effects of temperature on electrical resistance, **temperature** would be the **independent variable** which **you control** and **electrical resistance** would be the **dependent variable** which you **measure**.

4) The results are **turned into numbers** — the scientist looks for **patterns** and **cause-and-effect** relationships.

5) This method has been developed and used by **social scientists** to look for **social** causes and effects.

> Forming a hypothesis and testing it with an experiment is how science works, according to the hypothetico-deductive model.

There are Three Kinds of Experiment

1) **Lab experiments** are done in a **controlled environment**. The researcher **changes** the **independent variable**. The researcher observes the effect on the **dependent variable**. The researcher usually uses a **control group**, which is **left alone** to see what happens if you **don't do anything** to the **independent variable**. This method is often used by psychologists.

2) **Field experiments** are a response to the criticisms of lab experiments. They take place outside of the lab in **real social settings**, and those involved are often **unaware**. This method is used by **interpretivist** sociologists.

3) **Natural experiments** are not set up artificially. An example would be **twin studies**, but these are quite rare.

Strengths of lab experiments

1) The **researcher** has **control** over the experiment.

2) You get **quantitative** data.

3) You can **replicate** the research.

Limitations of lab experiments

1) It's **hard to reproduce real social situations** in a lab — lab experiments are **artificial**.

2) It is **difficult to isolate single variables**. **Social behaviour** is influenced by **many factors**.

3) There are often **moral** and **ethical** issues in lab experiments.

4) People may feel **intimidated** or **act differently** in the lab.

> Twin studies are where you study genetically identical twins in different situations, to see whether something's caused by genetics or if it's caused by socialisation.

> Researchers can measure things in a biased way if they have expectations about the results.

Strengths of field experiments

1) They're done in **natural social settings** and are more like **real life**.

2) They can show the **hidden meanings** of **everyday social interaction**.

Limitations of field experiments

1) You **can't control the variables** like you can in lab experiments.

2) If people **know they're being studied** they may **change** their **behaviour**.

3) There's an **ethical problem** in carrying out experiments when the subjects **aren't aware** that they are taking part in an experiment.

When People Know They're Being Studied, They Sometimes Act Differently

1) When people are more **interested** in something, they **try harder**. They may try harder at what they're doing because they know they're being observed and want to appear in a good light. This is called the **Hawthorne effect**.

2) People usually have an idea of what kind of **response** the **researchers want**. People often either give the researchers the **response they think they want** or the **exact opposite** — depending on whether they want to please the researchers or whether they want to be stubborn.

3) People usually try to show themselves in the **best possible light**. They may say they **wouldn't commit crime** when **really they would**. They may say they **recycle all their rubbish** when **really they don't**.

4) These effects mean data from experiments may not be **valid**.

Secondary Data

Statistics are a Source of Secondary Data

Official statistics are a source of secondary data. They're produced by local governments, central government and government agencies.

1) **Hard statistics** are **objective**. Politicians can't fiddle with them. Statistics on births and marriages are hard statistics.

2) **Soft statistics** are more **subjective**. Politicians can fiddle with them. Statistics on **crime**, **poverty** and **unemployment** are soft statistics. In the 1980s and 1990s, the government **changed the method** used to **measure unemployment** over 20 times.

3) **Social Trends** is a collection of **regular government surveys** published every year. It's a **great source** of **secondary data**.

4) The **census** is a survey of every household every 10 years. Every household has to fill in the form **by law**.

5) The **British Crime Survey** looks at victims of crime. The data is collected by a questionnaire.

Non-official statistics are statistics collected by organisations other than the government. For example:

1) **TV ratings** collected by the **British Audience Research Bureau**.

2) **Surveys** carried out by **special interest groups**, such as charities.

3) **Surveys** carried out by **sociologists**.

Documents and Mass Media are a Source of Secondary Data

1) A document is **written text**. Documents can be **personal** — like **letters**, **diaries**, **autobiographies**, **memoirs** and **suicide notes**. Documents can also be **official**, like **school records**, **health** records, **church** records and **social work** records.

2) Documents can be **expressive** — more to do with **meanings**, like a **suicide note**. Documents can be **formal** — like **official documents**. **Interpretivists** prefer **expressive** documents because they're a big source of **qualitative data**.

3) **Max Weber** used **historical documents** when he was studying how the **religious** beliefs of Calvinism brought about a **social change**. **Michel Foucault** used **historical documents** to analyse changes in **social control** and **punishment**.

4) **Content analysis** is a method of **systematically** analysing a communication (e.g. a speech, film or letter) to understand its **meanings**. It is often used to study the mass media e.g. research by the Glasgow University Media Group.

5) There are **problems** with documents. They can be **difficult to understand** if they're old. They might be **fakes**. They might contain **lies** — especially personal documents.

Sociologists Compare Different Secondary Documents

1) Sociologists look for **similarities** and **differences** between secondary documents. They can compare different **times**, different **cultures** and different **groups** within society by looking at secondary data.

2) Researchers can analyse real social behaviour and make comparisons without having to set up artificial experiments.

3) Durkheim used this **comparative method** in his famous 1897 study of suicide. He looked at the rates of suicide in different European societies. He found that the suicide rate was **consistent over time**, **but varied between societies** and varied for **different groups** within society.

Practice Questions

Q1 Name two advantages of field experiments over laboratory experiments.
Q2 What is the Hawthorne Effect?
Q3 What is the difference between hard and soft statistics?

Exam Question

Q1 Explain what is meant by the term 'independent variable'. (2 marks)

Anyone up for an experiment on how people cope with being millionaires...

If you're not really into science, this business about dependent and independent variables might seem a tad confusing. Don't be too confused — just remember that the dependent variable is the one you measure to see how it's changed. All the stuff on secondary data is fairly straightforward, I reckon — it's about what kind of secondary data sociologists use.

Interpreting Data

You can interpret, analyse and evaluate data in lots of different ways. **These pages are for AQA and OCR.**

Check Data's **Reliable**, **Valid** and **Representative**

Valid = data is a **true picture** of **what you're measuring**.

Reliable = you can use the **same method again** under the **same conditions** and get the **same results**.

Representative = the **sample** has the **same proportions** as the **population**.

Look for **Correlations** and Patterns in **Quantitative** Data

Correlation is where one variable is related to another.

% GCSE attainment by parents' socio-economic classification, 2002

	5 GCSE grades A*-C	1-4 GCSE grades A*-C	5 GCSE grades D-G	1-4 GCSE grades D-G	None reported
Higher professional	77	13	6	...	3
Lower professional	64	21	11	2	2
Intermediate	52	25	17	2	4
Lower supervisory	35	30	27	4	4
Routine	32	32	25	5	6
Other	32	29	26	4	9

Published in *Social Trends 34 (2004)*. Source: Youth Cohort Study by the Department for Education and Skills

If you were **analysing this data**, you would have to:

1) See **what the table's about**. The **title** tells you that this table is about how **educational achievement** is related to **parents' socio-economic position**.

2) Find out **where it's from**. It says *Social Trends*. This is a collection of government research. It's possible that there could be political **bias** here.

3) Look for a **correlation** between the variables. In this table, high socio-economic class seems to go with lots of GCSEs at grades A*-C.

4) Identify **patterns** in the data — it says that children with parents in higher socio-economic positions achieve a **higher percentage** of top grades. Those with parents in **routine** occupations achieve a **higher percentage** of **grades D-G**.

5) Ask if the data is **valid**. The relationship you can **see** might not be the **only one** there. There's a **correlation**, but you can't conclude that the parents' socio-economic class is the **cause** of their children's attainment level. Some sociologists would say that **material deprivation** is the cause but there might be **other causes** that the table just doesn't show.

6) Find out about the **sample**. It's from the **Youth Cohort** study, which has a **large** sample — so you could make **generalisations** about the **population** as a **whole**.

7) Find out about **how** the data was collected. The Youth Cohort study gets its data from school records. You could repeat this study again and get the same results.

The appendix of Social Trends tells you that the Youth Cohort study had 35 000 respondents.

If you've got a <u>hypothesis</u> about educational achievement and class, you can use the figures to <u>test it out</u>.

Question the **Method** and the **Sample** with **Qualitative** Data

"I always leave the quiet ones to just get on with their work. Girls are OK in the class too. It's the boys you have to be tough on. They are usually the troublemakers."

Imagine you got this quote from an **unstructured interview** with a teacher. You would have to:

1) Ask yourself whether the interviewee might have said it because of something to do with the **method**. A **different method** might produce a **different response**, so it might not be very **reliable**.

2) Ask yourself if it's **really what the interviewee believes** or whether they said what they **thought** the **interviewer wanted to hear**. This quote might not be a **true reflection** of how this teacher really acts.

3) See if the sample is **representative**. The research might use a **small** or **untypical sample** — which doesn't tell you much about **teachers in general**.

4) Find out **who carried out the research**. A researcher might have a particular **political** or **sociological point of view**. They can present the research in a way that suits their theories. This is **bias**.

5) Figure out what it **means**. The quote tells us something about processes like **labelling** that go on in schools.

Interpreting Data

Analyse *Official Statistics* — *They're Not as Objective as they Seem at First*

Official statistics are a **really useful** source of **existing information**. Some sociologists love them because they're **cheap** and **available** (fnar, fnar...). With **official statistics**, you can look at **trends** over **time**. The sample sizes tend to be **huge**, so at least you know they're **representative**. Official stats are sometimes your **only source of information**. There are some **problems** with official statistics, though — they don't always **measure** what they **say** they measure.

1) **Positivists** like official stats — they think official stats are a source of **objective, reliable** data. They **analyse** the relationship between social **variables** and look for **correlations** and **cause-and-effect relationships**.

2) **Marxists** say that **official statistics** are **government statistics**. They think all official stats are **politically biased** to serve the **interests of the ruling class**, and **designed** to **avoid political embarrassment**.

3) **Interpretivists** say that **official statistics** are **not hard facts**. They are **not as objective** as they **seem at first**. Interpretivists say **statistics** are **social constructions** and don't tell you about **meanings** and **motives**.

> **Example** — **crime statistics** don't tell you an **objective figure** of how many **crimes** are committed.
>
> The police **don't know about all crimes** that are committed. Some criminals get **let off**. Some people **don't trust the police** enough to **tell** them about a crime. Some people might not **realise** they're a victim of crime. So — there's crime that we **plain don't know about** if we use **official statistics**.

Analyse *Content* of *Documents* and the *Mass Media* — but *Take Care...*

1) Traditional **quantitative content analysis** produces **statistical data**.

2) For example, you can **count** the **number of times something happens** in a **TV programme** — like the number of times girls are in a passive role.

3) The research tends to be **reliable, easy to obtain** and you can **make comparisons**.

4) The problem is that the **researchers' interpretations** may be **biased**. Researchers **might not agree** on exactly what counts as a "passive role", for example.

5) You still have a lot of **explaining** to do even if you have a **clear result** like "ethnic minorities are under-represented in TV programmes". You have to explain **how** and **why**.

> **Qualitative analysis** (e.g. semiotic analysis) looks for **themes** and **meanings** in media and documents. **Interpretivists** prefer this method because it **uncovers hidden meanings**. It's more **valid** than quantitative analysis. The downside is that the researcher can **interpret** the sources in **different ways**. It's not very **reliable**.

John Scott (1990) thinks sociologists should be **really careful** when **analysing secondary sources**.

1) Documents might **not** be **authentic** — they might be **fakes**.

2) They might **not** be **credible** — the author might not be telling the **truth**.

3) They might **not** be **representative**.

4) They might be **difficult to understand** — full of **old-fashioned** meanings.

Practice Questions

Q1 How are the methods used to analyse quantitative data different to those used for qualitative data?
Q2 Name a strength of official statistics.
Q3 How would interpretivists criticise official statistics?
Q4 What does John Scott (1990) say about analysing documents?

Exam Questions

Q1 Explain what is meant by the 'reliability' of a set of data. (2 marks)

Q2 Examine the advantages and disadvantages of official statistics as a source of data for the sociologist. (20 marks)

I'm looking for patterns in an Argyle jumper...

Case studies don't always include numbers, but it's useful to know how to deal with them if you get them. Always look at how data's collected, the sample size, bias, validity and reliability. Don't get validity and reliability confused, will you. People seem to get them mixed up in the exam, and it'll lose you marks.

Limitations of Research

Research has its limits — it can't tell you everything. Here are all the pros and cons of different kinds of data.
These pages are for AQA and OCR.

Primary Data is Collected First-hand — it has Good Points and Bad Points

The researcher collects primary information first-hand — they find it themselves. You could use methods like **interviews**, **questionnaires**, **observations** or **experiments**. You gather quantitative or qualitative data.

1) Primary data is obtained from **first-hand research**. It doesn't rely on **another sociologist's research** and you can carefully **choose your method** to make your data as valid and reliable as possible.

2) Primary data is always **brand new** and **bang up to date**.

3) **Some methods** of getting primary data can be **expensive** and **time-consuming**.

4) **Some methods** may put the researcher in a **dangerous situation**.

5) **Some methods** may be **unethical** if you don't give **informed consent**.

6) The **researcher's own values** may mess with the research process. This creates **bias**.

7) You **can't always get access** to the group you want to study.

Secondary Data is Existing Information — it has Pros and Cons

Secondary data sources include **official statistics**, **diaries**, **letters**, **memoirs**, **emails**, **TV documentaries** and **newspapers**. You gather the data together and analyse it, but you don't generate the data.

1) You can **quickly** and easily collect secondary data.

2) You can **easily** use **secondary data** to **compare different societies**.

3) With secondary data you can study **past events and societies**. You can **compare past** and **present**.

4) You don't have to worry about **informed consent**.

5) The **existing data** may not be **valid** or **reliable** — you're **stuck** with the way the research was **originally done**.

6) Documents may not be **authentic**, **representative** or **credible**. Official statistics can be **biased**.

7) You **might not be able to find** the information that you need from existing data.

8) **Your values** don't influence the **collection** of the data (though they might influence your **choice of sources**), but the **researcher's values** might have ruined the validity of the **original research**. **Your values** can get in the way of **how you analyse** the data.

Quantitative Data Can be Reliable but Not Very Valid

1) With quantitative data, you can **test your hypothesis** and look for **cause and effect** relationships.

2) You can **compare** your statistics against existing statistics, and look for **trends over time** and between societies.

3) It's **easy** to **analyse tables**, **charts** and **graphs** — especially line charts, bar graphs and pie charts.

4) You can **repeat** questionnaires and structured interviews to **test reliability**.

5) Quantitative methods allow **large samples**, so the findings can **represent** the **general population**.

6) **Statistics** can **hide reality**. **Categories** in **interviews** or **questionnaires** can **distort** the truth.

7) Statistics don't tell you anything about the **meanings** and **motives** and **reasons** behind behaviour — there's not much **depth** and **insight** into **social interaction**.

8) Statistics can be **politically biased**. The method may have been chosen in order to get the "right" data.

Qualitative Data can be Valid but Not Very Reliable

1) **Qualitative sociological data** gives **insight** into **social interaction**. It's a **detailed description** of social behaviour.

2) Qualitative data lets you find out the **meanings** and **motives** behind behaviour.

3) You don't have to **force** people into **artificial categories** like in questionnaires.

4) Qualitative methods let you build up **trust** and research **sensitive topics**.

5) Qualitative methods are **difficult to repeat** — they **aren't very reliable**.

6) The research is often on a **small scale** — so the findings might not **represent** the whole population.

7) **Positivists** say qualitative results **lack credibility** because they're **subjective** and open to interpretation.

8) The **researcher** can get the **wrong end of the stick** and **misinterpret** the group or individual they're studying.

Limitations of Research

Sociology is More Subjective than Traditional Science

1) **Objective knowledge** is the **same** no matter what your **point of view**. **Objective** methods provide **facts** that can be easily **verified** or **falsified**. Objective research is also **value-free** (see below), and doesn't have any bias.

2) **Subjective knowledge** depends on your **point of view**. **Subjective** methods give data that **can't** be easily tested. Subjective research requires **interpretation**.

3) Sociology is **more subjective** than the physical **sciences**, but it aims to be at least partly objective.

Positivist Sociology tries to be as Objective as Possible

1) **Positivists** (see p. 102) think sociology should be scientific and analyse social facts. Social facts can be **directly observed and measured**, e.g. the number of followers of Christianity in Britain.

2) Positivists look for **correlations in data**, and **cause-and-effect relationships**. To do this, they use **quantitative** methods like **questionnaires** (see p.107) and **official statistics**, which are **objective** and **reliable**.

1) **Interpretivist sociologists** (see p. 102) reckon **sociology doesn't suit scientific methods**.

2) They try to understand human behaviour from the point of view of the **individual**, so they use methods that let them discover the **meanings**, **motives** and **reasons** behind **human behaviour** and **social interaction**.

There's Debate over whether Research can be Value-free

1) **Value-free research** is research that doesn't make **value judgements** e.g. judgements about whether the things it researches are **good** or **bad**.

2) Value-free research doesn't let the **researcher's own beliefs** get in the way. For example, questionnaires mustn't ask questions that **lead** the respondent towards a particular answer.

3) In order for this idea of **value freedom** to work, the researcher must **interpret** all data **objectively**.

4) Value freedom means that the **end use** of the research **shouldn't matter**. Research should come up with knowledge, and how that knowledge is used isn't up to the researcher.

Some sociologists say **sociology can't be value-free**.

1) The decision to research in the first place is **value-laden** — someone has to decide that the research is worth spending money on. Some say that research which the **state** or **businesses** want to see is most likely to get funding.

2) It's difficult to **completely avoid bias** and interview effects (see p.108).

3) Some Marxist and feminist sociologists **deliberately choose research** with an **end use** that they **approve** of. They believe that sociology **should** make **value judgements** about society and **suggest** ways it could be **better**.

Practice Questions

Q1 Give two strengths of primary data.
Q2 Give two criticisms of qualitative data.
Q3 How are interpretivists different from positivists?
Q4 Why do some feminists reject the idea of value freedom in sociological research?

Exam Question

Q1 Examine the problems some sociologists may find when using qualitative data in their research. (20 marks)

Research can't tell you everything...

When you discuss a method in the exam, try to include some examples of studies which used it. This shows the examiner that you understand what kind of research the method works best for. It'll also give you a chance to show off your wider sociological knowledge, which always goes down well with the examiners — it might even get you a few extra marks.

Mixed Methods

All research methods have strengths and weaknesses. Some sociologists combine different methods — they want to combine the strengths of all the different methods and overcome their weaknesses.
These pages are for OCR — but AQA students will find them useful extra background.

Methodological Pluralism became popular in the 1970s

The two main traditional approaches to sociological research are positivist and interpretivist (see p. 102).
To recap:

1) **Positivists** believe that sociology should be **treated like a traditional science**, so they have favoured **quantitative** research methods that produce **numbers and statistics**.

2) **Interpretivists** believe that sociologists should try to understand the emotions and thoughts of individuals. So they usually prefer **qualitative** research methods.

1) **Paul Feyerabend (1975)** was one of the first people to try to reconcile the positivist approach and the interpretivist approach, suggesting that sociologists should be willing to pick **whatever methods are most appropriate**. They should **combine quantitative and qualitative methods** as necessary, and even **change methods** during the process of research if the study calls for it.

2) Feyerabend's ideas contributed to the development of **methodological pluralism** — studying society using a **mixture of methods** instead of having to **declare one in advance**.

3) Methodological pluralism has become the **most common approach** to sociological research.

Triangulation is When You Combine Methods or Data

1) Triangulation is when sociologists combine different methods or data to **get the best out of all of them**.

2) Triangulation can **combine** quantitative methods and qualitative methods, e.g. questionnaires and unstructured interviews.

3) **Triangulation** gives a more **detailed picture** than when you only use **one method**, so it's more **valid**.

4) When you triangulate, you can **check different sets of data against each other**, so it's more **reliable**. You can even triangulate between data produced by **different researchers**.

5) Triangulation combines the **strengths** and the **weaknesses** of different types of data.

6) It can be **expensive** and **time-consuming** to do the same research with lots of methods.

7) Sometimes, it's **not possible** to use triangulation — e.g. you might only be able to use **one method**, or there might not be very many **different kinds of data** for what you're studying.

Harvey and MacDonald (1993) list **three kinds of triangulation:**

1) **One researcher** uses **two or more methods.**
So the results from one method can be checked against the results from another.

2) **Two or more researchers** use **the same method.**
So the results obtained by one researcher can be checked against the results obtained by the other.

3) **Two or more researchers** use **two or more methods.**
So researchers and methods can be checked against each other.

Here are two examples of studies which used triangulation:

Eileen Barker (1984) studied the Moonies

The Moonies are a religious organisation, also known as the Unification Church. Barker used **in-depth interviews, overt participant observation** and **questionnaires**. She used questionnaires to test out hypotheses that she'd thought of after doing the interviews and observations.

Mac an Ghaill (1994) studied masculinity

He used **overt participant observation** and **interviews** with young straight men and young gay men.
He **discussed ideas** about what made a man masculine.
He didn't just observe the young men and try to figure out what they thought.

Mixed Methods

Mixing Methods makes it More Likely that Some are Fit for Purpose...

1) A method is 'fit for purpose' if it is **capable of giving useful results**.

2) For example, if you were studying people's experiences of crime, a **questionnaire** given to a **large sample** should produce useful results. So for that study, a questionnaire is **fit for purpose**. It wouldn't make sense to try to do **participant observation** — you'd have to follow people for a **very long time** and the act of observing would probably **decrease the probability of them becoming a victim** of crime. So for this study, participant observation is **not fit for purpose**.

3) It's not always obvious which methods are going to be fit for purpose **before a study begins**. Using **mixed methods** can be an advantage — if one of your methods turns out to be **not fit for purpose** during your study then you could still be able to collect useful results from **the other methods**.

> ### Dobson *et al* (2001) studied childhood disability and family life
>
> They used a mixture of **diaries**, **questionnaires** and **focus groups**. However, when they organised a focus group on **categories of disability**, they found that the various children had such complicated medical histories that they **couldn't be categorised**.
>
> So, that particular focus group turned out to be **not fit for purpose**. But Dobson et al still managed to complete their research because that focus group was just **one of several** methods they were using to obtain data.

...but Makes it Harder to Analyse Data

1) Trying to find patterns is more difficult when you have to simultaneously analyse lots of **different kinds of data**. Sometimes it isn't clear how the results of different tests **relate to one another** and sometimes it's just difficult to **think about all the results at once**.

2) But successful use of mixed methods usually leads to **increased validity** and **increased reliability** because each set of data is **checked** against all the others. It's very unlikely that all the methods will be **invalid** in the same way. If any one is **unreliable** then it won't **affect the outcome** of the study as strongly as if it was the **only method** used.

Practice Questions

Q1 What is meant by the term 'methodological pluralism'?
Q2 How does triangulation help to ensure validity?
Q3 What do Harvey and MacDonald identify as the three kinds of triangulation?
Q4 What is meant by 'fit for purpose'?
Q5 How do plural methods affect fitness for purpose?

Exam Questions

Q1	Explain what is meant by the term 'triangulation'.	(2 marks)
Q2	Suggest two reasons why sociologists might use mixed methods.	(4 marks)
Q3	Examine how using mixed methods can improve sociological studies.	(20 marks)

Oops, my revision's just done some Bermuda triangulation...

Mixed methods are really helpful — if you do end up picking a method that turns out not to be fit for purpose, then it's unlikely to matter as much. They increase the validity and reliability of your data. Triangulating different methods can be complicated, but you can triangulate between different researchers to reduce the possibility of mistakes. Which is fun.

Application of Research Methods to Education

These pages give some examples of research into the sociology of education. **These pages are for AQA only.**

Rosenthal and Jacobson (1968) Tested Self-Fulfilling Prophecies

1) **Rosenthal and Jacobson (1968)** went to a school in San Francisco and gave every student an **IQ test** that they said could predict **intellectual blooming**. They kept the results **secret**.

2) They took a **random sample** of 20% of the students and **reported to the school** that the students in the random sample had been identified as the **bloomers** — those who were likely to show the **biggest gains** in IQ during the year.

3) A year later they went back to the school and **retested** all the students.

4) The results of the two IQ tests showed that the students they'd **randomly identified** as bloomers had made the most **intellectual progress** in the year between the tests.

5) They concluded that the teachers must have been communicating a **positive label** to this group — that they had successfully created a **self-fulfilling prophecy**.

Advantages of Rosenthal and Jacobson's research method

1) The children were researched in a **natural, real-life setting** — giving a greater chance of **validity**.

2) Studying IQ creates **quantified data**, which makes the patterns easy to assess.

Disadvantages of Rosenthal and Jacobson's research method

1) The children and teachers may have acted differently because they **knew they were being observed**.

2) **Misleading** the teachers at the school is arguably **ethically incorrect**, because it involves **deceiving** some of the subjects of the study.

3) Rosenthal and Jacobson were unable to **control all the variables** — there are many factors which could have **contributed** to changes in IQ over the year besides the treatment of students by their teachers.

4) The entire study relied on **IQ tests**, which some sociologists criticise as a **bad measure** of intelligence — e.g. they claim that IQ tests are **culturally biased** in a way that favours some people.

Paul Willis (1977) Studied Anti-school Culture

1) **Paul Willis (1977)** studied a group of 12 working class boys as they made their **transition from school to the workplace**, using a mixture of **observation**, **group interviews** and **individual interviews**.

2) He found that the group had formed an **anti-school culture** that **rejected trying hard** in favour of **disruptive behaviour**. The group had decided not to try to **achieve qualifications**, even if they were **intellectually capable**.

3) Willis found that they transferred the same **anti-authority culture** to their **workplace**. Most of them found work as shop-floor staff in factories.

4) Willis claimed that their anti-authority nature was something they **created themselves** and not something that was **transmitted to them** by school or society.

Advantages of Willis's research method

1) Most human interactions are **instinctive** and best studied in **real situations**. Willis used **direct observation** to see how the group acted in school and in their workplace, **group interviews** to see how they acted in each other's company, and **individual interviews** so that he could get an idea of what each subject was like on their own.

2) Individual interviews gave Willis a chance to **build a rapport** with the boys, allowing him to gain an **in-depth understanding** of their behaviour.

Willis's work is an example of a mixed method study (see pages 118–119).

Disadvantages of Willis's research method

1) A sample of just 12 working class boys is **unlikely** to be **representative**. It would be misleading to generalise about all working class boys from these results.

2) However, performing the same study with a larger group of boys would be **very expensive**.

Application of Research Methods to Education

William Labov (1972) Assessed Linguistic Deprivation

1) **Bernstein (1971)** (see p. 59–60) suggested that "**linguistic deprivation**" is a cause of **underachievement** of **working class and ethnic minority children**.

2) **William Labov (1972)** tested Bernstein's theory using **informal, unstructured interviews**.

3) Labov discovered that when **black working class children** were interviewed by a **white person** in a **formal interview**, they **became tense** and **spoke nervously**, appearing to be **linguistically deprived**.

4) When they were interviewed by a **black person** in an **informal setting**, they became much more **articulate**.

5) So the **apparent linguistic deprivation** seemed to be a reaction to a **perceived hostile environment** rather than a genuine feature of the children's **communication methods**.

"Linguistic deprivation" means a lack of ability with Standard English. The theory is that working-class children tend to describe things in a condensed way and use more slang. This causes them to underachieve in education even though they may be expressing the same ideas as high achievers.

Advantages of Labov's research method

1) Informal, unstructured interviews are likely to offer greater validity than formal, structured interviews because they give the interviewer a chance to adapt their questioning to their subject.

2) **Sensitive or interesting issues** can be researched at greater depth in an informal interview because the interviewer doesn't have to stick to a **fixed questionnaire**.

3) The subject is more likely to be at ease in an informal situation, as the interviewer has a chance to build up a **rapport**. So they're less likely to hide information, potentially giving a greater insight into their thoughts and feelings.

Disadvantages of Labov's research method

1) All interviews depend on the questions and the skill of the interviewer. So results may be different from one interviewer to the next. This is known as "interviewer bias".

2) The possibility of "interviewer bias" also means that if the same study is carried out a second time then it can easily produce completely different results — it isn't reliable.

3) Data collected through informal, unstructured interviews is difficult to quantify — subjects may not have all been asked the same questions.

4) As the questions aren't all planned in advance, there is a risk that the interviewer will ask biased or leading questions, or just keep asking similar questions without realising.

5) The subject may give the reply they think the interviewer wants to hear to try to please them, possibly without realising that they're doing it.

6) Unstructured interviews are time-consuming and relatively expensive.

Practice Questions

Q1 Describe Rosenthal and Jacobson's research method.
Q2 Give two disadvantages of Rosenthal and Jacobson's research method.
Q3 Describe Paul Willis's research method.
Q4 Give two advantages of Willis's research method.
Q5 Describe William Labov's research method.
Q6 Give three disadvantages of Labov's research method.

Exam Question

Q1 Suggest an advantage and a disadvantage for sociologists of using direct observation. (4 marks)

So many studies, so little time...

It's unlikely that these specific studies will come up in the exam — but you do need to understand how sociological methods can be applied to education. There's more about the AQA exam on pages 124–126.

Application of Research Methods to Health

These pages show how some of the methods can be used to research health. **These pages are for AQA only.**

The *English Longitudinal Study of Ageing* Explored *Ageing, Health and Class*

1) The **English Longitudinal Study of Ageing (ELSA)** was set up by **Michael Marmot**. It follows a group of **over 8,500** people from all social classes who were **born before 1952**.

2) The ELSA is partially funded by **central government**.

3) The subjects have had to fill in a questionnaire **every two years** since **2002** about their health, work, experience of healthcare, cognitive abilities and income. In 2004, the questionnaire was combined with **a visit from a nurse** to measure things such as **blood pressure** and **lung function**.

4) A new report on the study is **published** after every set of questionnaires.

5) In 2006 the study showed that people in their 50s from the **poorest 20%** of the population are over **ten times** more likely to die than those in the **richest 20%**.

6) It also showed that there is a **strong relationship** between levels of wealth and **mortality and morbidity**.

~ Longitudinal studies are ones that follow the same group of subjects over a long period of time.

Advantages of Marmot's research method

1) Marmot has generated a **huge amount** of **quantitative data**, which is helpful for **scientific** and **positivist** research.

2) **Longitudinal studies** are the most **reliable** way to analyse **changes over time** as they eliminate the possibility of **different sample groups** each being **unrepresentative** in **different ways**.

Disadvantages of Marmot's research method

1) Longitudinal studies are **very expensive** and **time-consuming** — long-term funding is essential.

2) Some of the original group inevitably **leave the study** as time progresses — either **by choice** or just because they **die** or become **impossible to contact**. This affects the **reliability** of the research.

Dalrymple and Appleby (2000) Studied the *Attitudes of Epileptics*

1) **Jamie Dalrymple and John Appleby (2000)** used **anonymous questionnaires** to investigate the accuracy with which people suffering epilepsy **reported seizures** to their GPs.

2) Their questionnaires asked for **quantifiable data** and were filled in by **122 respondents** from **31 practices**.

3) They found that **one sixth** of their respondents **hadn't reported** a recent seizure to their GP.

4) They also found that patients who had experienced a recent seizure were also likely to be **suffering from depression** due to reasons such as **loss of driving rights**, **loss of employment** and **fear of discrimination**.

Advantages of Dalrymple and Appleby's research method

1) The use of questionnaires from patients that Dalrymple and Appleby had **never met** meant that the study was **detached**. It eliminated the possibility of **interviewer bias**.

2) The use of **quantifiable** data made it **objective**.

3) The study was **quick** and **cheap**, but collected results from a **large number** of people.

4) The fairly large size of the study means that it was likely to be **representative** of all epilepsy sufferers.

Disadvantages of Dalrymple and Appleby's research method

1) Questionnaires are **inflexible** and there is no real opportunity for **follow-up questions**.

2) Questionnaires depend on respondents **telling the truth**. Some may have been **embarrassed** about not reporting seizures, so may have **deliberately provided untruthful answers**.

3) **Interpretivists** think that questionnaires are **too detached** to produce **valid results** — they think that they don't provide a **true picture**.

Application of Research Methods to Health

Quirk and Lelliott Observed Acute Psychiatric Ward Patients

1) **Alan Quirk and Paul Lelliott** studied **acute psychiatric wards** in London hospitals. Their data was collected over **three years** of **participant observation** starting in the year 2000.

2) Alan Quirk **immersed himself** in the life of the ward, taking part in activities including **occupational therapy**, **ward rounds** and **treatment sessions**.

3) He often sat in TV rooms and corridors to try to **observe** what was going on and to **talk to patients**.

4) The study produced a large amount of **qualitative data** about how patients **interact with each other** and with **medical staff**.

5) One of the conclusions they drew was that **Goffman's 1961** characterisation of mental health institutions as total or closed institutions is no longer relevant — patients **maintain contact** with the outside world, tend to only stay for **short periods** and there is a **high turnover** in medical staff.

Advantages of Quirk and Lelliott's research method

1) Their data is likely to be **valid** — they gained a **large amount** of data, and had time to develop a **thorough understanding** of the interactions between patients and staff.

2) Their method gave them **access** to a group that is **difficult** to research with other methods.

Disadvantages of Quirk and Lelliott's research method

1) The study took **three years**, making it **time-consuming** and **expensive**.

2) It's unlikely that a **shorter study** with the **same methods** would produce reliable results because of the difficulty of **being accepted** by the group being studied.

3) It can be difficult to get **consent** from hospital trusts and their **ethics committees** for research of this nature due to the **unpredictable** and **dangerous environment** of acute psychiatric wards.

4) The research cannot **be repeated easily**, meaning that it **lacks reliability**.

Practice Questions

Q1 What is a longitudinal study?
Q2 Give two disadvantages of a longitudinal study.
Q3 What were the advantages of Dalrymple and Appleby's use of questionnaires?
Q4 What were the disadvantages of Dalrymple and Appleby's use of questionnaires?
Q5 Describe the research methods of Quirk and Lelliott.
Q6 Give three disadvantages of Quirk and Lelliott's research methods.

Exam Questions

Q1 Explain what is meant by 'validity' of data. (2 marks)

Q2 Suggest two reasons why sociologists might use questionnaires. (4 marks)

This last question's for one million — would you like to ask the audience...

Studying lots of people seems to mean either using questionnaires, which are very detached, or spending a great deal of money on interviews. And the latter may only produce qualitative data, which isn't always helpful for scientific analysis. In some cases it may not really be possible to do either, and sociologists like Quirk just have to observe as much as possible.

Do Well in Your AQA Exam

The next three pages are all about how to do well in AQA exams. So don't bother reading them if you're doing OCR.

These pages describe what the sample exam papers for the new specification are like. We can't predict exactly what the new exam papers will be like though — there may be a few changes. So it's important that when you take the exams, you **read the instructions and questions really carefully**. Don't assume they'll always follow the same pattern.

Unit 1 *is worth* **40%** *of the AS-level*

1) The **Unit 1** exam is **1 hour** long. It's worth **60 marks** — **40% of the AS-level** or **20% of a full A-level**.

2) **Unit 1** has **three topic areas**: 'Culture and Identity', 'Families and Households', and 'Wealth, Poverty and Welfare'.

3) There's **one section** about **each topic area**. You only have to do **one** of these sections. It might sound obvious — but make sure you **choose** an **area** which you have been **taught and revised**.

4) Each section has **five questions**.

5) There are usually two **items** (short texts about the topic) to **read at the start**. The items usually highlight some of the **themes** or **theories** within the topic. Some of the questions will **refer to the items** — so you **have to read them**.

6) The first **three questions** are likely to be **short-answer questions** worth about 2, 4 or 6 marks. The next **two** questions are likely to be **longer essay questions** worth about 24 marks each.

Unit 2 *is worth* **60%** *of the AS-level*

1) The exam is **2 hours** long and it's worth **90 marks** — **60% of the AS-level** or **30% of a full A-level**.

2) **Unit 2** covers **three areas**: 'Education', 'Health' and 'Sociological Methods'. All students study 'Sociological Methods' and at least one of 'Education' and 'Health'.

3) The exam has **two sections** — not three like you might expect. This is because **'Sociological Methods'** is **combined** with the 'Health' and 'Education' topics. The two sections of the exam are called: **'Education with Research Methods'** and **'Health with Research Methods'**.

4) You only have to do **one section**. You have to answer **all parts** of the section you choose. Again, make sure you **choose the topic** that you have **been taught and revised the most**.

5) Each **section** contains **nine questions**.

- The first four questions are worth **40 marks**, and are about either 'Health' or 'Education' depending on which section you're doing. You'll probably be given an **item to read**. The exam advises you spend **50 minutes** on these questions.

- The fifth question is usually worth **20 marks**, and requires you to **apply** knowledge and understanding of **sociological research methods** to the topic of 'Health' or 'Education'. You're advised to spend about **25 minutes** on this.

- The next four questions are usually worth **30 marks**. Like the fifth question, these focus on **sociological research methods** but you can use knowledge from **any area of sociology** to answer them. You're advised to spend about **40 minutes** on these.

You Get Marks For...

AO just means 'Assessment Objective'

You Get Marks for:
AO1 — Knowledge and Understanding shown through Clear and Effective Communication
AO2 — Application, Analysis, Interpretation and Evaluation

Short-answer questions are questions that **don't require an essay** or a **detailed description** for their answer — they're all the questions that are usually worth 2, 4 or 6 marks. They mainly test **AO1 skills**.

Essay questions and questions requiring **more detail** test **AO1 skills** *and* **AO2 skills**. They're usually worth 20 or 24 marks.

For **AO2** marks you need to do things like:

1) **Evaluate** a theory / study / method — discuss its **strengths and weaknesses**.

2) Present **alternative** explanations / interpretations of findings.

3) **Identify** and **evaluate** social trends.

4) Organise your essay so that it's got a **coherent argument** and **structure**.

5) Use **evidence** to **back up** your points.

And don't forget about the basics:
- Write as **neatly** as you can.
- Use good **grammar** and **punctuation**.
- Check your **spelling** — especially of words to do with sociology.
- Make sure you **answer the question**.

Do Well in Your AQA Exam

Here are some Hints for Short-Answer Questions

1) If you're asked for **two** things, give **two** things. **Not one**. Not three. Or four. Five is **right out**.
2) If you're asked for two things, spend **equal time and effort** on **both**. You **won't** get as many marks for a **lopsided** answer.
3) Give **examples** from **sociological studies** and from **statistics** to **back up** your points.
4) Refer to **theories** like Marxism, functionalism and interpretivism — but **only** if they're **relevant**.
5) Use the **number of marks** as a **guide** for **how long you should spend on each question**. The more marks a question is worth, the longer you should spend answering it.

Here are some Example Exam Questions and Answers

A Couple of 2-mark Questions and Answers to Show You What to Aim for:

(01) What is a pilot study? (2 marks)

(01)   A pilot study is a small-scale study carried out before the main research to test the method being used. For example, a researcher might give their questionnaire to a small group to ensure the questions can be easily understood.

Explain the term

Give a short example.

(01) What is meant by 'labelling theory'? (2 marks)

(01)   Labelling theory is the idea that the labels given to people affect their behaviour. For example, someone labelled in school as 'disruptive' may internalise that label and start to believe it, causing them to actually become disruptive.

A Couple of 4-mark Questions and Answers to Show You What to Aim for:

(07) Suggest two ways in which industrialisation affects the family. (4 marks)

(07)   Family structure changes as a result of industrialisation. Nuclear families become the norm, instead of extended families. Talcott Parsons argued that this is because the nuclear family is better suited to industrial society.
   Roles within the family are also affected. In pre-industrial society, men and women usually work together in the home. In early industrial society, many men leave the home to work, for example in factories. Women are more likely to remain working in the home.

Don't waste time writing more reasons — two is enough.

(02) Suggest two ways in which an individual might be socialised into femininity. (4 marks)

(02)   The family can socialise girls to behave in a feminine way, for example through verbal appellation. They might call a girl "pretty", "sweet" and "lovely", whereas a boy might be called "a big, strong boy" and "a cheeky monkey".
   The media can act as a secondary agent of gender socialisation. For example, Angela McRobbie argued that magazines aimed at teenage girls reinforce conventional ideas of femininity.

Briefly mentioning relevant studies is good.

Here are a Couple of Example 6-mark Questions and Answers:

(02) Suggest three reasons why boys achieve slightly less highly than girls in education. (6 marks)

(02)   Traditionally "male" employment sectors such as heavy industry and factory work have declined. It can be argued that this has left boys with greater uncertainty over what they can aim for in life — some are disillusioned and feel no incentive to work hard at school.
   The number of female teachers has increased. This means that boys have fewer role models at school than before, which arguably means they are less likely to try to push themselves to achieve.
   The trend is also likely to be partly self-perpetuating. Boys are considered to be underachievers, so some teachers negatively label them. That negative labelling can become a self-fulfilling prophecy, causing boys to continue to underachieve.

Don't waffle at the start. Get straight in there with your suggestions.

(08) Suggest three ways in which children are treated differently than adults in modern UK society. (6 marks)

(08)   Children are banned from buying many harmful substances, such as alcohol and tobacco. This represents an extra protection for children — it works in addition to the various laws that govern adults.
   Children are not expected to work and are financially supported by their parents. This is different from most adults, who are required to earn enough money to support themselves.
   Children are also protected by the state from abuse by their parents or carers. So the state offers additional protection to children in the family, above the protection that other members of society receive.

A new paragraph for each new point makes it clear you've suggested three things.

Do Well in Your AQA Exam

Here's an Example *20-mark Question* and *Answer*:

Here's an example of a **longer exam question** based on a short **text**. It's the kind of question you'll get in the **Unit 2 exam** — it combines sociological methods with another topic.

---

05   For this question, you need to apply your knowledge and understanding of sociological methods to a specific area in the topic of 'Education'.

You should read Item B and then answer the question below.

> **Item B: Investigating social class and educational achievement**
>
> Sociologists have studied the extent to which there is a link between social class and standards of achievement in education. For instance, Willis (1977) investigated how an anti-school subculture among 12 working class boys contributed to low educational achievement. More recently, Willmott and Hutchinson (1992) studied the link between deprived social backgrounds and an increasing number of children leaving school with no GCSE passes in inner-city Manchester and Liverpool.
>
> Sociologists researching this topic have been interested in finding the reasons behind patterns of achievement. They have investigated the effect of negative labelling on students, and the extent to which cultural differences between social classes affect educational achievement. Other research has focused on material deprivation as a factor affecting education.

Read the text carefully. It'll give you ideas for what to write about.

Using material from Item B and elsewhere, assess the benefits and drawbacks of **one** of the following sociological research methods in the study of social class and educational achievement:

EITHER   unstructured interviews
OR   official statistics

(20 marks)

---

(05)   Unstructured interviews take the form of an unrestricted, free-flowing conversation between the researcher and subject.

Give a brief description of the research method you're discussing.

A key benefit of using unstructured interviews for researching social class and educational achievement is that they allow the researcher to build up a rapport with the interviewee. This makes the interviewee more likely to open up and be honest in their answers, resulting in valid data. Another advantage of unstructured interviews is that they allow the researcher to follow up any ambiguous or unusual responses, to gain greater clarity and detail. Unstructured interviews are most appropriate for interpretivist research which is focused on empathising with individuals and discovering the motivations and emotions behind their behaviour.

Some sociologists argue that differences in educational achievement by social class are a result of cultural differences in attitudes. Unstructured interviews are a good way to research individuals' attitudes. For example, Willis (1977) used a range of methods, including unstructured interviews, to research the male, working class anti-school subculture referred to in Item B. The boys in this subculture had very negative attitudes towards education and were disruptive in school. The unstructured interviews allowed him to build a rapport with the boys and gain an insight into their motivations and beliefs. This opportunity for rapport wouldn't have been possible using quantitative methods, for example official statistics or questionnaires.

Apply the information about methods to specific studies.

Another advantage of unstructured interviews for researching this topic is that it is a sensitive and subtle approach. For example, Labov used this method when investigating whether "linguistic deprivation" might be a factor in working class children underachieving in education. A different approach, such as formal, structured interviews, may have been intimidating to the interviewees.

On the other hand, there are some disadvantages of unstructured interviews as a research method. The results are not reliable. For example, if another sociologist repeated Willis's research with a different group of working class boys, they would probably get different results. The research sample tends to be small because it's a time-consuming and expensive method. For example, Willis used a sample of only 12 boys. It's difficult to generalise from the results, because answers tend to be specific to individual subjects. This also makes it difficult to make direct comparisons between one interviewee and another.

Discuss both strengths and weaknesses.

Positivist researchers would find alternative methods more appropriate, for example a survey of a large sample would be more likely to provide reliable, quantitative data that could be used to make generalised conclusions. An investigation such as Willmott and Hutchinson's into a possible correlation between social deprivation and educational failure might be easier to research using a positivist approach.

In conclusion, unstructured interviews are a useful research method for the topic of social class and educational achievement to some extent. In particular, they would be appropriate for interpretivist sociologists researching individuals' attitudes, motivations and emotions. They would be less useful for large-scale research.

Sum up with a short conclusion.

Do Well in Your OCR Exam

Pages 127-129 are all about how to do well in the OCR exams. So don't bother reading it if you're not doing OCR.

These pages describe what the sample exam papers for the new specification are like. We can't predict exactly what the new exam papers will be like though — there may be a few changes. So it's important that when you take the exams, you **read the instructions and questions really carefully**. Don't assume they'll always follow the same pattern.

You'll sit an exam on Unit G671 'Exploring Socialisation, Culture and Identity'...

1) This exam tests '**Exploring Socialisation, Culture and Identity**'. This topic includes material about **sociological research methods**.

2) This exam lasts **90 minutes** and is worth **100 marks**. It's **50%** of your AS-level.

3) You'll get **pre-release material** — a text that you are given **in advance** and expected to read **before you go into the exam**. The text will be roughly 2 pages long. It will be an **overview** of a piece of **sociological research** — including information about the research **process / methods** used.

4) There are **four questions** on the exam. They'll be based on the pre-release material. You have to **answer all four**.

...and one on Unit G672 'Topics in Socialisation, Culture and Identity'

1) This exam also lasts **90 minutes** and is worth **100 marks**. It's **50%** of your AS-level.

2) The exam includes questions about four topics — sociology of the **family**, sociology of **health**, sociology of **religion** and sociology of **youth**. You may not have studied all of these topics, but you should know **at least one** of them.

3) There are **eight questions** on the paper — **two for each topic**. You **answer any two** of the questions. It doesn't matter if you pick two questions on the **same topic**, or two questions on **different topics**.

4) It's likely that each question will be broken into two parts — **part (a)** and **part (b)**. You have to **answer both parts** of the questions you choose.

You Get Marks For...

AO just means 'Assessment Objective'

You Get Marks for:
1) *AO1 — Knowledge and Understanding. You need to show you understand a range of sociological theories, debates, studies, methods and terms.*
2) *AO2 — Analysis, Evaluation and Application. You need to show an ability to discuss the strengths and weaknesses of theories, concepts and studies.*

All the usual Exam Tips apply

1) If you're asked to make **two** points, make **two** points. **Not one**. Not three. Or four. Five is **right out**.

2) If you're asked for two things, spend **equal time** and **effort on both**. You won't get as many marks for a **lopsided** answer.

3) Give **examples** to back up your points, e.g. sociological studies or statistics.

4) Refer to **sociological theories** like Marxism, functionalism and interpretivism — but only if they're **relevant**.

5) Use the number of marks **as a guide** for **how long** you should spend on each question. The more marks a question is worth, the longer you should spend answering it.

And don't forget **the basics**.
You get marks for the quality of your **written communication**.

- Write as **neatly** as you can.
- Use good **grammar** and **punctuation**.
- Check your **spelling** — especially of words to do with sociology.
- For longer answers, remember to write in **paragraphs**. **Link** paragraphs together **smoothly** so that your answer **flows**.
- Make sure you **answer the question**.

Do Well in Your OCR Exam

A Short **Example Essay** to Show You What to Aim at:

This one is the kind of thing you could get for a 17-mark question in the 'Topics in Socialisation, Culture and Identity' paper.

> **5(a)** Identify and explain two ways in which religion affects contemporary society. (17 marks)

Refer back to the question in your answer.

Religion can affect contemporary society by influencing people's sexuality and by influencing gender roles.

Some religious groups promote a dominant norm of heterosexuality and marriage, which limits and regulates people's sexuality. For example, the New Christian Right in America argue, from a fundamentalist Christian viewpoint, that liberal reforms allowing people more freedom and control over their sexuality (for example, gay rights) are causing a moral decline in society. They believe people shouldn't have sex before marriage, and they promote abstinence to young people. They promote their views to society through mass communication, for example television and Christian publishing.

Other fundamentalist religious viewpoints also try to influence and regulate the sexuality of their believers. For example, under traditional Islamic Sharia law, homosexuality and adultery are heavily punished. In some modern Middle Eastern societies, for example in Saudi Arabia, Sharia law is still used, and has a strong influence on society.

Another way that religion can be argued to affect contemporary society is through influencing gender roles. Many feminists argue that religion acts as an agent of social control, passing on patriarchal ideologies which reinforce the male domination of society. Many churches support and promote conventional family values with traditional roles for women as wife and mother. This encourages women into a passive role. The radical feminist Mary Daly argues that Christian teachings, imagery and hierarchy contribute to this. For example, St. Paul's letter to the Ephesians says, "Wives submit to your husbands" and the central female image in Christianity is of Mary the mother. Modern church hierarchy often excludes women, for example women can't become Catholic priests.

In conclusion, some religions directly and indirectly try to influence the social norms of what is acceptable in society in terms of individuals' gender and sexuality. This influence is perhaps strongest in more religious households and communities within society as a whole.

Give examples to support your points.

Give TWO ways.

Put in a short conclusion.

A Longer **Example Essay** to Show You What to Aim at:

This one is the kind of thing you could get for a 24-mark question on the 'Exploring Socialisation, Culture and Identity' paper.

> **3** Explain and briefly evaluate ways that primary socialisation might construct gender identities. (24 marks)

Primary socialisation takes place in the family, during the child's early years. It is a major force in the social construction of gender, but it is by no means the only important force.

Gender identities are ideas of what it is to be a man and what it is to be a woman. Along with gender identities go gendered norms of what behaviours count as masculine and what behaviours count as feminine. Most sociologists agree that gender is socially constructed: a product of socialisation.

There is evidence that children are gendered by their family from birth. This is their primary socialisation. Studies comparing adult reaction to a baby dressed in blue and introduced as a boy and the same baby dressed in pink and introduced as a girl show very different reactions. The "boy" was described as "big", "strong" and "lively" and the "girl" was described as "sweet" "beautiful" "quiet" and "good".

Ann Oakley (1974) described four ways in which primary socialisation constructs gender. 1) Manipulation — girls are put in pretty dresses and boys are allowed to get more mucky when they play outside. 2) Canalisation — children are directed to play with toys that the parents consider gender-appropriate, e.g. dolls and toy hoovers, building bricks and toy planes. 3) Verbal appellations — girls are called "pretty" and "good", boys are called "cheeky" and "strong". 4) Boys and girls are exposed to different activities. For example, boys often help out with gardening and DIY, girls often help mum with the housework and childcare. This teaches children what men's work is and what women's work is. Oakley said that by the age of five most children have a good idea of what appropriate behaviour for their gender is.

On the other hand, there are other ways, apart from primary socialisation, in which gender identity is constructed. By the age of five, the groundwork of gender socialisation is done, but the process isn't over — secondary socialisation also has a big effect on children. Education treats girls and boys differently. Labelling theory says that labels given to an individual by others affect their behaviour, and can turn out to be self-fulfilling prophecies. Girls are usually labelled as more studious and more compliant than boys. Boys are labelled as disruptive, and often prove to be so. However, boys' disruptive behaviour is likely to be not solely due to negative labelling by teachers. Primary socialisation may have already directed boys to be boisterous and girls to be calm.

Some sociologists also say the hidden curriculum in education passes on gender stereotypes. Girls tend to choose more arts subjects and boys tend to choose more science subjects. The advice that teachers give about subject options may transmit gender stereotypes.

Peer groups in school also have a big effect on gender socialisation. Children are ready to criticise behaviour they consider deviant — insufficiently masculine or insufficiently feminine. Mac an Ghaill found that young men were extremely concerned about masculinity to gain status in their peer groups. He also found that they saw academic achievement as effeminate. Mitsos and Browne thought that this was because education is highly feminised, and therefore does not provide role models for boys. However, if primary socialisation had not already irreversibly socialised children into genders, the fact that the teacher is a woman would not impact upon a male pupil in the least.

Another factor which affects children's views of gender is the media. The media have a huge effect on the transmission of ideologies about gender. Advertising perpetuates an image of women as concerned with their attractiveness, and their ability as a homemaker. Many films portray women as in need of rescuing by men. Children see media images and are affected by them.

In conclusion, primary socialisation is very significant in the construction of gender identity, and is the first influence on children's ideas about gender. However, as the child grows older, other factors are also important in shaping their gender identity, for example the media, their peer group and their education.

A02 marks for choosing a study to support your argument.

A02 marks for analysing and interpreting the study.

A02 marks for giving alternative explanations.

A01 marks for knowledge of a debate about socialisation.

A02 marks for choosing a study to support your argument.

Evaluate — give alternative explanations.

Do Well in Your OCR Exam

Before you sit the exam on **'Exploring Socialisation, Culture and Identity'**, you will be given some **pre-release material** to read. This will be a **synopsis** of some **sociological research** — and you'll be asked questions related to it in the exam.
Here's an **example** of the **kind of text** you'll get (the real thing will probably be a bit longer).

Asian Children at home and at school

Bhatti G. (1999) Routledge

This ethnographic study concerned the experiences of Asian children. Bhatti wanted to explore the relationship between home and school. At the time the research was carried out, in the late 1980s, British Asian communities had been established for over twenty years. Previous studies had portrayed the Asian communities as 'encapsulated', that is to say, most people's needs were met within the community and there was little contact with, or influence from, wider society. This was less likely to be true of the younger generation, who were attending compulsory education.

She also wished to question the statistical evidence, which suggested that children from Indian backgrounds did well in education, while others, especially Bangladeshi children, did worse. Bhatti wanted to see if the reasons for this difference were related to factors other than ethnicity. For example, was Bangladeshi underachievement due to their predominantly working-class backgrounds.

The children who formed Bhatti's sample all attended a mixed comprehensive school in the south of England, which Bhatti calls 'Cherrydale School' in 'Cherrytown'. She had been living in Cherrytown for two years, and selected Cherrydale partly because of informal conversations with parents she met through her part-time job in community education. After a one-hour interview with the Deputy Head, she was given permission. The fact that Bhatti was a qualified teacher and had taught in a secondary school contributed strongly to her being given access to the school.

The data was collected between 1987 and 1989. In school the main method was detailed interviews, supplemented by participant observation in classrooms. Bhatti also collected information through casual conversations with children. She kept detailed field notes. Questionnaires were also used for the school research.

The majority of the parents could not read or write English and some could not read or write Urdu or Bengali, so questionnaires were not used with them. To explore the children's home experiences, Bhatti used a sample of 50 families, interviewing one or both parents in their homes, making at least two visits to each family. The content of the interviews was negotiated, and Bhatti used a tape recorder when the respondents agreed, making notes when they did not.

The children of these families comprised 25 boys and 25 girls, from years 9, 10 and 11 and the school's sixth form. She chose this group because she wanted to study children who were old enough to talk articulately about home and school. 44 of the families were Muslim families from Bangladesh and Pakistan. 6 of the families were Indian — 4 of these were Hindu and 2 were Sikh.

The sample contained almost all of the Bangladeshi children in the school, half the Indian pupils and about a third of the Pakistani children. In total at Cherrydale, about 10% of the pupils were Asian. All of the children in the sample were from families where the father was in a working class occupation, or was unemployed.

Over the two years, Bhatti spent about two and a half days per week in the school. As a young Asian woman, Bhatti was seen differently by different groups within the school. Because of her age and ethnicity she was able to build strong rapport with the children, including truants and 'deviants'. For many of the parents, who knew her to be bilingual, she became a trusted point of contact and advice. Many teachers were suspicious of her at first, since they knew she was a researcher but did not know what she was researching. However, her presence was gradually accepted.

The research found that the parents felt that they lived in two worlds, because they maintained strong connections with their countries of origin. They had a high level of respect for teachers, but felt that they were not properly informed about their children's progress at school. They tended to have little understanding of the schooling their children were experiencing.

The children felt a strong tension between the home and school worlds because there were so few points of contact. For example they would often destroy letters home from school because they did not expect their parents to be able to understand them. They could not talk with teachers or non-Asian friends about family visits to the Indian subcontinent, though these were an extremely important aspect of their home lives.

You could **have a go** at answering these sample exam questions as part of **your exam preparation**.

1)	Define the concept of socialisation. Illustrate your answer with examples.	(8 marks)
2)	Outline and explain how any two agents of socialisation influence social class identity.	(16 marks)
3)	Explain and briefly evaluate why ethnic identities are changing.	(24 marks)
4)	Using the pre-release material and your wider sociological knowledge, explain and evaluate the use of mixed research methods to research Asian children's experiences of home and school.	(52 marks)

So, what's your favourite sociological term?

Glossary

absolute poverty Not having the essentials needed for life — food, warmth and shelter.

achieved status Status you get by working for it.

anomie A state of confusion where the norms of society break down.

ascribed status Status you have from birth.

Bourdieu, Pierre French sociologist who came up with the idea of cultural capital.

bourgeoisie What Marx called the capitalist class.

capitalism An economic system where employers buy workers' labour in return for wages, and sell the things the workers make for profit.

class Division of society based on how people earn money.

collective consciousness The shared values and norms that hold society together.

communism A system of government which is theoretically based on a classless society and where private ownership has been abolished.

conform To go along with society's norms and values.

conjugal roles Husband and wife roles — who does the paid work, who does the washing-up etc.

consensus A shared agreement.

cultural capital The skills and cultural know-how that children learn from their parents.

cultural deprivation theory This theory says working class culture makes people disadvantaged.

culture A way of life, a set of norms and values.

deferred gratification Working and waiting for a while until you get your reward.

delinquency Bad behaviour and social disruption. Includes criminal behaviour and plain annoying behaviour.

desacrilisation Religious and spiritual beliefs ceasing to have a place in society.

deviant Something that goes against society's norms and values. Deviant behaviour is behaviour that society doesn't approve of.

discourse Any kind of discussion or talk about something.

Durkheim, Emile (1858-1917) French founding father of sociology. He thought that different parts of society had different roles, like the organs of the body.

ethnic group A group of people with a common culture — language, religion and way of life.

ethnocentric Centred around the values and interests of one particular ethnic group.

ethnography The description of the way of life of people based on observation, interviews, case studies etc.

extended family Three or more generations all living together — grandparents, aunts, uncles etc.

false consciousness Marxism says that workers are in a state of false consciousness about their place in society. Workers don't realise how unfair it is. If they did, they'd start a revolution.

false needs Herbert Marcuse said that workers are fed the idea that they "need" fancy goods that they don't really need at all.

feminism Belief that women are disadvantaged in society, and that women and men should have equal rights. Feminist sociologists think that mainstream sociology has ignored the lives of women.

folk devil A scapegoat for things going wrong in society.

functionalism The belief that everything in society exists for a reason.

gender Masculinity and femininity. Sociologists say that gender is a social construction. Being male or female is the biological sex you're born with, while masculinity and femininity are identities you're socialised into.

Hall, Stuart (b. 1932) British sociologist, big on studying ethnicity and popular culture.

hegemony The domination of one group of people over another, or of one set of ideas over another.

hidden curriculum The social norms and values that are taught at school, but not as part of the regular curriculum. Includes conformity, respect for authority and other cultural values.

hierarchy A system which ranks people according to status. Any system where you have a boss in charge of people is a hierarchy.

household A group of people who live together. They needn't be related.

hypothetico-deductive model Where you come up with an idea (a hypothesis) and do experiments to test if it's true or not.

iatrogenesis The appearance of health problems caused by the medical system.

identity An individual's concept of themselves. This can be related to class, gender, ethnicity.

ideology A set of ideas and beliefs.

infrastructure The economic structure of society.

institutional racism When the policies, attitudes and actions of an institution discriminate against ethnic minorities — sometimes unintentionally.

institutions of society Established laws, practices and customs, e.g. the family, religion, the education system, the healthcare system.

internalised norms and values Norms and values that have become part of who you are and the way you think.

interpretivism A sociological approach which focuses on the actions and the thoughts of individuals. Also called **interactionism**.

Glossary

longitudinal study A study done over a period of time.

Marcuse, Herbert (1898-1979) German Neo-Marxist sociologist who had the idea of false needs.

Marx, Karl (1818-1883) German social theorist who wrote *Das Kapital* and came up with the somewhat influential theory about power being the control of the means of production.

Marxism The belief that society is divided into the bourgeoisie, who own the "means of production", and the proletariat, who do the work. The bourgeoisie or capitalist class exploit the workers, and arrange society to keep the workers down. Most of the profit from the work that the working class do is kept by the bourgeoisie.

mass media Newspapers, TV, magazines, radio, Internet — media that lots of people use and consume.

master status A label has master status when it's the most important thing about you and it rules how other people view you and how you behave.

means-tested benefit A benefit that you can only get if you can prove you're poor enough.

meritocracy A system where the best (most talented and hard-working) people rise to the top.

moral panic A fear of a moral crisis in society. Moral panics are usually linked to "folk devils". The mass media have a big role in stirring up moral panics in modern society.

Murray, Charles American New Right sociologist who believes that there's an underclass who are too dependent on benefits.

non-conformity Not going along with society's norms and values.

norm A behaviour that's considered normal in a particular society, e.g. queuing, wearing clothes, making some eye contact when talking to someone.

nuclear family Mum, dad and children living together.

Oakley, Ann Feminist sociologist who studied housework and gender socialisation.

Parsons, Talcott (1902-1979) American functionalist sociologist who wrote about the structure and functions of society.

patriarchy A society where men are dominant. Feminists often describe male-dominated societies and institutions as "patriarchal."

peer groups Groups of people who all have the same status in society.

pluralism The belief that society is made of lots of different parts, and that each of those parts gets their say, via democracy and a free market.

positivism A theoretical point of view which concentrates on social facts, scientific method and quantitative data (facts and figures).

postmodernism A movement that emphasises a mix-and-match approach to values, and which says there isn't a single objective truth.

postmodernity The world after the modern age — with flexible working, individual responsibility and people constructing their own identity.

qualitative methods of research Methods like unstructured interviews and participant observation that give results which tell a story about individuals' lives.

quantitative methods of research Methods like surveys and structured interviews that give results which you can easily put into a graph or table.

reliability Data is reliable if you can do the same research again and get the same results.

rite of passage A growing-up ceremony that young people do to prove they aren't kids any more.

secularisation When religion becomes less important.

self-fulfilling prophecy When people behave in the way that they know others have predicted.

social construct An idea or belief that's created in society, and doesn't come from a scientific fact.

social democrats People who think the state should redistribute wealth, and that there should be a strong welfare state paid for out of taxes.

social policy Things that governments do that affect society, e.g. raising taxes, having a free healthcare system, allowing schools to run their own budgets, changing divorce laws.

stereotype A generalisation about a social group — often inaccurate and insulting.

stratification The way society is divided up into layers or classes.

stratified sample A sample with the same proportions of gender or class or age as the population you're studying.

subculture A group who share values and norms which are different from mainstream ones.

superstructure The cultural structure of society.

symmetrical family A family structure where conjugal (husband and wife) roles are shared.

third-way politics A political viewpoint that combines elements of right wing self-sufficiency and left wing social democracy.

triangulation Combining different methods and data to get the best results.

universal benefit Benefit that everyone gets, whether they're rich or poor.

validity Data is valid if it gives an accurate picture.

values Beliefs or standards shared in a society.

vocational education Education aimed at a particular job.

Weber, Max (1864-1920) German academic, considered father of modern sociology.

Willis, Paul (b. 1945) Sociologist who studied working class boys and their anti-school subcultures.

Index

Index

Index